Walking Point

My Experiences as an Infantry Soldier in Vietnam

By Richard Ropele

Introduction

"My Turn in the Barrel" was a phrase that was coined during Advanced Individual Training (AIT) at Fort Polk Louisiana as part of the training during the Escape and Evasion course. During the course orientation, the cadre let it be known that if you were captured by the aggressor force, they would be realistic in their interrogation in extracting information (your unit number, where they are deployed, what is their strength, etc.). One of many methods described to us as a way to "interrogate" the prisoners, and actually used on some of my friends in the company that were captured, was that the aggressor forces would put them into a metal barrel, close the lid, then pound on the sides with sticks and pipes.

The point being that anything done by this "enemy" would be a cake walk compared to what the VC would do if you were captured in Vietnam. Needless to say, my companions and I worked hard during this training exercise to avoid being captured. You definitely didn't want a turn in the barrel.

Fortunately, I was never a POW. But anyone who has ever been involved in combat remains in a type of confinement because of experiences and memories – categorized today as Post Traumatic Stress Syndrome (PTSD). Some people are more confined and constrained than others. Sometimes, even the most insignificant of incidents, an odor, or a song, or the sight of something can trigger a series of thoughts that can indeed "put you back again in the action". Those of us that are lucky enough NOT to have our names on the Vietnam Veterans Memorial Wall have taken a "turn in the barrel" and we survived.

As life continues, our job now is again to make our contributions to the well being and protection of our families and to society, the same way we were trained to make our contributions to the well being and protection of the men in our squads.

I started writing this manuscript off and on during the 1980's (obviously more off than on because it's been about 48 years in the making). It has been difficult to bring it to conclusion because it means that I have to 'get back in the moment' to correctly recount a situation. Some of the memories are difficult to deal with when they come to the surface. I could have died that day in January, but I didn't and I wonder if these past 48 years are what my Heavenly Father envisioned in exchange for my life.

I don't know exactly why, but I feel a compulsion to get the words, thoughts and deeds that are in my head down on paper. I certainly wasn't a major "jungle fighter". I was just an ordinary guy, put into an extraordinary situation, and like many of my fellow veterans, just tried to do my best in the situations that arose.

I don't look at this account as providing a "sense of closure" (which is an overused, 'pop physique' phrase today) to a significant chapter in my life's instruction. It's a chapter that provides another dimension to my life and character. My hope is that by documenting these experiences and thoughts, I can more clearly understand my role in life today, my responsibilities to my fellow man, and my reasons for being on this earth. Additionally, my family may get a clearer understanding of how my character and thoughts were influenced.

Quite often I wonder why I didn't get killed that night in January of 1968. It's amazing how often this thought goes through my head. Why didn't the fragments from that explosion penetrate into my head, instead of into my leg and foot? I was so close to that explosion. I can still see the flashes of reds, blacks, and yellows. I can still smell the acrid odor of the burning powder. I can still hear the voices of Don Prien (Doc) and Henry Pickett as they took its full force.

These are memories that can't be purged - I don't want them purged. These memories, while not always pleasant, nevertheless will always be with me and they will continue to have a major influence on my character, in the decisions I make, and how I raise my family. Hell, this experience shaped my character and my outlook on life almost as much as the influence and example that my Mom and Dad provided.

I had the great honor to associate with some of the greatest men of my generation, men of valor, men of courage, men of commitment. Men who answered their country's call. Men who are real life American heroes.

This whole episode began as a great adventure. Here went little Ricky Ropele, my first time leaving home, going out as a boy, into a man's world. I would be doing something no one else in my entire family had done. I served as a combat infantryman in the Armed Forces of the United States of America during a time of war. I would actually be living in a John Wayne movie.

If I had to come away with one thought to sum up these experiences, it would be:

> There are countless millions of people alive today throughout the world because of the sacrifice and dedication of the men and women of the United States Military. Honored and great are they that wear the colors of the United States of America
>
> I'm proud and honored to have been a part of this great cause of preservation.

IT WAS A GREAT ADVENTURE.

Self Portrait

Summer time in Southern California in 1967 was the best place in the world to be. The temperature is always in the upper 80's, the sun is out, the surf is up, the beach is just a short stroke away. I had a job where I made pretty good money. I had a new car. I had very little responsibility in the world. I was only responsible for myself. What could possibly spoil this perfect picture?

New car

In the Summer of 1966, I decided I wanted another car. The 1966 model year cars were about to come out, so the 1965's would be reduced in price to make room. My present car, which was my very first car, was a 1961 Chevrolet, 2 door, automatic transmission, 283 cu in V8 (their small V8) engine. It was a nice car, but not exactly a babe mobile. I wanted the kind of car that fit my image as a hot, young buck.

I found the car I wanted at Selman Chevrolet in Orange and I traded the 61 Chevy in for a brand new 1965 Chevy Malibu. Now, this car was hot - forest green exterior, black leather interior, bucket seats, a 327 cu in V8 engine, 4 speed on the floor transmission. This car was hot - and I sure looked good in it. Mom and Dad co-signed a loan for about $3000.00 (I think) that was financed through the bank. I made the payments - I had my job and a new car. I was in "fat city". Life was good. I drove this car until I left for basic training at Fort Ord in the summer of 1967.

When it came time to leave for the Army, Dad and I decided that it didn't make sense to sell the car, after all, I was only going to be gone for a short 12 months. I figured I would need it at my next duty station when I finished my training or when I got back from Vietnam in a year (little did I know that it would be much sooner). So we parked the car in Mary Davenport's garage. The Davenports were lifelong friends of Mom and Dads and they just lived across town in Santa Ana. My Dad said he would go over there weekly and drive the car around to keep the battery charged.

Good Job

I started working at ITT Jabsco Pump Company in Costa Mesa full time during the first semester I was on academic probation (in the fall of 1966, I think). I started as a clerk in the Receiving department, then drove a truck up to Los Angeles to deliver and pick up the materials from our suppliers. It didn't take much of this to understand the importance of going to school and getting an education. However, my vision of the future was clouded by this freedom that I had and because of the money that I made to still place much importance in school. However, the next semester I was back at Santa Ana College and working part time at Jabsco, first in the print shop and then eventually in the inside sales department taking phone orders. I thought a career in sales or advertising would be a good path to follow and adjusted by course of study to Business Administration. It was the job at Jabsco that provided me with the money to buy a car.

While at Jabsco, I was recruited to play basketball on the company team. I had been playing basketball ever since the 6th grade and always played on school teams. However, in high school, I was under 6 feet and wasn't good enough to make the school teams in my senior year. I grew a couple inches after high school and peaked at 6 '3", and at 165 pounds, was fit to play the center position. You have to remember, in those 60's, 6"3" was tall for that time. We played in an industrial league and played a couple times a week at Costa Mesa High School. Good times. . . . another part of that perfect summer in 1967.

Brother and Father Classified 4F

My brother Don received his notice to report for his draft physical, I think in 1965 or 1966. He reported for his physical (because failure to report was against the law - draft evasion), and he took a letter from Dr. Donaldson attesting to his lifelong condition with asthma. Don had had asthma all his life – I remember there were periods where he could hardly catch his breath at night. I assume that after a physical examination and probably a telephone call to Dr. Donaldson by the Army doctors, he was excused and subsequently classified 4F (physically unfit to serve). Don used to jokingly say that the women and children would have to go first before they would take him.

My Dad was drafted in 1942 (after he and Mom were married) and he completed his time in basic training. Mom has pictures of him and her when she went up to visit him at Stanford. Subsequently, he was given a medical discharged because he suffered from migraine headaches. My Dad was born in 1913 and Mom said his migraine headaches were the result of his being infected during the influenza epidemic of 1917. Dad was subsequently classified 4F.

My Dad is a good honest man who would have pulled his weight in the war had he been able to serve. It must have been very hard on him during that time. My Dad was drafted in 1942 and went through training at Fort McArthur and at Camp Haan (which is now March Air Force Base and Riverside National Cemetery). In one of his letters to Mom he said he felt he could contribute by being a plumber/pipefitter and work in the defense industry.

Those headaches must have been pretty powerful because during World War II, the country needed every able bodied man. I remember some of his headaches when I was a boy. He would disappear into the bedroom for 3 days, the curtains closed tight to keep out as much outside light as possible. The only time he would come out would be to go to the bathroom. I remember him saying that his headaches were so severe it hurt just to touch his hair.

Messed Around in School

I was attending Santa Ana Jr. College (now, Rancho Santiago Community College) during this time. I graduated from Santa Ana High School in June of 1963 and began college in September of that same year. Now, two years later, I was on academic probation in the latter part of 1966 and because I didn't pull my grades up and I was excused from school for the next semester. As a result, I lost my school draft deferment (which was classification 2S) and reclassified as 1A (prime choice). I spent the next semester working full-time at ITT Jabsco Pump Company in Costa Mesa.

Leaving the House

The Vietnam war was hot and heavy in 1967. President Johnson made commitments to increase the troop strength to over 500,000 men, totally involving the entire country in the war. I knew that I was a prime candidate for the draft and if I didn't buckle down and pay attention to school, I would be one of those directly involved.

But you know how it is, you never think it could happen to you, that somehow you would be overlooked in this mass mobilization.

Well, it didn't take the Government long to realize that I was now available, because in May of 1967, I received my draft notice instructing me to report for my physical examination and if qualified physically, to take the oath of allegiance on 21 June 1967.

I can only imagine what my Mom and Dad must have been feeling knowing what they and the country experienced in World War II. They understood more than I what the possibilities for me could be.

This mass mobilization of troops certainly was not to provide clerks and supply people. The military required additional ground forces, infantry soldiers, the "get down and dirty" ones for service in Vietnam. It was very likely that those drafted now would become infantry soldiers. I had strong feelings about wanting to carry my share of the load in service to my country, but I was also aware of the distinct possibility that my life would be in jeopardy during that service.

The reality of my long-term situation didn't escape me. There was no doubt in my mind that I would be going to Vietnam. I wasn't aware of any physical limitation that would prevent it. No sir, I was a prime choice, grade A quality. However, there was always a glimmer of hope that maybe it, just maybe, I would luck into a situation that wouldn't put me in a direct combat role.

I don't know about you, but I had always wondered about things like war. I would see romance in the movies where the good guy always conquers the bad guy, gets the girl, and is only wounded in the shoulder. I grew up with innumerable John Wayne war and cowboy movies where he would do extraordinary things to save others - always coming out unscathed. Maybe that would be me this time.

But, never mind the potential danger - when you're young you think you are invincible and you don't look beyond the moment. I figured a lot of other people went into the Army and came out all right - so how hard could it be. There's a fascination that grip's a boy's imagination. I always wondered how I would conduct myself and react in these kinds of situations. Well, now I was going to get the chance to find out.

Little did I know that the events that would unfold over the next two years would change my entire philosophy on life, that the episode of cheating death would affect almost every decision I would make. In retrospect, I am able to see how these experiences still affect aspects of my daily decisions.

The 21st of June, 1967 loomed large, exciting and mysterious in my life. This was an opportunity to leave home, to be out in the world on my own. There was an element of excitement when I thought about the future. The great adventure was about to begin

My instructions were to report to the parking lot of the Santa Ana Bowl, at 8th and Flower at 6:00 a.m. to be bused to the processing center in downtown Los Angeles for our induction physical examinations and processing into the Army. I asked my brother Don to take me to the bus because I didn't want to go through a public emotional display with Mom and Dad. It's not like they would get hysterical or anything, but I knew they probably grasped more of the reality of the situation than I did and the possible outcomes, so it might be difficult for them to be there.

Additionally, if I were to die in Vietnam, I wanted Mom and Dads' last memories of me to be one that is within the walls of our home and not in some dark and lonely parking lot in Santa Ana. I knew they were more concerned about my future than I was at this time.

I don't remember much about how Don and I said good-bye. We were not a physically demonstrative family, so I'm sure we didn't hug. Maybe, we shook hands, but I think it was more of a ". . . well, I'll see you later, huh . . " type of farewell.

The bus ride to Los Angeles was fairly uneventful. I always use the joke that I was the one that scratched those grooves in the freeway roadway with my fingernails as they strapped me kicking and screaming to the back of the bus, but that's just a joke. I went willingly - and as I look back, I would do it again if my services were required.

The Physical Examination and Swearing In

We arrived at the processing center, located in a seedy part of downtown Los Angeles, around 8:30 am. It was here we were to receive our preinduction physical examinations and if we passed, to take our oath of allegiance to become full time members of the United States Army.

The physical examination provided an opportunity for that glimmer of hope to rise. Maybe they will find something wrong that will disqualify me and I'll be sent home. I knew it wasn't likely, I was always physically fit. I played basketball in high school, we surfed constantly throughout the year, and never had a sports injury. Deep down inside I knew I would qualify 100%, but maybe, just maybe . . . .

We were assigned lockers and told to strip down to our undershorts and T-shirts, put into groups and told to follow the different colored lines painted on the floor to the different medical stations throughout the building. I was in the yellow line group.

> They took blood samples to check for different things. AIDS wasn't a concern in those days but I suspect they were looking for venereal diseases (VD). VD wasn't an outright rejection, those individuals were excused and their physicals were rescheduled after seeing their personal physicians for treatment.
>
> They checked for hernias - "turn your head to the right and cough".
>
> Color blindness - We looked through a small foldout book that contained letters and numbers hidden in different colors of dots. If you were color blind, you would not be able to see the number or letter. Color blindness is a reason for rejection.
>
> Vision Test - Lack of 20/20 vision was not a reason for rejection. The Army was more than willing to provide glasses if you needed them.
>
> Hearing Test

The physical exam lasted most of the day. If they discovered a problem, they usually took that person out of the process to visit personally with a doctor. I remember one guy passing out while we were standing in one of the lines. They said he had been taking some pills throughout the day

I just followed the yellow line and went through the process (a little intimidating to be interviewed in your underwear). It didn't surprise me that I passed.

Lunch was provided at a restaurant around the corner from the building. We were given a ticket which we handed to the cashier before going through the buffet line. We were 'strongly encouraged' to return after lunch. I don't remember anything extraordinary about the food or the restaurant. After lunch, we continued with the examination.

Around 2:00 pm, all of us who passed were gathered in this large room, four or five lines of 10 to 15 guys each in each line for the swearing in ceremony. We were told to raise our right hand, to repeat the oath and take one step forward. I don't remember all the words of the oath, but I do remember words like:

> ". . . allegiance to the United States. . . . defend against all enemies, foreign and domestic. . . "

I repeated the oath and took my one step forward and from then on I belonged to the United States Army for the next two years (whoa, 720 days to go). As a result, I became the first Ropele man to serve a full enlistment in the United States Armed services.

Around 3:00 p.m., several buses from Continental Trailways arrived at the front door. We all piled in and left for Fort Ord.

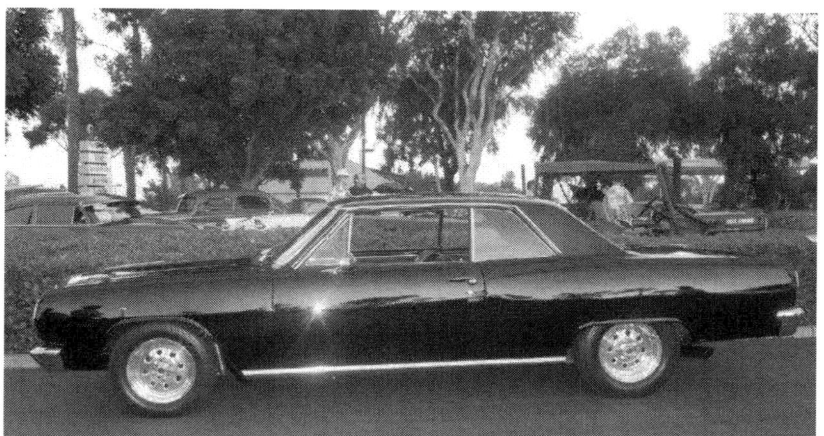

This is not my 1965 Malibu, but it's just like it. Mine was forest green and while I was in Colorado, I put on Keystone mags. It had a 327, 4 speed on the floor, bucket seats, black interior. My first new car, paid about $3000.

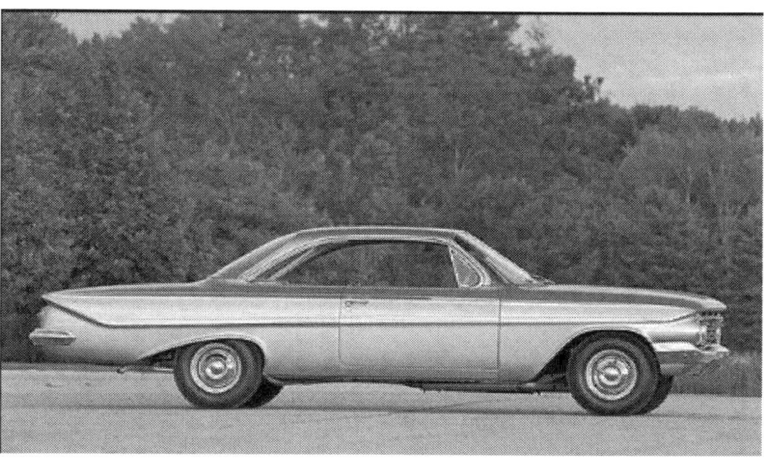

This is a 1961 Chevy – it's just like my first car. 283 V8, automatic, bench seats

Fort Ord Reception Center

Cultural shock at its peak. Just a few short hours ago I was a carefree young buck, the biggest decisions I faced were whether I should go to the beach after work or just drive around and try to pick up on some girls. Now, I'm in an organization that will teach me to "be all that I can be". But, so far, riding on this bus, being in the Army is not so bad. I figure plenty of other guys have been in this same position. If they could do it, I certainly can also.

Now, I'm riding up Highway 101, wondering how all this is going to play out.

Welcome to the Army – Fort Ord Reception Center

Somewhere along the way, the bus pulled into a restaurant and the U. S. Government bought us dinner. Otherwise it was a straight through trip arriving at the Fort Ord reception center around midnight on the 21st of June 1967. Everyone was awake by this time and we just sat there waiting for someone to tell us what to do next. We didn't have to wait long, almost immediately the door flew open and this big black guy in an Army uniform, wearing a campaign hat (i.e., a "Smoky the Bear" hat), leaps into the aisle way and begins shouting:

> "YOU'D BETTER GET OFF THIS . .#$!!#. . BUS RIGHT NOW. WHAT DO YOU THINK YOU'RE DOING, YOU'RE IN THE ARMY NOW. GET YOUR . .#$!!#. . OUT OF THOSE SEATS AND MOVE IT. . . I'M NOT YOUR MOTHER YOU KNOW . . . I MEAN MOVE IT, RIGHT NOW, MOVE IT, MOVE IT! "

Why is he talking to us like that? I didn't know what his problem was, or why he was so excited, but I knew we had better "move it". Little did I know that this would be the style of communication for the next eight weeks. We scrambled off the bus like our pants were on fire. Once outside, we milled around like sheep until they shouted us into several lines and columns (i.e., a "formation") and walked us into a room. There we began filling out reams of paperwork.

I don't remember specifically which papers we processed, but I suppose it would be things like personnel information (i.e., name, address, birth date, next of kin, etc.), insurance papers, saving bonds cards, and other things. It took two or three hours to complete. The DIs checked everyone's papers whenever we turned them in before moving on to the next one. We're talking about 100 to 150 guys in this room. It took a long time.

About 2:00 a.m. they formed us into several groups, and assigned us to barracks to get some sleep. I don't know how they arranged the groups, but we were put into groups of 48 guys. They then "marched" us someplace that issued blankets, pillows and sheets and moved us into some barracks for the night. Everyone just covered up with their blanket on the bare mattress and crashed until morning. Little did we realized that morning was so close

The next day, our second day in the Army, began at 5:00 am.

The First Weeks Processing

After 2 hours of sleep, someone came onto the floor at 5:00 am shouting and screaming like the guy on the bus the previous night:

> ". . . GET UP YOU MISERABLE MAGGOTS, WHERE IN THE . . #$!!$. . DO YOU THINK YOU ARE, YOUR MOMMA IS NOT HERE ANY MORE, YOU ARE IN THE ARMY NOW, GET UP AND GET OUTSIDE, I MEAN NOW, YOU . . #$!!$., MOVE IT, MOVE IT. . ".

Whoa, mom never got me out of bed like this. Just like on the bus, everybody started scrambling and moving as fast as they could. As no one changed their clothes from the night before, it wasn't much of an effort to get outside and get lined up.

This was my introduction to Sgt Henley, our Drill Instructor and his two Assistant Drill Instructors, Cpl Weddendorf and Cpl Cuneo.. Sgt Henley was a tall slim black man. Spoke at the top of his lungs. He would be our leader for the next 9 weeks. Cpl Cuneo was a thin lanky white guy, looked a little 'pasty faced' and soft. Cpl Weddendorf was also about my size but had a 'hard edge' look about him.

We lined up in some random order, 4 lines of about 12 people each. Sgt Henley and the two Cpl's shouting instructions about standing at attention, right face, left face, marching, etc. We acted just like you'd expect of a bunch of guys trying to do things in unison.

After breakfast that first morning, they "marched" us off to get our clothing issue. "Marching" is not very descriptive of the way in which we moved about on this second day of our Army careers. Herding of sheep is more like the way we were moved around.

The reception center was the original part of Fort Ord. All the buildings were wood frame structures, built during World War II (approximately 50 years old). The walls were exposed through the studs and the ceiling exposed through the rafters. These were very basic quarters. Bunk beds were arranged in two rows on each floor with the foot end facing the center aisle.

This would be the last day that I would wear civilian clothes for the next six months. I don't remember what we did with the clothes we wore up there. We must have packed them away somewhere. We were in the Army now and we were to wear only Government issue clothing (hence the term GI issue). Our everyday clothes were called "fatigues" (I guess because we were always tired). Anyway, the basic uniform issue consisted of:

Boots (2 Pair)	Fatigue Pants (4)	Fatigue Shirts (4)
Underwear	Undershirts	Socks
Caps	Regular Shoes (2 Pair)	Dress Jacket
Dress Shirt	Tie	Dress Shoes
Dress Cap	Dress Socks	Duffel Bag
Laundry Bag	Summer Dress Uniform	Winter Dress Uniform

Back at the barracks, the assistant Drill Instructors taught us how to pack our new wardrobe into our footlockers and into our wall lockers. The Army is very precise on how things are done and everybody's foot locker is packed exactly the same way and clothes are hung in your wall lockers in exactly the same order for everyone. This was only the beginning of the Army way of doing things – part of losing your individuality and becoming part of a unit where you're interchangeable with anyone else.

On the morning of the third day, we took a series of tests - tests on general intelligence and knowledge. Everyone thought the Army would use these test results to place you into a Military Occupation Status (MOS) best suited to your skills. We all hoped that we would show significant intelligence such that they would want us to be in communications, or be a clerk, or something other than in the infantry. MOS 11B10 was the infantry MOS. This was one of those situations where you hope against hope. We certainly didn't get drafted because we were good at stringing telephone lines and such. The military needed fighting soldiers for the war in Vietnam and we were it.

The afternoon of the third day we marched to the barber shop. We all knew it was inevitable that a buzz cut was on the horizon, but it was still a shock to see yourself. We sat in the barber chair and the barber took about 15 seconds on each man, zip, zip, zip, front to back and we were done. All of a sudden here are 48 guys and all their hair is less than 1/4 inch long. So now, we're all dressed alike and we all look alike.

There was one guy who looked like Buffalo Bill - he had long blond hair flowing over his shoulders and a beard. He wore a fringed buckskin jacket. Someone said he worked at Knotts Berry Farm as one of the train robbers. For some reason, he didn't get his haircut that first day. The rumor was that it was something to do with his citizenship and whether he was legally in the Army. He really stood apart from the rest of us bald heads in the area. But after a couple of days, whatever problem must have been cleared up because he was given his haircut and uniform and blended right into the bald headed landscape.

Part of the orientation process during our week in the Reception Center was to get our shot records up to date. At this point the Army didn't know where anyone would be ultimately assigned, so every recruit went through the same series of vaccinations. I don't remember what we were vaccinated for, but there were about 6 or 8 shots we had to take over this week.

The process both times was the same. We would march over to the Infirmary (which was nothing more than another small wood frame building, with a couple of tables, chairs and gurneys) and line up in formation outside. We would take off our fatigue shirts, fold them and set them on the ground beside our right foot and roll up the sleeves on our undershirts to expose our shoulders, and stand there until it was our turn to file into the building.

Now picture this, 48 guys standing in 4 lines, all dressed alike, black boots, olive drab fatigue pants and white T-shirts, with both sleeves rolled over their shoulders, just waiting. Not only did you feel vulnerable, but you also looked really stupid.

Inside there were four guys administering the injections, two on each side about 3 steps apart. One pair for the left arm and one pair for the right arm. Each doctor, I assume they were doctors, was armed with one of those pneumatic guns that shot the serum into you with air pressure instead of with a needle. I walked between the first pair and ZAP ZAP, one shot in each arm, took 3 more steps and stopped and ZAP ZAP, another set of shots in each arm.

You know, I hate getting shots, but these didn't feel so bad. However, the next day, my arms were real sore, but it was OK. Several days later we went back for the second round. This time there were only two doctors. I got my one shot, but the other doctor's gun was out of serum.

This doctor kind of rolls his wrist off to the side, the gun pointing out into the open part of the room, puts in another bottle and while still pointing the gun across the room, squeezes the trigger. I swear, a stream of serum shot 15 feet across the room and hit the far wall, looking like the stream of water coming out of a hose. He turned and pressed the gun against my arm and ZAP.

I swear, I felt this medicine go into my arm, out the other side and across my chest. Man, it really hurt. I think it was tetanus.

The Mess Hall

One thing about the Army, they don't skimp on food. We were given 3 square meals a day. Breakfast was served between 5:00 and 6:00 am, lunch between 11:30 and 1:30, and Dinner between 4:30 and 6:00 p.m.. As I recall, the food was pretty good.

The Mess Hall was a long, single story, wooden building located central to our barracks. One third of the building was the cooking and serving area and the remaining two thirds was the dining area. It wasn't big enough to accommodate everyone at the same time, so people would move in as others would move out.

At meal time, each platoon in the Company would line up outside the Mess Hall. Each of us would have to cross the ladder bars (we know these as "Monkey Bars") before you could go into the Mess Hall. The Army never passed on an opportunity to work on our physical conditioning.

The food was served on metal trays. You walked cafeteria style through the serving area and the cooks would put the food on your tray, you would grab napkins and silverware, then find a table in the dining area. Milk was available in a self service dispenser out on the floor.

After eating, you went outside and scraped your tray into a trash can, then stacked the tray. This was the meal time process for the next five months. Fort Polk was the same way.

The First Weekend

This first Sunday I was feeling so low, so far from home, so alone. I knew that my brothers Don, and Rod, Jeff, and the rest of the Monroys would be going to the beach at San Clemente for the day and here I was, 350 miles away locked in on this Army post. Hell, I can't even walk around and see the rest of the post. I can't even leave the company area.

All of a sudden it dawned on how 'far away' I really was. Two years is a long time when it's only the first day. 729 days to go and I'll be home and at the beach with the rest of my family. Oh crap.

There had been outbreaks of spinal meningitis at Fort Ord over the last several years, so all new recruits were confined to their company areas. During my entire training process, we could only go somewhere as a full platoon. Our uniforms had a white band sewn above the left pocket identifying us as basic trainees. Even on our "off times", we could not leave the immediate area around our barracks.

I was lying on my bunk this Sunday afternoon when the Assistant Drill Instructors (ADI's) Weddendorf and Cuneo came in to jerk us around. They walked through the barracks and generally harassed the troops. They stopped at my bunk and told me that I would be one of the trainee squad leaders and handed me some temporary Corporal stripes to wear on the sleeve of my uniform. I had 10 guys assigned to my squad.

A trainee squad leader was one of those good news/bad news situations you fall into in your life. The good news is that I wouldn't be doing any KP or Guard Duty, but the bad news is that I would be held responsible for the performance of these guys. They selected me because I was one of the bigger guys in the platoon (at the time I was 6"3" tall and weighed 180 lbs).

We stayed at the reception center for one week and then moved up the hill to the basic training facilities - our home for the next 8 weeks.

Barracks at Fort Ord reception area. Obviously, built during World War II, Fort Ord was one of the primary training base on the West Coast. I got these pictures off the internet recently, as Fort Ord has been closed and sold by the military in the 1990s (that's why the windows are boarded up). Millions of men went through Fort Ord in preparation for Vietnam.

This is another view of the barracks. One platoon was housed in each building in bunk beds. Each soldier had a bed, a foot locker and an open locker for his hanger clothes

Fort Ord - Basic Training

Haircuts and Candy

As basic trainees, we were not allowed free access around the Post because of the outbreaks of spinal meningitis problems in previous years. That meant, we couldn't even go across the street from our barracks to the Post Exchange (PX) when we wanted to buy something. All movement during basic training was made with the entire platoon, otherwise we were confined to the company area, which was the lawn area in front of and behind our barracks.

As part of the Army method of molding us fresh troops into a working combat unit, the concept was that all soldiers are created and treated equal. Part of that equality was that everyone dressed and looked as much alike as possible. One method of accomplishing that concept was to ensure that everyone had the same haircut.

Across the street from our barracks, the PX and barber shop were combined into one building. Every Saturday afternoon, just before releasing us for the rest of the day and Sunday, Sgt Henley would march us there for our weekly haircut and purchases from the PX.

The entire platoon would line up for formation after lunch and march across the street and line up in back of a building that housed both the PX and the Barber Shop. Sgt Henley would send us in groups of 4. It would only take about 30 seconds to get our butch haircut refreshed to its 1/4 inch level. That 30 seconds included sitting in the chair and getting the cape thrown over you. The barber had a vacuum affair attached to his clippers, so as he cut, the hair was sucked into the waste container. When he was done, he was done.

We could then exit through the PX and buy some candy and stuff - all told, we had about 15 minutes a week.

Living in the Barracks

Being a squad leader gave me certain privileges not available to the other guys in the platoon. One advantage was that I did not have to live in the squad bay with the rest of the platoon. The squad bay slept about 40 guys in bunk beds that lined each wall of the room. As you can imagine, 40 people in one room would always be loud. I shared a two man room just down the hall from the squad bay with Wayne Persall, another squad leader. Wayne was kind of a dork, but he was OK.

One of the projects Sgt Henley gave us to get us to start working together as a unit was to keep a certain portion of the barracks floor waxed to a mirror like shine. He taped off a rectangle in the center of the bay about 4 tiles wide and about 25 feet long. We had to polish this piece of the floor by hand every day and night - we certainly couldn't walk on it. This project was one of the inspection points the Company Commander rated us on during his weekly inspections of the barracks.

Because of the closeness imposed upon us by the meningitis control there was a lot of potential for problems, especially in the barracks. So we had to find some sort of diversion. Sgt Cunningham provided us with that diversion.

One of the standard rules was that anytime you were in the hallway and would encounter an NCO or an Officer, you would shout "ATTENTION", and plaster yourself against the side wall of the hallway and let them pass. Depending on how these people felt at the time, they would either pass you by, or take the opportunity to get in your face about something:

> " WHAT'S YOUR FIRST GENERAL ORDER, SOLDIER?" or "NAME THE THREE MAIN PARTS OF THE M14 RIFLE, BOOT".

Anything they thought that we were supposed to know, they would ask us. Usually, if you didn't know the answer, or if you didn't answer fast enough, you would be ordered down to the floor for push-ups.

All this dialogue was done while shouting as loud as possible, both by the NCO and yourself. Even counting the push-up was done while shouting. If you weren't loud enough, they would sing out, ". . . I can't hear you soldier".

Just down the hall and across from my room lived Sgt Cunningham. Sgt Cunningham lived in the barracks and was a brand new buck sergeant. He was kind of small in stature and he didn't have that imposing bearing of some of the other seasoned DIs.

Those of us trainee leaders got together and decided to have a little fun with Sgt Cunningham and give a little harassment back to the NCOs by getting on Sgt Cunningham. I would leave the door to my room open just a crack so that I could see towards Sgt Cunningham's room. When I would hear the rustle and noise of his door as he was leaving, I'd get up and position myself by my door and would wait until he was right in front. Then, I'd swing the door open, spring out into the hallway, and scream "ATTENTION" as loud as I could and plaster myself against the hallway wall.

Sgt Cunningham would follow the usual pattern of screaming and shouting and I would end up doing some push ups. When he was done with me, I would go back into my room and close the door. He would continue down the hall for about 3 steps and when he was in from of the next door, Paul Corr or Del Holland would swing open their door, spring out into the hallway, and scream "ATTENTION" as loud as they could and then plaster themselves up against the hallway wall.

True to form, Sgt Cunningham would get in their face and the whole process would repeat.

Sgt Cunningham would be beet red with rage about this time. When he was done with them, 3 more steps and Kalil or Armstrong would be next; ". . . ATTENTION", etc. What a great time, we had a ball. We did this to him off and on for about two weeks. I think he finally moved into some other quarters somewhere else on the post.

During the week, Army life was busy and exciting. But, on weekends, it was difficult to keep the homesick blues away. Usually our weekend would start on Saturday afternoon around 2:00 p.m.. We couldn't go anywhere because of the meningitis control, so we were forced to hang around the company area.

Several times during basic, Mom and Dad would come up on a Sunday and we would "picnic" on the lawn behind the building. Mom would bring a big bowl of tuna and crackers, or tuna sandwiches, sometimes she would cook a turkey and bring up the slices of white meat for sandwiches.

I remember those warm July Sundays, looking out the window towards Monterey bay and feeling so lonely and far away.

Physical Training (PT)

One of the many purposes of basic training is to take a bunch of "out of shape" city boys and build them into a physical specimen of manhood. Everyone in the platoon was at such a different level - we had some who were obviously associated with athletics to some who never got off the couch. I was in the former group. I have been involved in sports all my life.

I went into basic at 6'3" tall and 180 pounds. Besides the daily calisthenics of jumping jacks, push ups, etc., we ran. We ran everywhere we went. Now this wasn't like running the 100 yard dash. We always ran in formation, it was called double time. For qualification, we had to run the mile.

Fort Ord's main purpose was to prepare individuals for the Army, so their athletic fields were not always at the top of their priority lists. When we ran the mile for qualification, the tracks were nothing more than an oval track plowed out by a bulldozer. Most weren't very level and most had long stretches of loose sand - sometimes it was like running on the beach.

About every two weeks we would march to one of the PT fields, strip off our fatigue shirts and run the track in our long fatigue pants, boots and T-shirts - not exactly a track uniform. But by the end of basic I could run the mile in under 6 minutes.

Tear Gas Training

"Wait till you get the gas. . . . ". This was one of the taunts by the guys in the barracks behind ours. They were about two weeks ahead of us in the training cycle and would take every opportunity to let us know that an upcoming activity would be a tough assignment. "Wait till you get the gas" was their way of telling us that tear gas training would not be a pleasant experience.

Tear gas training, like all the components of the basic training curriculum, we spent one or two 4 hour sessions in the classroom learning about the equipment associated with the process - in this case, we had to become familiar with the construction, design, and use of the gas mask. If there was the possibility of being attacked with gas by the enemy, you wanted to be sure that you knew how to get that mask on before you were overcome by the effects of the gas. Once the classroom training was complete, we then put the training into action in the field.

Field training was conducted in a small wood frame building several miles from our barracks. We were issued our gas masks from Supply and the platoon jogged to the training area. The purpose of this exercise was to experience firsthand the effects of tear gas and to develop confidence that your equipment and training would protect you.

We were instructed to put on our gas masks, walk into a building and line up against one wall. Several of our ADIs were already inside wearing their masks. On a table in the center of the room was a tin can turned upside down holding several smoldering tear gas tablets. The room was filled with a cloud of tear gas. You could feel a slight tingling sensation on those sensitive portions of your exposed skin. But with the mask on, you could breathe OK.

As ADI would walk up to each of us, we would have to take off our mask, shout our name, rank, and serial number, then put our mask back on. When PFC Weddendorf came up to me, I took a deep lung full or air, took off my mask, and shouted:

Ropele, Richard A, Private, E2, Serial Number US 56. . . . . . " Then I was out of air.

All the time, my eyes were stinging and tears were running down my face, I could feel a burning sensation on my freshly shaved face, and inside my nose. I gulped a lung full of the tear gas clouded air to finish: US56707489.

I put my mask back on, blew out the air I had to clear my mask, and the ADI moved on to the next guy. My eyes burned, you know like bad smoggy air only 100 times worse. I had my mask on and couldn't rub them.

After our squad was finished, we left the building and removed our mask and gulped breath after breath of fresh air, we rubbed our eyes and skin. The burning and stinging effects of the tear gas lingered for about 30 minutes. It was not a pleasant experience.

Tear gas does not deprive you of air, it does make it difficult to breathe, but its primary purpose is to irritate your eyes and skin. In AIT, CS gas training would be the real test. However this experience taught me that my gas mask was an effective tool and I knew how to make it work.

Pictures

Upon graduation from Basic Training, we would be given a 5 x 7 inch picture as well as a "yearbook" of our training.

The 5 x 7 picture was taken one afternoon after a typical morning of training, which usually consisted of running or crawling through the mud, dirt, or yuck of Fort Ord. Around 2:00 p.m., we went back into the barracks to get our pictures taken for our "Yearbooks".

We were told to put on only our Class A shirts, ties and coats and come back down to the dayroom for pictures. We didn't have to worry about the entire uniform because the pictures would only be from the waist up. So here we were, wearing our dirty fatigue pants and boots and the upper part of our dress uniform, shirts untucked waiting in line for pictures - everyone dirty and smelly from a day of training.

Whenever I see that picture, I marvel at how good I look and know how dirty and scummy I am just below the camera angle.

Graduation from Basic Training in August 1967

Bayonet Training

Rifle training also included learning how to work with the bayonet. Hand-to-hand combat was a real possibility and you had to understand how to win with the weapons you had. Bayonet training consisted of learning and passing basic moves:

The Thrust: While holding your weapon at the ready position (barrel pointing slightly upward, butt down against your right hip), you step forward on your left front foot and with your arms you jab the bayonet forward into the mid-section of your opponent.

The Parry: While holding your weapon in the ready position, you use the bayonet to deflect your opponents thrusts away from your midsection - kind of like sword fighting, except the sword weighs 5 pounds.

The Butt Stroke: While holding your weapon in the ready position, you step forward with your left foot to parry an opponent's thrust and swing the butt of the rifle around into your opponent's body or head. The butt stroke is most effective coming off a thrust move and sweeping the butt of the rifle in an uppercut motion into your opponent's chin.

We would check out our M14's and bayonets from the Armory, run to one of the workout areas, separate enough so we didn't stick to each other and practice all the basic moves in unison. Occasionally, we would get the practice field that had the stationary dummies and we could do all the moves against the dummy. But our most frequent training was with the pugil sticks.

Pugil sticks are wooden sticks about 4 feet long and padded on both ends with a boxing glove like device. Sgt Henley decided that training would be more intense if the men in the squad were matched against their squad leaders. So each of us squad leaders would put on a football like helmet and square off in the pit to take on each member of our squad..

As the squad leader, I knew that these guys would be gunning for me and would ultimately want to get in a good butt stroke. But neither one of us intended to get pounded by the other, so the training took on an intense approach, just like Sgt Henley intended.

I decided that right from the start, I would take an offensive approach. Each time someone would thrust, I would counter with a parry and either thrust back into their face or try to sweep a butt stroke across their head. It didn't take very many guys to get the idea that I wasn't going to be their target.

Things got a little heated as I worked my way through the 12 guys in the squad. I don't recall getting the short end of the stick very often. I wasn't going to let myself get beat up, just to be a nice guy.

Marksmanship

Marksmanship training began about our third week with familiarization of the M14 rifle. The M14 is a 7.62 mm, semi automatic, shoulder fired weapon of the infantry soldier. This weapon was the standard issue preceding the M16. Training began by taking the weapon everywhere we went. In the morning formation, we would fall out at 5:00 a.m. with our weapons and web gear, stack our weapons and go to breakfast. Come back to the formation after breakfast, pick up our weapons and march or run off to the day's activities. Wherever we went, the M14 was with us.

Certain protocols were always followed during training. If you were walking (i.e., marching) with your weapon, you carried it resting on your right shoulder ("right shoulder. . arms!)", if you were running with your weapon, you carried it at port arms ("port. . . arms!)(i.e., at a 45 degree angle across your chest). As physical fitness was one of the major purposes of basic training, we always ran to the rifle range. The rifle range was located about 2 miles from our barracks, next to the Coast Highway on the way into the city of Monterey.

As a way to foster unity and solidarity within the platoon, Sgt Henley said that if anybody fell out of the run to the range, the rest of the platoon would run in circles around the parade grounds (which was about the halfway point) until the stragglers caught up. It didn't take too many times circling the parade ground for us to realize that everyone had to pull their share of the load in order for the platoon to prosper.

But you always had someone who would try, someone who didn't care about the rest. In our platoon, that guys name was Thomas Utter. Utter would last for about the first 200 yards, then step to the side and start walking. So it was decided that we squad leaders would run at the back of our squads to "encourage" everyone to keep up the pace.

The first time Utter started to drop out, someone would grab his weapon, a couple of others of us would grab the suspenders on his web gear and hold him up and pull him along with the rest of the platoon. Utter was too fat and lazy to even try, even with all this help, so Charles Anderson would run behind him and kick him in the butt to give him more "encouragement". Utter was a loser from the get-go. We ran many circles around the parade ground because of him.

Being at the rifle range was always a difficult experience because you were so near to the real world, yet so far. While on the post, everything was Army, the people, the vehicles, the buildings, everything. But at the rifle range we were right next to Pacific Coast Highway, on the beach.

Keep in mind that this was in July, the summer sun is out, kids are out of school, people are going to the beach. It was very difficult to see all these people zipping by in their cars going about their usual business-not giving us a second thought. That's what I was doing only a month ago. It made me feel so far from home.

The first week or so, we were taught the basics of shooting, the prone position, the sitting position, standing and shooting from a foxhole. The targets were about 100 meters downrange towards the ocean (the military always talked about distance in meters - a meter is 39 inches - just 3 inches longer than a yard.).

The next week, we were permitted to load up a magazine and fire in bursts. Those people that run the range were always careful to account for all the ammunition and to ensure that no one took any live rounds back to the barracks with them. The 7.62 mm is comparable to a .30 caliber. It is a big gun and can do a lot of damage.

One morning at the range, they brought out hot chocolate. I knew I shouldn't have any because I hadn't properly cleaned and scrubbed my canteen cup, but I figured that the heat from the hot chocolate being hot would sterilize it and clear out any germs. WASN'T THAT A STUPID THOUGHT?

Montezuma caught up with me that evening and he extracted his revenge for the next two days.

Graduation and Reassignment

One morning during morning formation sometime during our last two weeks of basic training, we were notified of our next assignments. One of the DIs stood on the steps of the Company Headquarters and read off names of our next duty stations. As he would read the name and a duty station, he would then identify the "slogan" for the Post, like "Fort Sill Oklahoma, 'Home of the Artillery Support Headquarters', etc.

When he got to my name, he read; "Ropele, Fort Polk Louisiana, Infantry". Oh crap, There goes my hope of going to clerk typist school. From there on out, whenever one of the DIs would ask, ". . . WHERE ARE YOU GOING NEXT ROPELE?" I'd always have to shout, ". . . . FORT POLK, HOME OF THE TIGERS", then make a growling noise like a tiger.

On the Saturday afternoon preceding our graduation from basic training, Sgt Henley said to us that we could forgo our weekly haircut because our families and friends would be coming up for graduation. . Wow, two weeks to work with. It was really funny watching all of us in the bathrooms that following week trying to pull our 1/4 inch butch length haircut into a part.

Graduation from basic training was on Saturday, 25 August 1967 at 1:30 p.m.. Mom and Dad drove up for the occasion. The ceremony consisted of dressing in our Class A uniforms, listening to some remarks by the Training Commander and marching in review in front of the Post commander and our families. It lasted about two hours. The post commander spoke, but I don't remember anything he said.

Everybody was given a pass until 10:00 p.m. that night. Mom and Dad and I went to a seafood restaurant in Monterey for dinner. This was the first time I was able to leave the company area and the Post since 21 June. I don't remember specifically anything we talked about. They got me back to the barracks around 10:00 p.m.

That next day at Fort Ord was a busy day, packing duffel bags, turning in all the equipment we had been issued so that we could transfer to our next duty station. Everybody in the platoon knew where they were going, so there was lots of conversation about our futures. We all had an inkling of our destiny, had already been given their orders for our next duty stations and that afternoon we were bused to San Francisco and I boarded a chartered commercial plane for Louisiana.

Tom Utter was the guy during basic that wouldn't perform. He was the guy Anderson was kicking along the way to the rifle range so he would keep up running with the platoon.. When we left for Fort Polk, Utter was mowing the lawn in front of the barracks laughing about; how he was getting out of the Army and that we were going to get our butts shot off.

I saw him in a car stereo shop in Santa Ana during 1970 and he was talking about how he was going to go back in the Army and "kill me some gooks" because he had a brother killed in Vietnam. What a loser! Blowhards are everywhere you look when there is no possibility of the occurrence happening

Acting Corporal Rick Ropele, summer of 1967.
Mom and Dad came up a couple of times as
We had Sundays off. We'd sit on the lawn behind
the barracks and just visit. My Dad took all these pictures

A summer Sunday afternoon at Fort Ord - 1967

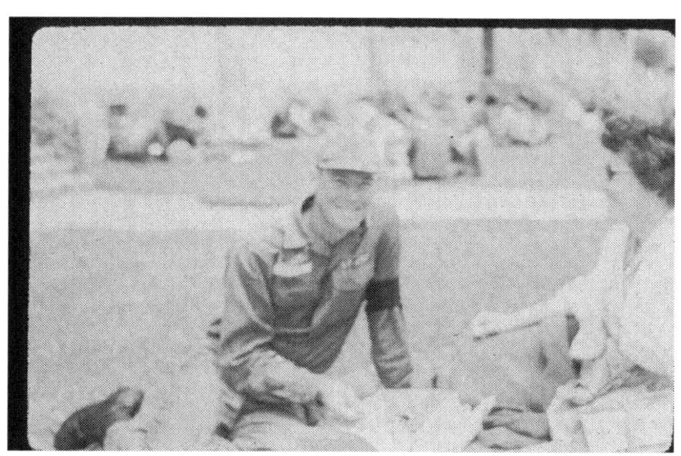

Lunch with Mom. She would have been about 50 years old then

Dad and I at Fort Ord, in the summer of 1967. Dad would have been 54 years old then. A good man who taught me a lot of things that directly contributed to my survival in Vietnam

Graduation from basic training – August 1967

Pass in review during graduation ceremonies from basis training – August 1967. I'm in the center of the picture, behind Les Kalil, the trainee platoon sergeant, leading my squad

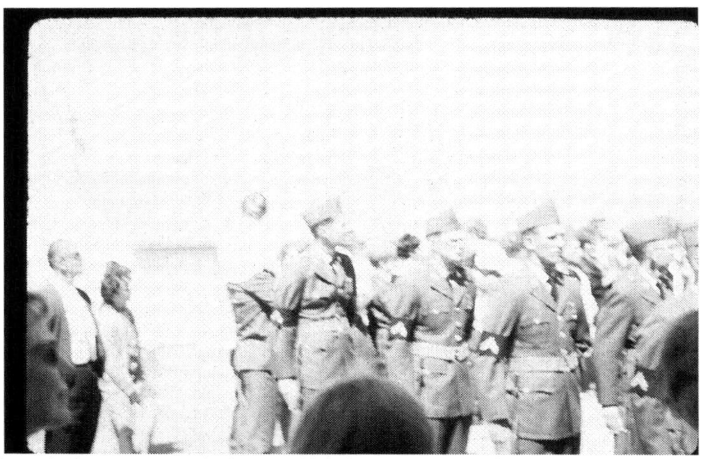

After the graduation ceremony, we had to assemble in the company area before being released for the evening. That's me in the back of the platoon and I think that's Mary Davenport standing there

Graduation day with Mom, latter part of August 1967.

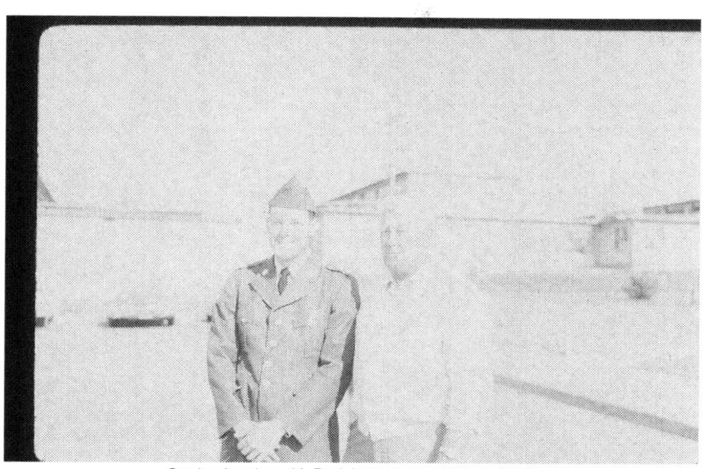

Graduation day with Dad, latter part of August 1967.

More Fort Ord pictures that my Mom and Dad had

Fort Ord graduation and my Dad and I at Uncle Buds house in Tulsa after AIT at Fort Polk. The trip with Dad was what I always referred to as my 'farewell tour' before going to Vietnam. It was possible that this would be the last time anyone would see me alive.

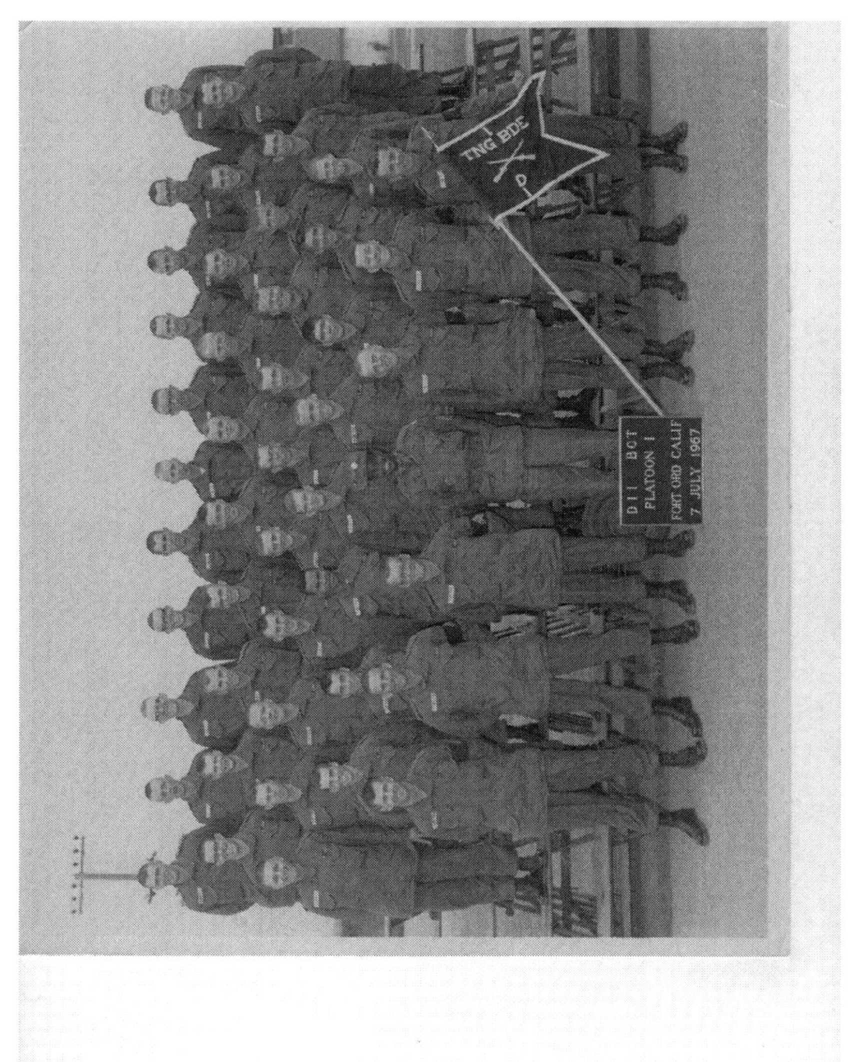
TNG BDE
D
DIT BCT
PLATOON 1
FORT ORD CALIF
7 JULY 1967

Fort Polk - Advanced Individual Training (AIT)

Welcome to Fort Polk

Our plane landed at some airport in the morning and we boarded buses for the ride to Fort Polk. If I ever thought there was a chance to get out of the infantry and into something relatively safe, that thought was beaten into the ground the minute the bus pulled into the post. Greeting us at the main gate was a billboard that read:

Welcome to Fort Polk, Louisiana

Tiger Land.

Birthplace of The Combat Infantryman for Vietnam

Oh crap, that pretty much makes it final. I might as well kiss the dream of going to clerk typist school goodbye.

Physical Conditioning

One of the purposes of Fort Polk was to ensure that our physical condition was at its peak because in just another 8 weeks we'd be running around the jungles of Vietnam, so we ran everywhere. Every day at 5:30 a.m. after formation, we would march away from the assembly area in formation and run about a mile before breakfast. We always ran in formation, usually singing some dirty cadence song to help everybody to keep in step.

Every morning the Company Commander, a Major Somebody, would run along with us. The Company Commander was 100% Army. He was a Vietnam combat veteran. He wore a Combat Infantryman's Badge (CIB) and combat jump wings. He was one of those ". . . been there, done that . . . " kind of soldier, the kind of guy you want in charge of your training.

He would wear a fresh set of starched jungle fatigues each day and would literally run circles around us. I mean literally, he would run circles around us as we ran forward in formation. He would run along the sides backpedaling as we ran forward, slide across the back of the platoon, up the other side and across the front of the formation, all the while encouraging us to put forth our best effort.

> ". . . let's go men, pick up the pace men, don't let Charlie get to you because you're not in shape, come on men , step it up . . .Charlie in shape, you need to be in better shape". . . .

He was in great physical shape and in turn made sure we had the opportunity to be in great physical shape.

One of our testing points while in training was being timed in the mile run. We would strip off our outer fatigue shirts and run in our fatigue pants, boots and undershirts. I remember running the mile between 6 and 7 minutes. This work paid off, I was in great shape by the time I left Fort Polk. I never experienced any physical problems in Vietnam keeping up with the rest of the platoon or carrying my share of the gear.

At Fort Polk, Army life became serious business. Fort Ord was kind of a lark, almost like going to scout camp, playing with guns, playing Army, that sort of thing. But at Fort Polk, I had to develop a different attitude. This was the last stop before the big one. Here I was, little Ricky Ropele, a gun in his hand, on his way to the war zone - it's time to get serious.

KP - Kitchen Police

KP was a real ordeal at Fort Polk. I never had to pull duty at Fort Ord because I was one of the trainee squad leaders, but how difficult could it be? Get out of the everyday activity, sit back in the kitchen all day long, eat all the snacks you could find. It has to be a piece of cake (no pun intended, but it shows how clever I am).

About 3:00 a.m., the night NCO wakes me up, I dress, and shuffle off to the mess hall. The mess hall is a single story wooden building next to our assembly area and feeds only our Company. The Mess Sergeant meets us at the back door and immediately begins yelling and screaming instructions and bragging about how we don't know what work is until we work for him.

I thought, "what's this guys problem"? A little too much caffeine already? Little did I know that this was normal behavior for all the cooks on the kitchen staff. I saw similar behaviors from all the mess hall personnel throughout my time in the Army.

The morning effort is to prepare for breakfast. Now, we didn't have anything to do with the food preparation - we were the clean-up crew. The Cooks cooked and we cleaned, and cleaned, and cleaned. After the 6:00 a.m. breakfast, we washed all the dishes, all the cooking pots and pans, all the serving area and dishes, all the tables and chairs and mopped the floors.

After the 10:00 a.m. and 2:00 p.m. trash pick-up, we washed all the trash cans.

After the morning clean-up process, we began preparing for lunch. Just like in the movies, we had to peel potatoes. There was this cylindrical rotating machine that would hold about 18 potatoes at a time and it would take off most of the skins. We then had to peel the remaining skin and dig out the eyes with a knife. This consumed a goodly portion of the morning.

After lunch and dinner we went through the same clean-up process as before. By the time our duty was finished, it was midnight when we were released to go back to the barracks to sleep until the 5:00 a.m. reveal. What a nasty detail. Luckily, I only had KP once.

Catching up on Sleep

Training at Fort Polk was constant and intense, both day and night. Every class and instruction period was painted as essential to survival. Seems the Army thinks that you should be able to function at peak efficiency irrespective of the amount of sleep you have acquired.

September/October in Louisiana is hot and humid. During the days we would attend outdoor classes on various subjects. It was especially difficult to stay awake after lunch and listen to the monotone voices of some of the instructors, whoa, Sleepville USA, next stop.

When you would doze off in the bleachers, the other DIs would make you get up and stand off to the side to listen. I was standing on the side listening to this guy talk about probing for land mines with your bayonet, how to mark a clear path, and the next thing I know, I'm asleep.

I found that if I positioned my body weight evenly over my legs, I could doze off until my body relaxed enough and I would lose my balance and startle myself awake. I would adjust my position and doze off again. The DIs were only paying attention to the group in the bleachers, so I could do this without fear of being caught.

Escape and Evasion Training

Escape and Evasion training was a short 2 or 3 day training course designed to teach you how to move around and take care of yourself if you got separated from your squad. We had discussions on the Geneva Convention and the rules for treating prisoners, we discussed our responsibilities if we were captured by the enemy, the Code of Conduct. The training culminated with our running a night Escape and Evasion course.

At 2:00 or 3:00 p.m., we were driven out into the boonies where they had constructed a typical Vietnamese village. We were divided into groups of 4 or 5 people, given a chicken, some knives, kindling and matches and told that was our last meal until breakfast the next morning. I was with Tom Jordan, Ed Cahill, and Ted Smith.

We gathered up some fire materials to start our fire, killed and cleaned our chicken and cooked it. As I recall, it wasn't too difficult and the chicken didn't taste bad at all. Fortunately, my Dad had taught me how to clean and prepare birds for cooking when we were quail or dove hunting. The most distasteful part is removing the feathers, they stick to everything, and birds smell really bad when you're cleaning them.

Around 6:00 p.m., they gathered everyone for an orientation to tell us what the rules were for tonight. We were to leave in our groups of four starting at 10:00 p.m., with groups leaving in 15 minute intervals. The only equipment we could take with us was our canteens and a compass. We were to travel northward for about four miles to the end of the course, being on the lookout for and avoiding being captured by the aggressors. At the end of the course, there would be trucks to take us back to our barracks.

As this exercise is supposed to reflect real life, the aggressor's purpose is to capture and interrogate, to gather intelligence information about our unit, the number of people, location, arms, etc. According to the rule of the Geneva Convention, we are only required to give our name, rank and serial number, no matter what they do to us. But we all knew that prisoners were tortured by the enemy.

After the orientation we were sent back to our areas to rest until after dark and we took the opportunity to develop our strategy. We certainly didn't want to get captured and tortured. We knew the torture wouldn't be life threatening, but we had heard from other platoons that some guys get beat up pretty badly.

We decided that we would combine with another group shortly after leaving the orientation area. Whichever group that would leave first would wait just out of sight for the second group. Our rationale was that if we thought if we were to be set upon by the aggressor force, a group of eight guys could pretty much beat the crap out of them and not get captured.

We also designed ourselves a weapon, of sorts. We all hooked our full canteens near the end of our belts and wrapped the belts around our hand. If it became necessary, we would use the canteen as a club. A full canteen of water clubbing someone in the face would do more damage than your fist.

About 10:00 p.m., our group was released from the company area. About 25 yards into the woods we met up with the other group, took our compass bearing, and started off. The night was bright with a full moon showing.

We weren't sure where or when the aggressors would pop up, so we were serious about how we moved around. We walked in a single file column and we had a point man. About a mile into our trek, we saw a blacktop road cutting through the forest, across our path. Now it didn't take a college professor to figure that if the aggressors were anywhere, they would be waiting in the underbrush across this road. We had to cross about 40 yards of open terrain before getting into the woods on the other side.

We got down on our bellies and crawled near the road to check out the situation and see if we could hear anything. We had to figure out how to cross safely. We knew we had to cross the road and we knew they would be waiting for us. They also knew we had to cross the road. Question was, how were we going to do it without getting captured? We had already heard from other training companies that those captured in this course were beat up pretty badly by the captors.

We pulled back a safe distance and discussed our options. We decided that we would get as close as we could, then all jump up and race across. If we all ran at the same time we hoped that our large group would overpower their group of aggressors waiting on the other side, some may get captured, but most would get away.

We crept back to the road again and we were just getting ready to go across when, to our surprise, another group started crossing the road about 25 yards away from us. As we expected, the other side exploded with the aggressor force running and tackling these other guys. We jumped up and retreated back into the woods to watch and wait.

These other guys got captured. Some of the aggressors walked within 6 feet of our hiding positions, but didn't see us. They brought in a truck and took these guys away. We waited another 15 minutes then crept back to the edge of the woods to put our plan in effect. At the signal, we jumped up and bolted across the road and disappeared into the woods. If there were any aggressors, they didn't come after us.

Two miles later we finished the course, boarded the trucks and went back to the barracks for the night.

The next day we had a meeting in an auditorium where they recapped the results of the Escape and Evasion effort. Congratulation and cheers for the guys that didn't break under torture. Boos and hoots for the guys that cracked. The guys they captured looked pretty ragged - besides not having any sleep the night before, some had black eyes, split lips, swollen faces, and one guy had a broken finger. I guess they worked pretty hard on these guys.

CS Gas Training

CS gas training was one of the most frightening things I ever experienced during training. The purpose of going through this training was to be able to recognize when gas has been used on you and to be able to put on your gas mask quickly, without panic.

CS gas training took place way out in the boonies of Fort Polk. They had erected a large Divisional size canvas tent to contain the gas. We walked in wearing our masks to understand that the mask does provide the necessary protection against the gas, and then to reinforce the point, we were to take off our masks while in the tent to learn what it's like when you are being attacked with gas.

So we all lined up and walked in. When it was my turn, I took a big breath, tore my mask off and tried to shout my name, rank, and serial number. I got as far as my rank and ran out of air. I gulped in a big breath and nothing. . . , I couldn't get air, I tried again and nothing. I began to wretch and gag, the more I tried to breathe, the more nothing I got and only the gas in my lungs. It doubled me over. Oh crap, is this what it's like to drown?

Luckily, the drill instructor had me by the arm and was leading me outside and away from the tent. My eyes hurt, my chest hurt so bad I could hardly draw in a breath. I had snot running out my nose and down my face. Finally, I got some air. I never thought relief would feel so good.

Everybody who came out of the tent was in the same shape. You don't know what panic is until you can't get air into your lungs. I guess this is what it's like to drown. When you can't get air, when all you get into your lungs is this gas, this certainly was the lesson of the day - the gas mask protects and CS gas is a nasty way to die.

In Vietnam, there were always several people in each squad who carried two CS gas grenades. They were used before sending someone in to investigate a tunnel complex or some other closed building.

Weapons Training

Fort Polk was my introduction to the weapons of Vietnam. The M16 was the main focus of training and qualification as it was likely the weapon most of us would carry. But we also had familiarization training on the M60 Machine Gun, the M79 Grenade Launcher, the .45 caliber pistol (issued as the sidearm to the Grenadier) and the 3.5 inch Rocket launcher (i.e., the "bazooka").

The M16 is a .223 caliber, shoulder fired, semi automatic rifle. It has a black plastic/rubber stock and fore piece and loads from a 15 round clip. It can fire semiautomatic and with the flip of a thumb switch, it can fire fully automatic. In Vietnam, firing on full automatic was not the preferred method because of how quickly you could use up your ammo, but when the command was given to "rock and roll", that's what it was. It was sweet.

Like all weapons training, we had to fire for qualification on the range. Shooting at targets to achieve a mathematical score for training and qualification is an indication of how well you've applied the principles of marksmanship - "Snug the weapon into your shoulder, line up the sights on the bullseye, take a small breath and hold it, and squeeze the trigger". These are principles I learned from my father many years earlier. I shot sharpshooter (out of Marksman, Sharpshooter, or Expert).

But in Vietnam, you don't have the luxury of time to squeeze off a shot. In a firefight, you want to put out the most firepower in the shortest amount of time, obviously into the right area, so marksmanship is important. But marksmanship takes a back seat to getting the bullets into the target area.

You bring the weapon up to your shoulder, point to the muzzle flashes, and fire a burst, BAM, BAM, BAM - adjust your point of aim and fire another burst, BAM, BAM, BAM. You keep it up until your firepower overpowers their firepower. If you can see where the bullets are landing, say in the open ground, you "walk" them into the target, BAM,. BAM, BAM, again and again, remove one magazine, toss it aside, jack in the new one, and fire, BAM, BAM, BAM, over and over.

This is the life of the infantry soldier, and if you're better than the enemy, you live.

The M60 Machine Gun was awesome. It was designed to function as the heavy weapon at the squad level. It is 7.62 mm (close to .30 caliber) and fires full automatic, and is fed by linked ammo (this is the same weapon that Sylvester Stallone used in the first Rambo movie to shoot up the town). It is equipped with bipod legs, but also has a tripod mount for a more permanent installation. While in the field, the M60 was THE WEAPON when you stepped into a firefight. The machine gunner job was always to run up to front and lay down the heaviest fire. As squad members, we either humped the belted ammo across our chest like one of those Mexican bandits or you carried an ammo can strapped to your rucksack..

Familiarization consisted of a morning session learning how to field strip the weapon (i.e., tear it down and reassemble it) and cleaning it. You never knew what you were going to be assigned to do in the squad, so you paid attention when learning these weapons.

In the afternoon, we went to the range and fired. There were about 10 guns set up on tripods and each of us were given a belt containing about 30 rounds. When it was my turn, I loaded the weapon, aimed in the direction of the target, which was about 100 yards away and fired. What a weapon. That thing really spits out the heat.

The M79 Grenade Launcher is a single shot 40 mm shoulder fired weapon. It looks like a small shotgun (it's about 2 feet long) with a muzzle diameter of about 2 inches. The grenade is loaded, fired and arms itself about 15 feet out of the muzzle (I think based on the number of rotations). Once the grenade hits, it explodes just like a hand grenade.

The Grenadier is also issued a .45 caliber pistol. We had to learn how to disassemble and reassemble it. We also fired it for familiarization.

The 3.5 MM Rocket Launcher is a shoulder fired weapon designed to blow through enemy armor and bunkers (commonly referred to as a bazooka). This 3.5 Rocket Launcher was of World War II vintage and it was not likely that we would see any in Vietnam, but it was used as a training alternative because the M72 LAW Rocket was too expensive to use.

The LAW Rocket is a weapon about 2 feet long. The rocket is encased in a fiberglass tube and has a pull down trigger mechanism and a pop up sight. Once it's fired, you crush the tube and throw it away.

This 3.5 mm launcher was an open tube of steel about 5 feet long with a diameter of about 6 inches. You rest the tube on your shoulder, snug your eye directly into the padded eyepiece, and put the crosshairs on the target. It was really disconcerting to put it against your eye. If the weapon was like the other things we fired, the recoil would surely tear your head off.

But as the name implies, the rocket is launched from the tube and all the recoil goes out the back end of the tube. I sighted in on an old armored personnel carrier down range as my target and fired my rocket and waited for the explosion and the only thing I heard was the loud CLUNK of metal hitting metal. Apparently, because of the expense, the rockets we fired didn't have an explosive warhead.

Field Training Exercise (FTX)

The last week of AIT was a three day field training exercise designed to simulate life in Vietnam. We left the company area on Monday afternoon and returned Thursday night.

Dinner that first evening was brought out on trucks from our mess hall and consisted of liver, diced potatoes, and a vegetable. If I had known that this was the last hot meal for the week, I would have eaten all I could, even though it was liver (I HATE LIVER).

The next afternoon we were issued C-Rations for dinner that day. I'll never forget my first taste.

My main course was Ham and Lima Beans (a "B Unit" which was one of the worst). After a full day of hiking through the hills of Louisiana, carrying a full pack and humping the M60 machine gun, I wanted food and I didn't care how it tasted (little did I know).

I took out my P38, ripped into the can, and shoveled a heaping spoonful into my mouth. WHOA, talk about nasty things. Cold lima beans and ham fat in some kind of sauce. Can you imagine going into your cupboard and opening a can of lima beans and eating it straight from the can? Holy cow, that was awful. Where's that liver I hated so much yesterday?

We weren't issued heat tablets during this exercise, so we had to eat every meal cold out of the can. Some of the others weren't so bad, beanies and weenies, spaghetti and meatballs, others I can't remember. But you learn to make do with what you have.

Ted Smith and I were teamed up and issued the M60 Machine Gun. Everyone's weapon had blank adapters and everyone was issued blank ammo. We carried the weapon everywhere we went.

We went to various classes, things like probing for mines, or patrol tactics, type of booby traps, different things. We also went to one of the ranges and threw hand grenades.

.At night, we had to set up a perimeter, post guards and sentries and prepare for attacks from an aggressor force that roamed around. Outside of the C-Rations, it was like a camping trip.

Graduation from AIT

Completion of AIT didn't have the pomp and ceremony that we had at Basic Training. As I recall, after breakfast we dressed in our Class A winter uniform and assembled with the Company Commander to receive our orders for our next assignment.

Big Surprise, I got orders for Vietnam, as did most everyone else in the Company. Tom Jordan was sent to NCO school at Fort Benning, Georgia. We all were given a 30 day leave and I was ordered to report to Fort Lewis, Washington, on 22 November 1968 for processing to the Republic of Vietnam.

After being dismissed, we were free to make our way home. Some people went to the travel office to make arrangements for flights home. Ted Smith flew to his home in Stillwater Oklahoma. Tom Jordan, Ed Cahill and I piled in Tom's car and began driving to Oklahoma City. Tom and Ed were from Oklahoma City and I hitched a ride with them to meet Dad in Tulsa at my Uncle Bud's house.

Tom had a car because his father was a used car dealer in Oklahoma City and one weekend with only a local weekend pass, Tom flew home and drove back to Fort Polk in this red and white 1956 Chevy. He was not allowed to have a car during training, so he kept it hidden by moving it around the post until we completed AIT.

Fort Polk was located outside of Leesville, Louisiana, almost directly east of Dallas Texas. We alternated driving and drove straight through to Oklahoma City. I think we pulled into Tulsa in the early evening. Tom and Ed dropped me at Uncle Bud's house.

This was the last time I saw Tom Jordan. I remember seeing Ed Cahill on the road outside of An Tan village when we were on the bridge in detail sometime during January 1968. He was attached to some unit of the 196th Light Infantry Brigade, which had their base camp just north of An Tan.

Traveling with Dad

Ed and Tom dropped me off at Uncle Bud's house in the afternoon and Dad was there to meet me. This was the first time I had seen any family since I left Fort Ord in August.

Dad and I stayed with Bud and his family for about two days then we flew to Chippewa Falls and visited with Uncle Bill and Aunt Ernie and Grandma Ropele. I remember that it was raining cats and dogs when we left Tulsa. We changed planes in Kansas City. Being in the military, I was required to fly in my uniform so I think we got quite a bit of attention.

I enjoyed this time alone with my Dad. Although he never verbalized it, I think he was really fearful about my future. I know how I'd feel if one of my children was going off to war.

It was good to see the relatives again and to spend time with my Dad. It didn't occur to me during this trip, but this could be the last time that I see my relatives - or the last time they could see me. Was this my farewell tour? I hope not.

The EM club was right across the street from our company area. You can see that we're back in the World War II building style

Our barracks at Fort Polk – September 1967

Inside the barracks. My platoon was on the 2nd floor. Don't know who that is sitting on the footlocker

The mess hall. This is where I pulled KP for 20 hours

Don't remember who this guy is standing in front of the orderly room. But at Fort Polk, we could get weekend liberty and leave the post that's why we have civilian clothes

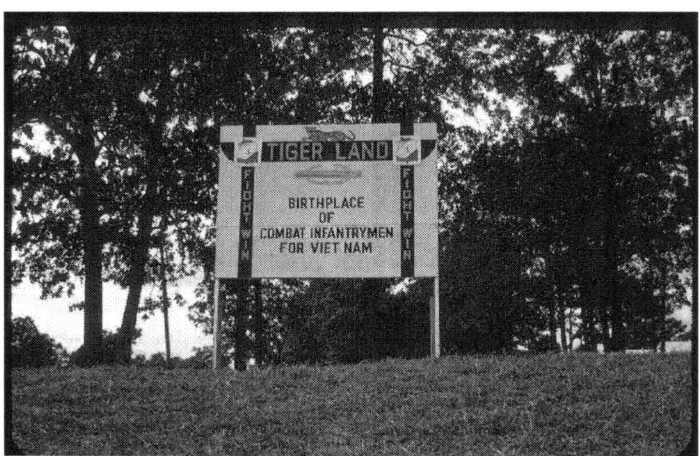

No doubt that we were here for an Infantry MOS – I guess the dream of going to clerk typist is just a dream

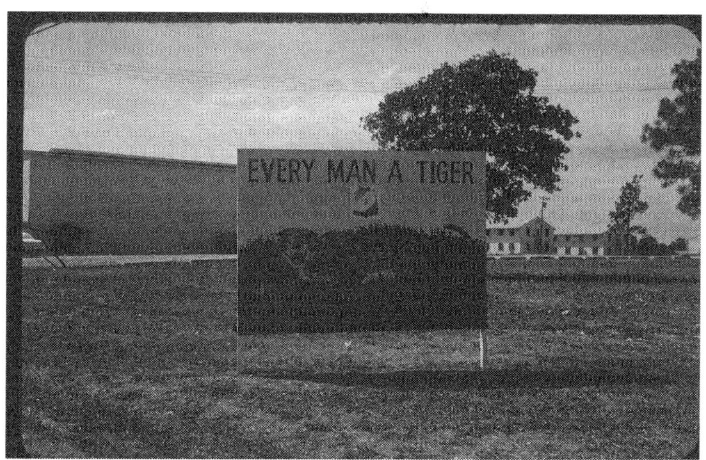

Signs around the post to inspire us

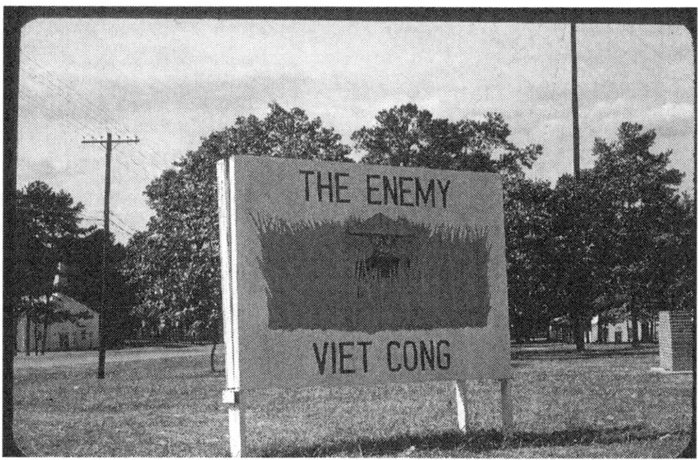

Signs around the post to inspire us

Signs around the post to inspire us

Signs around the post to inspire us

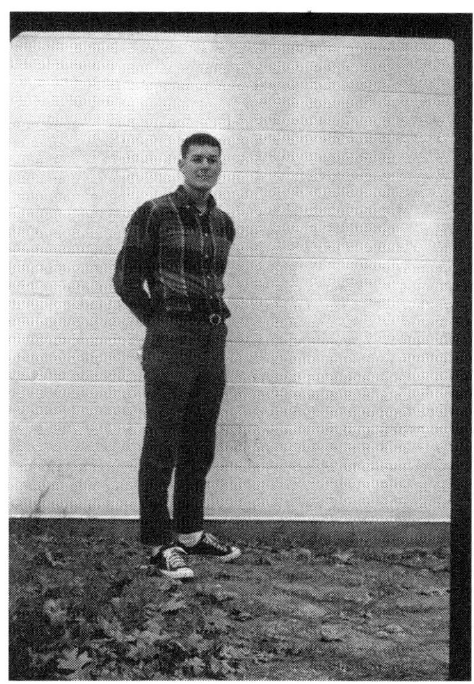

October 1967 taken at my Uncle Buds' house in Tulsa. Dad and I met in Tulsa after finishing AIT and we visited with Uncle Bud and his family, then flew to Chippewa Falls, Wisconsin to visit with Aunt Ernie and her family. I didn't connect the dots until years later, but could this visit be the last time my parents' family could see me alive if things don't work out in Vietnam? I dubbed this my 'farewell tour' – Not a bad looking stud.

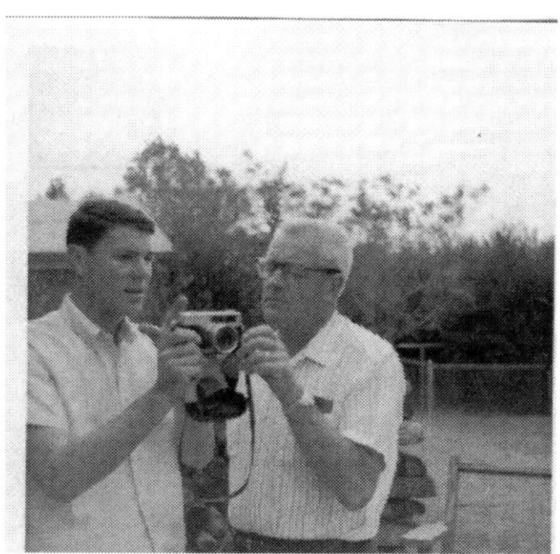

Dad and I in Tulsa in November 1967 on the Farewell Tour. Dad would have been 50 years old and I was 22. That's my 'Petri 7S' 35mm camera that I bought at the Fort Polk PX and left in my rucksack when I was medevaced from the bridge at An Tan. Never saw the camera again or my friends in the squad.

Back in those days, we took slides. I had two rolls of 36 taken on the flight over and in Vietnam that I sent home for Mom and Dad to develop. I didn't see them until some time in 1968 when I came home on convalescent leave from Fort Ord hospital. While at the bridge at An Tan, I took a number of pictures, but since I never go my camera back, I never saw those pictures

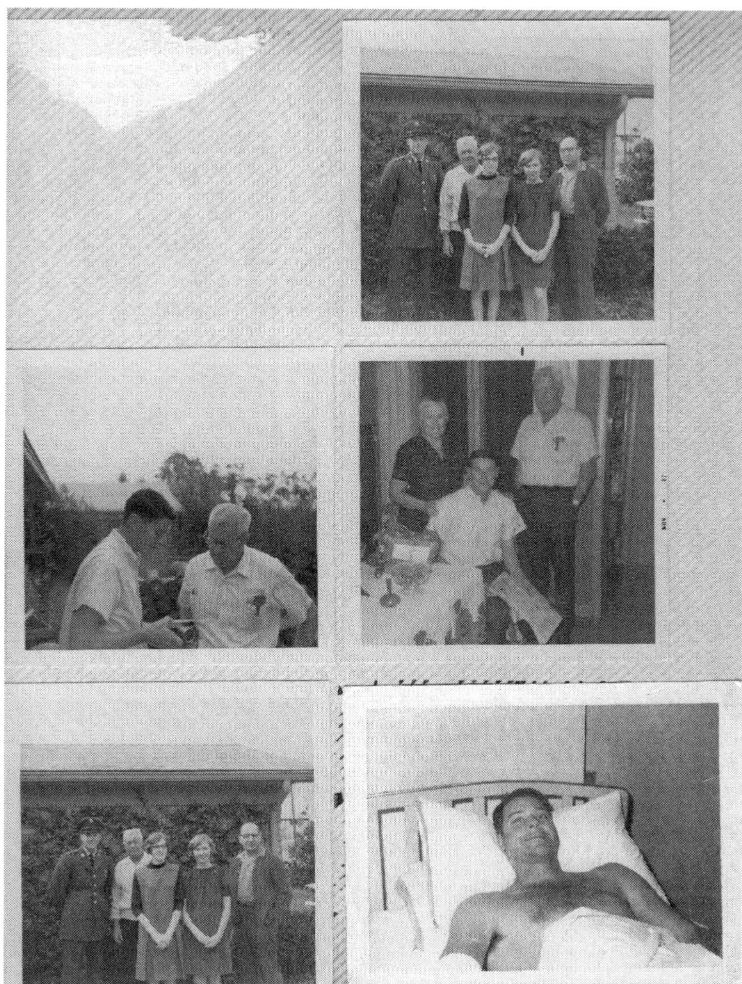

More pictures from the 'farewell tour'. That's my Dad and I with Uncle Bud and cousins Pam and Pat, Grandma Margaret while she was living in Chippewa Falls Wisconsin with Aunt Ernie (my Dad's sister). This is me in the hospital in Japan in February 1968 – this is the picture I sent to Mom and Dad when I notified them of the circumstances and the extent in which I had been injured.

Fort Lewis Washington

Leaving Orange County

I had orders to report to Fort Lewis Washington on Monday, 21 November 1967, no later than 11:59 p.m. I didn't want to be late, so I had Mom and Dad take me to the airport for a Sunday afternoon flight. Being where you're supposed to be, when you're supposed to be there is serious business in the Army - especially concerning those individuals on their way to Vietnam. The Army takes a real dim view of those people that are Absent Without Leave (AWOL). I wasn't going to take any chances of being late.

I don't remember much about what we discussed on the way to the airport, but I hope I wasn't acting too much like a macho smartass. I do remember thinking that this great adventure is about to begin. I hope I come back to talk about it.

You know, I never really had any major worries about losing my life - I knew it was a distinct possibility and I was concerned, but it wasn't an overriding thought. I rationalized that there were a lot of guys that have gone to Vietnam before me and they didn't get killed, so maybe I would be one of those lucky ones.

I don't know if that's a normal thought process, but that's how I handled the situation. I thought maybe I'll get wounded or something, but killed, no, I don't think so.

Fort Lewis Washington

I flew to Seattle/Tacoma airport from John Wayne airport on Sunday, 20 November, and stayed the night in a motel close to the airport. I had to report to Fort Lewis in the morning. November in the Pacific Northwest is cold and overcast. The sky was gray, the air was wet and looked like rain.

Fort Lewis was the West Coast gathering point for soldiers going to Vietnam and one of its purposes was to do the administrative things necessary for us to ship out to a war zone. I was assigned to a company and put in the barracks. I spent two days at Fort Lewis.

We had to fill out and update insurance papers, beneficiary forms, next of kin notification papers, etc. I turned in the basic issue of clothing that I got at Fort Ord and drew clothing for Vietnam.

We were issued jungle boots, jungle fatigues, olive drab boxer shorts, socks, and T-shirts. You certainly wouldn't want to be in the jungle with someone wearing white shorts and T-shirts - you would be a major target. We also got these little plastic clips to put on our dog tags so they wouldn't clink together.

The barracks were World War II style wooden buildings just like we had at the Fort Ord Reception Center and were heated by coal furnaces. Burning coal makes a particular smell and coal dust is everywhere, I suppose even in your lungs. Everything you touched had a layer of coal dust on it. I remember one morning grabbing the overhead rafter to swing myself out of the top bunk and when I put my hand on the sheet, it was instantly covered in black soot.

We were scheduled to ship out on 24 November. We dressed in our summer Class A khaki uniform (short sleeve uniform) and loaded into buses for the trip back to Seattle/Tacoma airport to board a Northwest Orient commercial jetliner. It didn't even register to me that today was Thanksgiving. We left Fort Lewis Washington on the first leg of our journey to Cam Ranh Bay, Vietnam. The route was through Anchorage Alaska stopping for fuel, then across the Pacific Ocean to Japan, and then down into Vietnam.

I guess I was now what the United States Army considered a finely tuned fighting machine. I was a "veteran" of five months, having completed basic and advanced infantry training. The five months had been a whirlwind of activity, excitement, anxiety, and apprehension. Today, I knew for sure where my future would be decided.

Now, on Thanksgiving day 1967, I was one of some 200 other soldiers on an airplane heading to Vietnam. I sat next to Ted Smith and John Harrold. Ted had a pocket chess set and taught me how to play.

Fort Lewis Washington – These are pictures that Rod took when he went up there for predeployment training before he shipped out to Iraq. Still using the World War II barracks

Fort Lewis Washington

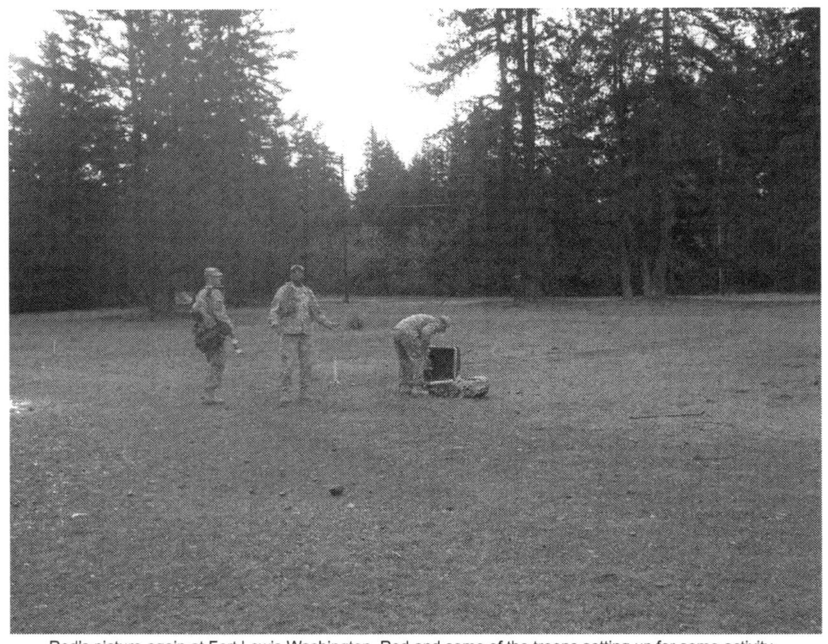

Rod's picture again at Fort Lewis Washington. Rod and some of the troops setting up for some activity

Thanksgiving Dinner in Anchorage

We left Fort Lewis Washington on the morning of the 23rd of November 1967. I was one of some 200 – 300 servicemen aboard a Northwest Orient 727 flight to Vietnam. I was 22 years old and this was the beginning of the 'biggest adventure' of my life. What did the next year hold in store? Where would I be 365 days from now?

Our plane stopped in Anchorage Alaska about 2:30 in the afternoon before crossing the Pacific for Japan. I assumed it was for refueling, as we had to disembark and go into the terminal. As you all know, airports are such depressing places to wait, and this one was no exception. It was practically empty. I think they must have had a minimum staff working because of the holiday.

While waiting, I took the opportunity to call home. I knew my family would be celebrating Thanksgiving, as usual with the Monroy family at Nana and Grandpa's house.

Nana and Grandpa are Monroy's grandparents. They lived in Tustin and I had known them all my life. My brother Don and I grew up with the Monroy kids, Jeff, Linda, and Rod. They are just like brothers and sisters, their parents, Betty and Larry are just like my parents. My folks established traditions for us for moments just like this. I knew what they were doing and I wanted them to know where I was and what I was doing. I talked to everybody, Mom and Dad, Don, Jeff, Rod, and Linda, everybody.

It was so good to hear the voices of my parents, my brother, and my friends. When I hung up the phone, I had a warm feeling all over, I could feel their love and concern for me. I felt so good, yet it was the classic good news/bad news scenario.

The good news was that I was able to reconnect with my family on this holiday, and the bad news was that I realized again just how far away I was. I felt so lonely, so far away, and with the future so uncertain, so vulnerable (hope I come out of this OK without too many scars).

During the refueling process, a snow storm blew in and closed the airport preventing us from continuing our flight until the next day. The military made arrangements for us to spend the night at the American West Hotel in downtown Anchorage and leave again the following day. John Harrold and I shared a room. It was after 5:00 p.m., by the time we were settled into our rooms. Because it was Thanksgiving, the hotel notified us that Thanksgiving dinner was being served in the dining room and we were welcome to eat our fill.

I was anxious to feel those holiday celebration feelings and enjoyment, John, and me and my "family of 727 companions" readily accepted the invitation. When you remember that we anticipated Thanksgiving dinner on the airplane (can you imagine, airplane food for Thanksgiving, holy cow). We feasted on turkey, mashed potatoes, and all the trimmings, pumpkin pie. You name it and the hotel served it. We ate and we talked and we relaxed. Those anxious feelings about our futures were temporarily put in the background.

It was after this dinner that I was privileged to be on the receiving end of an extraordinary act of compassionate service. You know, some life changing experiences happen boldly and noisily and you realize at the time that you won't be the same person after it's over. This is one of those experiences that came along simply and quietly. It's only later, when you have time to reflect, that you understand the deep and immense impact that has taken place in your soul.

John and I were leaving the dining room, walking down a corridor leading from the dining room to the Hotel lobby. We were going back to our room, watching a little television and going to bed, when I felt the touch of a child's hand in mine. I looked down into the eyes of a young boy, 5 or 6 years old, he grasped my hand tightly in his and began pulling me across the lobby while calling, "Daddy, Daddy, I got one, I got one".

It was then that I became more aware of the surroundings. The hotel lobby was filled with people, with families, children, people were everywhere. These were local residents of Anchorage. Unbeknownst to us, a local radio station had broadcast the news that a plane load of soldiers, bound for Vietnam, had been stranded for the night because of the storm. This station suggested that it would be a nice gesture if the residents of Anchorage would invite these soldiers into their homes for Thanksgiving dinner. And boy did these good people respond.

John and I had the good fortune to be "captured" by the Robert Cacy family. Like the other local residents in the hotel that night, the Cacy family interrupted their Thanksgiving celebration to drive downtown in a snow storm, to share their time, their meal and most importantly, their family with us.

They drove us to their home where we sat down and had a real family style Thanksgiving dinner, turkey, potatoes, dressing, gravy, just like the one my family was having at home. We didn't tell them we had just eaten at the hotel. The enjoyment of the evening was not in the food, but in the company and in their compassion for us. We ate, we talked, we laughed, we watched football - we did those things that families do when they are together during the holidays.

The evening was magical. Thoughts of our present circumstances and our immediate future were temporarily put into the background as we enjoyed the sacrifice and the graciousness of this good family. I felt like I was at home.

After dinner, they drove us to see some of the sites of Anchorage and returned us to our hotel about 9:00 p.m. After wishing us well, they left. Just as quietly as they came into our lives, they were gone, without fanfare. The next day we left Anchorage to continue our journey.

Every time I sit down to a Thanksgiving dinner, I ALWAYS remember this experience. Even to this day, even now when I'm writing these words, I can still feel that little child's hand squeezing mine and I can still hear those words that made me feel so at home, ". . . Daddy, Daddy, I got one, I got one . . .".

The Cacy family wrote the following letter to Mom and Dad.

> To the Ropele family.
>
> You don't know us, however we had the pleasure of meeting your son on Thanksgiving day. The plane he was on going to VietNam was grounded here in Anchorage at about 2:30 pm. There was a general appeal on the radio to invite the boys from the plane home for dinner. We were happy to have your Rick as one of our guests.
>
> He is certainly a fine young man. We were very pleased by his whole outlook with regard to going overseas. We have a boy on his way over there also. He is in the Navy. His ship is the USS Manley, a destroyer – He has been in the Navy a year. Rick said he had been in the five months – We lived in Escondido, CA in 1956 – 57 – 58. We are familiar with the area you live in. Rick was telling us of the big forest fire you had. My father in law had also mentioned it. He still lives in Escondido.
>
> Our prayers will be with Rick and the many others who are in Viet Nam.
>
> Sincerely,
>
> The Robert Cacy family.

I didn't realize until years later what an impact these people and their compassion would have on my life. I can't help but think how that scripture in Matthew 25: 35 – 40 applies:

35. For I was an hungered, and ye gave me meat: I was thirsty, and ye gave me drink: I was a stranger, and ye took me in:
36. Naked, and ye clothed me: I was sick, and ye visited me: I was in prison and ye came unto me.

37. Then shall the righteous answer him, saying, Lord, when saw we thee an hungered and fed thee? Or thirsty, and gave thee drink?
38. When saw we thee a stranger, and took thee in? or naked and clothed thee?
39. Or when we saw thee sick, or in prison, and came unto thee?
40. And the King shall answer and say unto them, verily, I say unto you, inasmuch as ye have done it unto one of the least of these my brethren ye have done it unto me.

I was "one of the least of these" that the savior spoke about. I was "hungered" and "thirsty" for that closeness that exists in families. I was in "prison" in the sense that my future was certainly not in my control. I was a "stranger" in Alaska on Thanksgiving, 23 November 1967 and the Robert Cacy family "took me in".

The Cacy family physically left my life that night of November 23rd, 1967, but there will always be a place in my heart for them as their extraordinary act of kindness continues to burn bright within my heart.

Extraordinary people.

Landing at the Alaska airport

The terminal at the Alaska airport

View from the hotel window of downtown Anchorage

View from the hotel window of the bay in Anchorage

View from the hotel window of the bay in Anchorage

Arriving in Japan

The next morning we awoke, had breakfast in the hotel restaurant and boarded our plane to continue the journey.

Several hours later, we landed in Japan, either to refuel or to change planes (I don't remember which). At any rate we again had to disembark and wait. I'm really seeing the world now – Japan, the mysterious orient. I'm halfway around the world. This might be the only time I get over here in my life. I want to get out and look around, see the sights. This is going to be cool.

But, when we got off the airplane, we didn't go into the terminal. We went into a large hangar- like place. There were soldiers all over, everybody sort of milling around. I don't think we landed at the commercial airport. This is either the Air Force base or the Northwest Orient maintenance area.

I didn't even see any real Japanese.

While waiting, I ran into Les Kalil and Dwight Mumm. Mumm was the ultimate "make love not war" hippie during basic training, but he was either dumber than a stone or the smartest guy there. After basic training, Mumm was sent to Artillery school at Fort Sill Oklahoma, and now here he was in Japan on his way to Vietnam. However, this time his foot was in a cast. He told me that during his 30 day leave after AIT, he had one of his friends break his foot hoping that would keep him from going to Vietnam. Obviously, it didn't work, because here he is - same as me.

After about a two hour layover, we boarded the plane again to continue our flight to Cam Ranh Bay.

Flying across the Pacific Ocean to Japan or to Vietnam

Flying across the Pacific Ocean to Japan or to Vietnam

Flying across the Pacific Ocean to Japan or to Vietnam

Flying across the Pacific Ocean to Japan or to Vietnam

Flying across the Pacific Ocean to Japan or to Vietnam. Look at that little island down there.

Vietnam Replacement Depots

Cam Ranh Bay Replacement Depot

Arriving in Vietnam wasn't the "eye opener" that you would have thought it would be. I envisioned tent city types of establishments, base camps they were called, that were carved out of the jungle, military people living in sandbag bunkers, Vietnamese people living in thatched huts. I figured every soldier would be carrying a gun all the time.

But, Cam Ranh Bay is like any military base, it was one of the largest American military complexes in Vietnam. From its look it could have been any military base back in the United States. Everywhere you looked there were military personnel, aircraft, buildings, and equipment. I didn't see any Vietnamese. Heck, we might as well have been back in Louisiana.

I can see why Fort Polk was so tailored to Vietnam training. Walking off the plane was like walking into an oven - the heat and humidity was absolutely intense, just like Louisiana.

I can't remember specifically how we were moved from the plane to our company area, but we were assigned to a replacement company, moved into a barracks complex, given a schedule for the next day's activities and told to wait until evening formation for more instructions. The barracks were wooden structures with tin roofs, protected by sandbags about 4 feet high on the outside. The insides were lined with cots, mattresses and lockers. Ted Smith and I selected our bunks and settled in until dinner.

Morning formation the next day was as usual. The platoon sergeant would call out the names of those individuals who would be transferring to their next unit. These guys would then be excused to go into the mess hall first, and then gather their stuff and leave that morning. The Platoon Sergeant would then stroll through the rest of the formation and randomly select people for different duties to be done that day.

I figured I didn't come to Vietnam to do KP work or to do somebody's "gofer" work, so after not being given an assignment that first day, Ted and I decided that we just wouldn't show up for morning formation tomorrow and we would go after the platoon was dismissed to find out if our names were called for reassignment – I wasn't going to wash a bunch of dishes.

If we got in trouble we figured we could plead ignorance. What could they do about it anyway, send us to Vietnam -we were already there.

So the next day when the company went to formation, Ted and I just walked around the area. We actually saw some Vietnamese working in the kitchen areas. Later we asked the platoon sergeant ". . . . hey Sarge, did you call Ropele or Smith, someone was talking and we couldn't hear very well". He groused around a bit about not paying attention and how that could get us killed, but then told us, yea in fact our names were called and we had been assigned to the Americal Division outside of Chu Lai and we would be leaving that afternoon.

We didn't have to worry about packing, as we never really unpacked. We weren't issued weapons. We were traced back to the flight line around 10:00 am, and climbed aboard a C130 for the flight to Chu Lai.

The C130 is the short haul, heavy cargo transport aircraft for the Air Force. It's designed to carry a lot of weight and use only a short amount of runway. Cargo and personnel are loaded from the back. The tail drops down and you can drive or walk up the ramp into the cargo bay. This plane is probably big enough to hold four army tanks.

We walked up the ramp, found a place on the floor, and sat on our duffel bags to wait for takeoff. The back end was filled with guys. The ramp was raised and we took off. Like all military aircraft designed for transport, the weight of the plane was reduced to ensure that maximum cargo could be loaded - therefore, there was no insulation between the fuselage and the engines - plus there was a two foot gap between the tailgate ramp and the top of the plane. With the roar of the engines and the air rushing in through the tailgate, it was noisy. You couldn't hear yourself think, let alone talk to anybody.

Chu Lai Replacement Depot

Fortunately, the flight from Cam Ranh Bay was only about an hour and we landed at Chu Lai air base. Chu Lai is a major air support base located in I Corps (the northernmost portion of the country). Regarding the origin of Chu Lai air base and An Tan village, I took the following from the book, "Vietnam War Almanac ", by Harry G. Summers, Jr.

> Located on the South China sea in Quang Tin Province, I Corps, Chu Lai was not even a town until the U. S. Marines constructed a major base there. When Marine Lieutenant General Victor H Krulak selected the site for an airfield, a naval officer accompanying him remarked that the place looked good but was not marked on the maps. Krulak replied that the name was Chu Lai but later explained: "I had simply given him the Mandarin Chinese characters for my name."
>
> A major port and jet-capable airfield were constructed there, It was headquarters for the South Vietnamese Army's Second Division, and at one time or another elements of the U. S. Marines First Division, South Korea's Second Marine Brigade and the U. S. Army's Americal Division were also stationed there. Chu Lai fell to the North Vietnamese during the Final Offensive.

After landing, we were loaded into the back of a deuce and a half (a 2 1/2 ton truck) and were taken to our final replacement depot. This place was a large two story wooden structure. It reminded me of an old frontier trading post. The upstairs was one large room lined with single beds; the windows were without glass and screens.

This was the first time I actually saw Vietnamese people in their natural environment. Were they all Viet Cong? Were they all waiting to kill an unsuspecting GI? Why doesn't someone give me a gun? I guess I'll have to wait to find out.

We still hadn't been issued weapons. Hope nothing happens.

One afternoon, I was looking out the window on the 2nd floor, watching people on the road that ran in front of the barracks. The women all wore similar attire - billowy leg black trousers and a kind of an ankle-length tunic top, that was split up to the waist. All of a sudden, this one lady in a group of 3 other women steps off the road into the field and squats down.

> "HEY, what's she doing over there? Was she planting a land mine? Was she planting boobie traps? Was she planting weapons to be used against us later that night?"

No, she was taking a crap. She squatted down, lowered her trousers and did her business right there in the wide open spaces. Holy cow, these people are really uninhibited.

Well, it's apparent that they do have the same biological functions as we do, and there are no public restroom facilities available out in the boondocks, so they do what they have to do. These peasants are very practical people. These are people who live in houses made of bamboo and palm fronds, homes that have dirt floors, people who fertilize their rice paddies with human excrement. Of course, they don't have public bathrooms.

We were only at this replacement facility overnight. The next day a bunch of us were loaded onto a truck and driven about 5 miles south on Highway 1 to the base camp of the 198th Light Infantry Brigade (referred to as LZ Bayonet). Ted and I were assigned to E Company of the 1st Battalion, 6th Brigade, of the 198th Light Infantry Brigade, of the Americal Division. There were about 30 guys assigned to various units there.

Flying into Cam Ranh Bay Vietnam

Flying into Cam Ranh Bay Vietnam

Flying into Cam Ranh Bay Vietnam

Flying into Cam Ranh Bay Vietnam

Flying into Cam Ranh Bay Vietnam

This is the C130 on which we flew from Cam Ranh Bay to Chu Lai

198th Light Infantry Brigade-Americal Division

Our base camp was located on a hill above a village that was called "Nook Mao" (I don't know the correct spelling, but this would be the phonetic spelling) and was known as LZ Bayonet. We were about 5 miles south of Chu Lai on Highway One. Base camp was built into the contours of the hills-all the buildings were wooden, some with sheet metal roofs, others were tent buildings (wooden floors and sides with tent roofs), administration buildings, mess halls, jeeps, trucks, roads, etc. There were guard posts and military police at all the entrances. Sandbag bunkers were built around the perimeter to protect the camp and the whole camp was ringed with barbed wire and razor wire (circumference of the camp must have been 5 or 6 miles).

The following was extracted from the book, "Vietnam War Almanac", Colonel Harry G. Summers, Jr., regarding the history of the Americal Division and its performance during the Vietnam war:

> The Americal Division was formed on the battlefield in World War II, deriving its name from the phrase "Americans in New Caledonia". an island in the South Pacific that it defended from Japanese attack. In October 1942 the Americal Division became the first U. S. Army unit of World War II to go on the offensive, taking part in the attack on Guadualcanal.
>
> During the Vietnam war it became necessary in February 1967 to reinforce Marine units operating in I Corps in Vietnam's northernmost provinces. Army brigades from the First Cavalry, Fourth Infantry and 101st Airborne Divisions along with the 196th Brigade served initially under a combat headquarters called Task Force Oregon until September 1967, when the Americal Division, as in World War II, was activated on the battlefield, releasing the divisional brigades to return to their parent units and in their place bringing together three previously independent units - the 11th, 196th and the 198th Light Infantry Brigades. The Americal Division (officially designated the 23rd Infantry Division) consisted of 11 battalions of light infantry (the Second and Third Battalions, First Infantry; the Fourth Battalion, Third Infantry; the First Battalion, Sixth Infantry; the First Battalion, 20th Infantry; the Third and Fourth Battalions 21st Infantry; the Fourth Battalion, 31st Infantry; the First and Fifth Battalions, 46th Infantry; and the First Battalion, 52nd Infantry).
>
> Its other combat elements included one armored Cavalry squadron (the First Squadron, First Cavalry, which had been and is again part of the First Armored Division), two armored reconnaissance troops (Troop E, First Cavalry and Troop F, 17 Cavalry) and an air reconnaissance troop (Troop F, Eight Cavalry); and six battalions of artillery - three with 105 mm howitzers (the Sixth Battalion, 11th Artillery; the First Battalion, 14th Artillery; and the Third Battalion, 82nd Artillery), two battalions with 155 mm howitzers (the Third Battalion, 16th Artillery and the First Battalion, 82nd Artillery); and the Third Battalion, 18th Artillery with 8-inch howitzers and 175 mm guns. The Division also had its own aviation group, with three battalions of assault helicopters and gunships and two companies of assault support helicopters. In effect, the division's air mobility was equal to that of the designated airmobile divisions (the First Cavalry and the 101st Airborne).
>
> The Americal Division fought continuously in the three southern provinces of I Corps; but as in World War II, elements of the division were dispatched to other areas, fighting at the side of U. S. Marine units along the DMZ and in other northern provinces in the I Corps area. Unlike most of the Army units in Vietnam, which battled Viet Cong guerrillas, the Americal Divisions combat operations were primarily against North Vietnamese regulars. The Americal Division less the 196th Infantry Brigade was deactivated in December 1971. The 196th Brigade remained in Vietnam until June 1971 and was the last U. S. combat brigade to depart Vietnam.

The Americal Division was awarded the Cross of Gallantry with Palm by the South Vietnamese government in recognition of its combat service. Soldiers of the division won 11 Medals of Honor for bravery on the battlefield. While overall casualty figures are difficult to obtain because the Americal Division was a composite unit, some 5,400 soldiers killed or wounded in Vietnam, the 196th Light Infantry Brigade suffered 6,610 soldiers killed or wounded and the 198th Light Infantry Brigade suffered some 5,555 killed or wounded. The 17,565 casualties suffered by these three brigades alone were more than four times as high as the 4.209 casualties the entire Americal Division suffered in World War II.

Although the Americal Division is no longer on active duty there is an Americal Division Veterans Association that publishes a periodic newsletter. Further information can be obtained from Mr. William L. Dunphy, 247 Willow Street, West Roxbury, Massachusetts 02132. The association also maintains a museum at Fort Devens, Massachusetts.

Introduction and Welcome

Upon arrival we were assigned cots in the platoon tent, given footlockers, and were issued M16s, web gear, and a basic supply of ammunition. This was the war zone and you didn't go ANYWHERE without your weapon and ammo. While in base camp, you didn't keep a round in the chamber, but you always kept the magazine in.

Initially, I didn't get a steel pot because they didn't have any in Supply. I felt very vulnerable for that first week until I was able to take one from some Vietnamese PFs. We found their living quarters under a bridge in the village of Bien Son and I took this helmet that was there. I figured the Americans originally issued it to the Vietnamese, and I was an American that needed it more than this guy, so I figured to hell with him.

Later that afternoon, we were taken to the Brigade Commander (I don't remember his name) where he welcomed us into his command, told us about our mission, then told us about his plans for running the outfit.

He proudly told those of us assigned to E Company that he had just formed E Company into his fifth line company and given them their own Area of Operation to work. Previously, E Company had been a support company and would only go out into the field if another unit needed assistance. But since he had received such a large influx of replacements, he decided that he could staff E Company sufficiently to function as a full-fledged line company.

I didn't know whether this was good news or not. To stay around base camp and only pull perimeter security at night would be real easy, but the alternative of which was not so good, was that whenever you were called out to the field, you knew you were going to get involved in a real heavy situation immediately. But like anything else in Vietnam, you adjusted your rationale in order to deal with your situation as best you can and hoped that it wasn't your time.

The 198th Light Infantry Brigade had just arrived in the country in October 1967, so even the "older guys" (defined as being in the country longer than us new guys – sometimes referred to "FNGs") didn't have much experience. I was assigned to the 4th squad, Ted Smith was assigned to the 2nd squad. My squad leader was Sgt Mouton. Douglas Dennis, John Hasbrook, Henry Pickett, Doug Radar and I were riflemen, John Haselbauer and some redheaded guy were the grenadiers and Willie Grissom was the machine gunner. Charlie Denning was the platoon sergeant and Lt. Livingston was the platoon leader. There were a couple of others in the squad, one being the radio man, but I can't remember their names.

Getting Acclimated

The first couple of days in base camp we would take "day trips" to acclimate us new guys to the weather, to the terrain, and to the people. They could be day trips, but we didn't know for sure, so we would have to load up with a full load, ammo, C-rations, put on our web gear, and rucksacks and work the local area.

We even had to hump extra ammo for the M60 machine gun. Everyone was given two bandoleers of machine gun ammo that we draped across our chest (just like the Mexicans bandits in those old cowboy movies). The way an infantry squad operates is that if the squad runs into some stuff, the machine gunner hustles up to the front of the column where he can provide the most intense fire support. Everyone then runs past his position and drops off their bandoleers.

This made for a full load. Machine gun ammo is heavy and uncomfortable. Not only do the bandoleers weigh on your shoulders (along with your rucksack and your web gear), but the tips of the bullets and the metal links on the belts dig into your neck and shoulders. But the discomfort is well worth the firepower the machine gun provides.

Our area of operation was typical of the northern coastal provinces, characterized by low rolling hills and valleys and rice paddies. The flat lands were cultivated into rice paddies. More inland, the hills were steeper and more dense with brush and trees. If you weren't following a trail or a road, walking through the brush could be a very "cutting" experience. However, it rarely did ever require a machete to hack a path.

The weather was always really hot and humid, it rained everyday. The watchword for an infantryman was to keep ;your feet dry. If your feet got wet and you didn't do anything about it, you could get all kinds of foot funguses and things. Between the rain and walking in the rice paddies, it was always a battle to keep your feet dry.

I remember the first couple of times it started to rain while out on patrol. Here we are, walking around the jungle and the rain starts. Back in the world, your first thought is ". . . I don't want to get wet, how can I keep myself dry, where can I go?" Obviously, in the jungle there is no place to go. By the time you took off your rucksack and got your poncho out and on, the rain had stopped or if it didn't once you started walking while wearing this rubber poncho, you got very hot and sweaty.

After going through this quandary several times and trying different rain devices, you came to the same conclusion that the "older guys" already knew that you were going to get wet. It's a lot of trouble to stay dry and sometimes, it's just not worth the effort. You knew that when the rain stopped, you would dry out in about 15 or 20 minutes.

So this is one aspect of life in Vietnam-if it rained, you got wet, when it stopped raining, you dried out. Wet or dry, it didn't matter, you still had to go about your business. If it rained at night, you got wet, if you could sleep wet, OK, otherwise you didn't sleep.

I tell others if they want to experience a night in Vietnam, try this: The next time it rains, go out into your backyard, crouch down into the bushes in your flower bed, stay awake all night in the rain and wait for somebody to walk by so you can shoot – because if someone was walking around at night and they weren't wearing any army uniform, they must be a bad guy and your job was to shoot them.

I remember one night laying on the wet ground, my helmet for a pillow, and covering up with my poncho trying to keep the rain off and trying to sleep. To this day, I can't stand being out in the rain, "I can't stand getting wet with my clothes on."

The people in the countryside were mostly farm villagers working the rice paddies immediately surrounding their village. They lived in thatched huts with dirt floors. They had chickens and pigs - small livestock. I never did see any large oxen. This is where the VC were during the day, kind of like our National Guard, only instead of doing their military thing on the weekends, they would do theirs at night.

There was a whole other class of people who lived in the villages along Highway One. These were the "commercial business people" who made their biggest living off the soldiers. Everything you could want was available in the towns adjacent to Highway One. These villages offered everything, radios, batteries, cigarettes, food, prostitutes, drugs, beer, etc.

Each village in the boondocks was basically an agricultural co-op working a rice crop. The village would be in the center surrounded by rice paddies usually with a road going into the center of the village. Each rice paddy was a rectangular shape, maybe 100 by 300 feet, with 2 foot high dikes to hold in the water.

One of the most critical things we learned during this brief acclimation period was where it was safe to walk. Sometimes the most attractive path was also the most deadliest. The VC were very good at planting booby traps.

It's human nature to walk the "path of least resistance." The VC knew this and would place their booby traps and landmines accordingly. When crossing a rice paddy, you never walked on the dikes surrounding the paddies. No matter how much you wanted to keep your feet dry, you always walked through the paddy, through the water, stepping over the dikes.

Sometimes this principle was difficult to follow. You were always changing your socks in an effort to keep your feet dry to avoid any foot disease. So if you could keep out of the water, that's what you wanted to do. But it's not a good idea. We hardly ever entered a village using their main road, not a safe thing to do. More often than not, we would come out of the jungle in a skirmish line formation and across the paddies.

Most of December 1967 was spent out in the field. We would come back into base camp for a day, maybe two, but would go right back out again.

Base Camp-Perimeter Security

I remember those first few nights in base camp. While waiting for the company to return from the field, we didn't have the luxury of just sleeping through the night. Every night around 5:00 p.m., several of us were selected and assigned to perimeter security - bunker guard as it was called.

The base camp was 2 or 3 miles in circumference and ringed with razor wire and sandbag bunkers placed every 30 feet. Each bunker was 6 feet square, sandbags piled up to 4 feet high, then open to the roof. The roof had a two foot overhang and was sheet metal covered in sandbags. Each bunker was manned by 2 guys all night who alternated between sleeping and guarding.

I remember my first night on guard and how alert I was. Apprehension doesn't even begin to describe the heights of my emotions and instincts. I was sure that tonight was the night of the big attack. You know how at night, every sound is amplified, every noise has a double meaning.

HEY, what's that over there? Did I hear something in the brush? I remember seeing the twinkle of lights in the bushes and thinking ". . . is that the VC signaling to one another" finally realizing it was only fireflies. It was a long night.

The jungle had been cleared back about 50 yards from the bunkers. We coordinated our field of fire with the bunkers on either side of us, checked our radio, set out and checked our claymore mines, and settled in for the night. You always had to check your claymores. The VC had a trick where they would turn them around, so when you fired them, you would be shooting back at yourself. Claymore mines were nasty, but effective weapons.

I don't remember who I was paired up with. Starting around 9:00 p.m., the NCO on duty would take our situation report (a "sit rap"). . "bunker 23, sitrap negative. . " was our usual response.

I remember another time, two black guys were in one of the bunkers, one on guard, the other asleep. The guy on guard thought he saw something, so he grabbed and fired a parachute flare. Unfortunately, he didn't stick the flare out far enough and when he popped it, the flare fired into the overhang in front of the bunker and ricocheted back inside.

The sleeping guy told me later that he awoke to his yelling and shouting and that this other guy was trying to beat out the flare with the barrel of his gun. Their bunker was lit like the noonday sun. These guys both bailed out of the bunker until the flare burned itself out.

Another night, some guys down the line from us were bored, so they took the C4 explosive out of one of their claymore mines and packed it into an ammo can. They inserted the fuse and led the wire back to their bunker. They then got on the radio and began talking like they saw something in front of their position. The guy in the next bunker didn't see anything, but said he'd shoot in the same spot they were going to shoot.

Next thing is this explosion when they detonated their ammo can bomb - KABOOM - followed by several rounds from their M16s. Boys and their toys, always looking to have fun.

Search and Destroy Missions

Search and Destroy was the phrase used whenever we went out into the field. The object was to search for the enemy and destroy his ability to continue the war. The phrase gives one a visual image of soldiers burning villages and destroying everything in their path, which was certainly not the case - far from it. Our mission was to find the VC and destroy them. The VC hid among the civilian population, therefore, we had to be careful not to hurt innocent individuals - and there were plenty of innocent people around.

As we would come upon a village, we would spread out in a line about 50 to 60 yards long, and advance upon the village across the rice paddies that usually surrounded them. The objective in spreading apart was for safety, ". . SPREAD OUT, SPREAD OUT, ONE GRENADE WILL GET YOU ALL. . . ", and to be able to watch the sides of the village to see if any VC ran out.

As we came in contact with the village, our line wrapped around it and everyone separated into teams of two or three people to round up the villagers and move them into the center of the village. When we had them all contained, we would post guards and the rest of the platoon would then go back through each of their huts searching for guns, explosives, tunnels, people hiding, etc. for any sign that would indicate that the people were hiding or supporting the VC. If we didn't find anything, we would move on.

Most of the time the people were scared. They had been fed tales by the local VC that the GIs would burn, loot, and rape their villages. If they were friendly with the Americans, the VC would extract revenge on them after the Americans left the area. Any way you put it, these people were between a rock and a hard spot.

Most of the time we treated the peasant population well, but there were always thoughts in the back of your mind:

> ". . . . is this smiling guy one of the guys that will be shooting at me tonight?"

We had all heard those stories of women and even little children tossing hand grenades into the backs of passing trucks. It was difficult sometimes to separate the good guys from the bad guys.

A lot of the villages were ringed with warning devices and booby traps. Whether it was done by the VC to alert them to the GIs when they came in or if it was done by the villagers to protect themselves from the VC, I didn't know. But it was a dangerous situation that you had to be aware of when approaching any one of the hamlets.

I remember seeing warning devices as simple as tin cans filled with rocks hanging from wires on bushes to make noise if someone scraped against the brush and booby traps deadly as hand grenades suspended within the bushes with trip wires attached to the pins.

This one day our assignment was to sweep this village and look for the bad guys. We had one platoon on a line on the south side and we came out of the jungle on the north side in a line across the rice paddies. The plan was that anyone running from us would be taken by the blocking force on the south side.

We came in on a line and went from hooch to hooch gathering the people into the center. Once all the people are in a ring, then we go back and search the huts looking for weapons, grenades, whatever. . . .

We had all the people from the village in the center. They were all squatting down the way they do, flat footed with their butts just inches off the ground. There were only women, old men and children. That was a 'clue' to us because there were no military age men there – did they run out the backside as we closed in?

I was part of the force guarding the people. This old man in the center had to wizz, so he just let it dangle out of his shorts and go all over the ground, where it ran on the feet of all the others. No one batted an eye.

We searched through all the hooches, and they only found an old woman hiding in some sort of bin in her hooch. Mostly, these villages contained women, children and old men, as the young men had been recruited to work for the VC.

Pacification Forces

Pacification Forces (PFs) were a lot like our National Guard. These were local Vietnamese who were given uniforms and weapons and were responsible for fighting the VC in their local area. The trouble with the PFs was that you never really knew what side they were on. Many times the local VC would be part of the PF force. You never really let your guard down around them..

The ones I saw were mostly equipped with World War II weapons. I've seen these guy carrying M1 Carbines and Garands rifles. Sometimes there was a camp where they all lived, but for the most part they seemed to hang around the villages along Highway One. I never really saw them do anything.

I remember seeing some PFs ride by on their bicycles - the only weapon this one guy had was a bandoleer of hand grenades across his shoulders - and these were the World War II "Pineapple" type grenades. I guess he was the guy with the best arm.

Somewhere in the Area of Operation – coming out of the jungle

Somewhere in the Area of Operation – coming out of the jungle

Somewhere in the AO. At one time, this was a good looking house, maybe a plantation owner's house. Why wouldn't someone move in there?

Somewhere in the AO

First Ambush

Setting up an ambush was a way of life each night when we were out in the field. Besides, working our area of operation during the day, the ambush was one of the ways we communicated to the VC that they didn't own the night (isn't that how cowards always get their work done - in the dark), that we were always around and they had to be concerned with our presence in the area day or night.

The purpose of any ambush is to kill anyone who is out at night. The premise was that if you were out after dark, you must be one of the bad guys. You're up to no good. If someone happened to walk into your ambush, you don't holler "halt" or "drop those guns", or anything, you immediately open fire and shoot them. In an ambush setting it's kill or be killed. My first time on an ambush was obviously a memorable experience.

Our company was out working our AO during the early part of December 1967. Sometime in the late afternoon, the company took a break and we spread out across an open area, fairly concealed from view. As usual there were sentries posted on the perimeters of our break area, but our squad wasn't assigned to perimeter security. We were assigned the ambush that night. After about 30 minutes, the company began moving out to set up their night defensive position (NDP). Our squad stayed behind, shielded in the undergrowth. In case our movements were being monitored by any local VC, we didn't want them to know that part of the outfit stayed behind.

We stayed concealed in our position for the rest of the afternoon and into the night. When it was sufficiently dark, around 7:00 p.m. or so, the squad moved out for the ambush site. I didn't have a watch, so the times are just guest estimates (the time of day wasn't important – it was just daylight or it was night. Our destination was an abandoned village near a river, about 5 or 6 miles away. Whenever we would walk anywhere, it was always in the single file column keeping a separation of about 3 or 4 feet in order to lessen the chances of multiple injuries if there were to be an explosion. As we would have a tendency to bunch up, Sgt Denning was always reminding us ". . . spread out, spread out, one grenade would get you all. . ."

When it was sufficiently dark, Sgt Denning got us together and said "Ropele, you're on point" and we took off. I don't recall being scared or apprehensive, it was just part of being a member of the squad – somebody had to do it and it must have been my turn. I was somewhat surprised as I had only been in-country for a couple of weeks, but that's the break.

The platoon sergeant would give me direction throughout the trek - he would say things like ". . . keep heading towards those trees, we should cross a path in about 300 meters, when we do, stop. If you come to a river, then we've gone too far, . . " or something like that. I didn't carry the map.

I remember the night was pitch black, there was only moonlight – there is no such thing as ambient light because everything around us was dark. Occasionally, a flare would be launched nearby and the column would stop and we'd all kneel so as not to give away our presence. I thought to myself, this is not like walking to the 7/11 to get a soda, this is big deal stuff.

This concept of the point man being out in front of the main column is rooted in the premise that it's better to lose one man than to lose the entire force. The point man is the first man in the single file column and generally walks about 30 feet in front of the rest. The point man's job is to provide an answer to the following question: is the trail we're following safe for the rest of the column to follow? He is the first alert - the first to walk into an enemy's ambush - the first to trip a booby trap that is strung across the trail - thereby saving the rest of the column. So, he's an early warning system that increases the safety of the rest of the squad.

In a convoluted sense, when living in a combat environment, we could easily rationalize that the point man was one of the safest positions in the column (the other being rear security). If the enemy were to ambush the column, they might stay concealed until the point man has gone through and the main body of the column is in the killing zone in order to be most effective. In that sense, the point man would be the safest position because he would be out of the primary killing zone.

So, now we're heading for our ambush site and we cut across a trail, which runs off to my right and leads to the outskirts of this village. Sgt Denning tells me to follow the trail and stop when I get to the outskirts of the village. All of a sudden, I'm walking up to hedgerows that outline places where people had hooches. I think to myself, "holy shit, we're walking right into someone's front yard". At this point, I start to get a little more tense and stop the column fearing we were walking into a thriving village - and it's really dark out (must be about 10 or 11 o'clock at night).

But thankfully, this place is abandoned, although it still has the look of a typical village without houses: house plots outlined by waist high hedgerows, with each plot having a front opening onto the trail we're following, sort of like a driveway opening onto a trail. Each house plot is about 50 feet across the front.

Sgt Denning consults his map and tells me the village is not populated and this is where we want to be and I move out again down the path towards the river.

As I go forward to the next hedgerow, I happen to look back to make sure the rest of the squad is still in sight and I see that the platoon sergeant is holding them up at the previous hedgerow - to make sure I make it past the next hedgerow. If I make it past the next one, then there is not ambush waiting for the squad, so it's OK for them to move forward.

I can understand and accept this concept of sacrificing one for the sake of many because I will sometimes be on the "many" side of the proposition. But, talk about being on your own.

So now, I'm walking on eggshells. I'm tense and strangely excited as we move through this area and I think to myself that this looks like a good spot for them to set up an ambush. I have my M16 at the ready, the safety is off, my finger near the trigger, I have a round in the chamber, and I'm ready for something to happen. The shit could hit the fan in the next couple of minutes.

If the VC is waiting to surprise us on this trail, I'm determined to do my best to see that they don't come out on top. Each time I successfully pass one hedgerow and approach another, I anticipate something breaking loose. Are they waiting just beyond the next hedgerow, or the next hedgerow or the next hedgerow. Am I walking right into it?

The reality of this war finally comes home to me. This is not camping in the woods, this is not hunting and playing with guns. I could get killed here. This is a big deal. But this is also my world now and this is the way life is tonight. It's my job as the point man, to be the insulator between the enemy and my comrades in the squad, so I press forward. They would do the same thing for me.

We walked through this area for about 10 minutes. Thankfully, nothing happens and the next thing I know I come to the edge of the river - we have arrived at our ambush site.

We set up our ambush next to a trail on the inside of one of these small hedgerows that runs parallel to the river. John Haselbauer, Douglas Dennis, and I are positioned on the left most side of the line, the rest of the squad to my right. Haselbauer is on the end, I'm next and Dennis is to my right. Willie Garissom, who carries the M60 machine gun is set up on the right most side of the line.

Haselbauer carries an M79, a 40mm grenade launcher which normally fires a fragmentation round that explodes upon impact - however the grenade is not armed until it's about 20 feet out of the barrel. It's not the type of weapons for close in work like this ambush. Tonight, Haselbauer loads his weapon with a shotgun type of round that will fire pellets directly from the launcher. We conceal ourselves behind some bushes lining the trail and wait for somebody to come along.

During an ambush, everybody is supposed to stay awake all the time. You can't have people on watch because by the time you see the enemy he is right on top of you - so everyone has to be awake and alert for the safety of the others. But the reality of the situation is that after working all day long, staying awake all night is very difficult - no matter what the danger level. I'm not sure how long we had to wait.

It must be around 2:00 a.m. `and I must have dozed off because the next thing I know I see people walking about 6 feet in front of me. I can't see faces, but I remember seeing people wearing plastic coverings in cape-like fashion for raincoats, and those conical bamboo straw hats (normally referred to as "coolie hats").

Oh crap, all of a sudden it's time to go to work. Here are these people in the middle of our ambush and strangely, the rest of the squad hasn't started firing yet. I'm wondering if they dozed off also. At the same time I realize that the only thing between me and these VCs is a bunch of bushes - and bushes can't stop bullets. These people are only 5 or 6 feet away from me. I reach over to my left and nudge Haselbauer to make sure he's awake and at the same time I bring my M16 up to my shoulder to start firing - and I hesitate.

Even today, I can remember my thoughts so clearly: - "Rick, this is the first time you're going to kill somebody", I visualize the whole scene, I see these bullets I'm about to fire tearing through their bodies, I see these guys fall dead to the ground. I wish someone else in the squad would fire first. At that very moment, I hear Haselbauer's grenade launcher misfire. Instead of hearing a loud blast from that 40mm, I hear "CLICK". The world's LOUDEST "CLICK"..

Oh crap, the metallic sound of his firing pin striking the primer is so loud - there was not any way they could not have heard it. It's now, kill or be killed, so I begin firing - BAM BAM BAM. . . several series of short bursts at these bodies walking in front of me. I swing my M16 from side to side, BAM BAM BAM again and again, longer bursts into the dark when I can't see a specific target.

I hear Haselbauer breaking open his weapon and closing it again and then he fires, -KABOOM- that grenade launcher bellows out next to me. I'm so relieved that I'm not the only one firing. I remember thinking and visualizing those shot shell pellets he's firing and the damage they'll do to these guys at such close range.

A 40mm grenade launcher is a single shot device. After the first round, Haselbauer has to break it open to reload another scatter-gun round and he fires again. He also loads grenades and fires his weapon like mortar exploding grenades 20 to 30 feet in front of us.

By this time, the rest of the squad opens up and the noise becomes deafening. Willie Garissom jumps into the middle of the trail and begins firing in the direction these guys are running. Man, that M60 roars. We all fire until we can't see anybody anymore. I can't see specific targets anymore, I fire into the dark at noises, at shadows, at anything that doesn't look like jungle, then the platoon sergeant calls for a cease fire. This whole episode lasts only about 10 or 15 minutes and then it's quiet all around us.

All of a sudden, the platoon sergeant hears something to our rear and throws a hand grenade in that direction. . . KABOOM, the grenade explodes with a sudden and deafening roar. I don't know where it landed - there is nothing but an open area between us and the explosion - I hope we don't get hit by the fragments. I think that they must be sneaking in behind us, but then it's quiet again. No voices, no running noise, nothing.

I'm thinking these guys are regrouping and coming back and to give us more fight. I think we ought to change positions (they know where we are), but the platoon sergeant says we stay where we are until light. It must have been about 3:00 a.m. now. So we wait and listen - nobody dozes off this time.

First light arrives about 6:00 a.m. and we start moving around to see the damage we've done from the night before. On the ground in front of me is some plastic sheeting, coolie hats, a few drops of blood - but no bodies. What happened to these VCs we shot last night?

As I start exploring around in the light, I notice that the trail we set our ambush on turns to the left about 15 yards beyond my position and slopes down at the river's edge in another 15 yards. I figure the VC must have ran down the trail when we opened up and jumped into the river to escape. That must have been the noise Sgt Denning heard behind us when he threw the hand grenade the night before. Anyway, we didn't have any confirmation, in bodies, that we did any damage to the local Viet Cong.

We stayed in this general area for the rest of the morning waiting for the rest of the company to join us. I was sent out with Dennis, to establish an outpost for perimeter security while we waited. We would come back periodically to touch base with the group as we didn't have a radio to talk among the squad. Several hours after leaving, I came back to the squad area and the others had two Vietnamese men hanging upside down by their feet from a tree.

I don't know how they found them or how they figured they were VC, all I know is, I see these two guys suspended from this tree by their feet and some of our guys are squatting on the ground burning their ID card. The platoon sergeant sends us back to the perimeter again. Later I hear some shots fired from the area where the rest of the squad is waiting - sounds like one, two, or three single shots, so I didn't get overly alarmed. Later I join up with the rest of the squad and these "prisoners" are gone and nobody is saying anything about them or where or when they left.

Several months later there was an investigation and some officer asked me what I knew of the situation. I told him the things I saw and heard, but I don't think anything came of it.

My personal opinion is I think the platoon sergeant was upset because we didn't have any bodies to show for last night's ambush and snagged these two locals to use as the body count. For all I know, they might very well have been VC from the previous night's ambush and they found them hiding in the bushes the next morning, but I don't think so.

What a rush that ambush was........8 guys all alone in the night jungle, away from all other support, one on one with the VC. First time I took the life of another......

DAILY STAFF JOURNAL OR DUTY OFFICER'S LOG

Page No. 2 No. of Pages 2

CONFIDENTIAL

Period Covered

Organization or Installation: Americal Division TOC

Location: CHU LAI, RVN

From: Hour 0001 Date 20 Dec 67 To: Hour 2400 Date 20 Dec 67

Item No	Time In	Time Out	Incidents, Messages, Orders, Etc.
38	1915		3/1, B/1/9, time 1736H, vic 983338. Eng'd 1 VC trying to evade UH1B. Res: 1 VC KIA (c). Aircraft developed engine trouble and crash landed. After landing observed 1 slaughtered buffalo w/2 VC beside it and eng'd. Res: 2 VC KIA. Blues were inserted and picked up crew at 1620H. Aircraft was destroyed. 1 US WHA (minor).
39	2020		3/4, A/2/35, at 1356H vic BS750550, secondary explosion when US tps threw a grenade into a trench. Res: 3 WHA (minor).
40	2031		3/4, R/1/14, at 1400H vic BS830274, rec'd SA fire and M79 rds. Res: 8 WHA (evac).
41	2035		198, E/1/6, 1947H vic BS525917, 1 element while moving to night location encountered 1 indiv coming fr S, told him to halt but did not. Eng'd. Res: 1 VC KIA (c), no ID card.
42	2110		3/4, LRRP-6 at 2010H vic BS839416 followed 6 males to a hootch and checked the hootch. Found 25 males [illegible] VC KIA (c), 1 M-1 rifle, 1 frag grenade, and doc's C/A. 3/4 is now engaging area with arty. Will send plt to area tomorrow to check. LRRP consisted of 6 EM and 1 LT.
43	2246		3/1, B/1/35 at 2201H vic BT193438, heard drums and bells, saw movement and saw tracer of poss .50 cal. Called in arty (194 rds). Res: 2 secondary explosions (1 large, 1 small). Two poss .50 cal MG sites, saw tracer fire at acft.
44	2300		3/1, B/1/35, at 1910H vic BT187441, eng'd 1 VC evading. Res: 1 VC KIA (c).
45	2300		DELAYED – 196th, C/1/46 at 192000H vic BT447053, ambush pl eng'd by unk # of VC w/HG. Res: 1 US WHA (minor).
46	2400		Opn WHEELER/WALLAWA cont'd w/light contact. 3/1 – A & B Co's w/10 PFs conducted cordon & search opns vic BT1142. C & D Co's w/25 NPFF conducted cordon & search opns vic BT0945. 4 co's conducted combat assaults beginning 0945H vic AT980340, AS015375 and BT041379 and BT002378. All LZs were cold. 196th cont'd S&D opns in zone w/3 Bns. Totals for W/W: 13 VC KIA (c), 1 WHA (minor). Sig event: At 2010H LRRP-6 (Duc Pho AO) followed 6 VN to hut vic BS839416 where meeting of 25 men was in progress. Hootch contained Russian flag and Ho Chi Minh picture. LRRP eng'd w/SA and 2 HGs, res 12 VC KIA (c), 1 M-1 rifle, 1 frag grenade, and doc's C/A. LRRP consisted of 7 men and was extracted at 2032H.
47	2430		JOURNAL CLOSED

This is the Tactical Operations Log (TOC Report) that reported our action that previous night.

Resupply chopper coming in

During my time in Vietnam, I didn't wear a watch. The time of day was not important, it was either daylight or it was night time., By the same token, which day it was, was unimportant. Monday, Tuesday, Wednesday, - didn't matter. The only way I found out when this action took place was because the TOC reports were made available.

Explanation: The Tactical Operation Center (TOC) is a collection of radio traffic from the units in the field back to the Operations Center at headquarters so that they know what actions are taking place in the AO. My Americal Division Verterations Association obtained these reports, had them digitized, and made them available to the association members.

This TOC report says: "On 20 Dec 1967, at 2035 hours, a unit of the 198th LIB, E Company 1/6th Infantry in the vicinity of BS525917 (a map coordinate) 1 element while moving to a night location encountered 1 individual coming from the south, told him to halt, but did not, engaged, result 1 VC KIA, no ID card".

Because of this encounter, I'm guessing that's where I didn't go in to see the Bob Hope show at Chu Lai.. I'm assuming that units out in the field were insurance against anything occurring while the show was going on. The picture of the chopper coming in, would have been my ride into the show, but it turned out to be a resupply of ammo, water, and C Rations.

Christmas 1967

One of the continual thoughts and topics of conversation we always fell into was about things that were going on "in the world"; like ". . .what are you going to do when you get back to the world. . . ", or ". . .when I get back to the world, I'm . . ." The definition of "the world" was any place back home, the place most of us had most recently left behind, where lives were normal.

We had to adopt a different kind of code of conduct than we had learned back home. It wasn't difficult to develop a "hard edge" – a different kind of normal.

Being an infantryman in Vietnam was a new world in and of itself and by necessity demanded a new thought process. At this point in life, Vietnam was "real life". It was difficult, dangerous, and required behaviors that were far from normal. It was absolutely mind boggling to know that I could be here in the jungle going out on an ambush every night for the expressed purpose of killing people and there are people "back in the world" worrying about the 5:00 p.m. traffic or whether they'll get their coffee hot enough in a restaurant. This is where the roots of PTSD evolve.

During this latter part of December, our conversations often dealt with the holidays; "what would you be doing if you were back in the world now", etc. The fact that we were in Vietnam and life was going on "normally" in the world" gave you that feeling of being very much "alone in the crowd.

Christmas Eve Ambush

This episode began on the 24th of December. The weathers was overcast most of the time with a constant drizzle in the air. We had left base camp three or four days previous to work our area of operation. The day prior to leaving base camp, I had just received a Christmas package from Helen Shives. The box was like a shirt box you get from the store and she had it lined with waxed paper and filled with chocolate fudge. It was a most welcome gift from a sweetheart of a woman and it was so appropriate during the Christmas season. A couple of us sat outside our hooch in basecamp and we ate it all in one sitting.

The Christmas truce just went into effect some days previous and we thought we would be treated to several days of relaxation - but we were wrong. The annual Christmas truce was just a "paper event" negotiated by the Governments. I don't think it was done so much to give the soldiers any relief from the war, but more of a propaganda ploy to display to the world the sense of fair play and honesty we Americans use in conducting our war business.

Logic tells me, why would the Vietnamese be concerned about Christmas? Christmas is a Christian holiday that celebrates the birth of Jesus Christ. The great majority of Vietnamese are Buddhist. They don't even believe in Jesus Christ.

So tonight, like every other night in the field, we prepare ourselves for ambush. The Platoon Leader meets with us to lay out the strategy for the ambush. We have a position a couple of miles away from the rest of the company next to a trail leading to a main village. He reminds us that we need to "adhere to the requirements of the Christmas truce" and instructs us that if we see anybody out, we're to shout "HALT", three times. If they don't stop, or if they open fire on us, then it's O.K.. to shoot back.

This look of disbelief came over everybody's faces and we all just looked at each other and said, "yea, right sir", and the Platoon Leader just smiled back - as if anybody in their right mind would put themselves in such a dangerous situation. The Platoon Leader knew perfectly well what was going to take place.

You have to understand the environment to know how foolish it would be to follow such an order. There were 6 or 7 guys out in the middle of the night, a long way away from any immediate help, and we're supposed to tell guys running around in black pajamas, carrying guns to "HALT" – I don't; think so!

Let's get real here for a moment; these VCs are out in the middle of the night because it's their job to fight against Americans - they don't go out unless they are well armed. They don't go out unless they intend to kill someone. If we were to shout at them, we would not only lose our element of surprise, we would also give away our position - an extremely dangerous thing to do. Everyone in the squad would be killed..

We left the company area to hold up until nightfall, then set out for our position. We set-up in an area off the trail that was surrounded on three sides by hedgerows with our backs against one hedgerow behind a small mound of earth. I thought we were too exposed and was quite concerned about shouting "HALT" in the middle of the night, in the middle of the jungle, to an armed enemy unless I had more protection between me and them. I intended to shoot first - then I would shout "HALT".

As we wait on the ambush, we have radio contact with base camp throughout the night. Their job is to coordinate any relief effort if we get into more trouble than we can handle. So, hourly throughout the night we make "situation reports" (a "sitrep", as we called it when speaking over the radio). Tonight at midnight, as we call in our "sitrap negative", instead of responding with their usual "report acknowledged", base camp responds by wishing us Christmas greetings. There are people shouting in the background, singing Christmas carols, and making general nasty comments about us being in the field and them being in base camp - these guys are having a mega-party.

It was scary to think that they were our link for further support,that we would rely on these drunkards to send us relief if we needed assistance. We were really lucky that night that nothing happened. My thoughts were that this is a really tough way to spend the Christmas holidays and if I make it back alive, I'm going to make the most of the holidays and my family.

What are the words to that Joni Mitchell song - ". . .you don't know what you got till it's gone. . . ". I didn't have to lose my life to realize that family and friends are what counts.

The next morning broke with the usual relief. It being Christmas morning, made it different than most. I thought that this was a unique way to spend Christmas - walking through the jungle looking for a fight with the VC. We joined up with the rest of company around 8:00 am to continue working our area of operation. Our destination that evening was LZ Chippewa, an artillery outpost.

This Christmas ambush episode is significant because it points out the quandary under which all soldiers serve - to operate strictly under orders from your superiors (today, it's called the "Rules of Engagement") or to use some form of common sense. To think that we would jeopardize our lives while on ambush, just to support the "truce".

It also points out how the Government can twist actual events just to generate a more favorable public response to the war. Not that I was ever an activist against the war, on the contrary, I was a firm supporter of my country and to my fellow veterans.. After I came back to the states, I was an active supporter of the soldiers serving in Vietnam. This episode contributed greatly to the difficulty I had in trying to regain my former self.

After I returned home from the war, I became very cynical of the Government, especially around the holiday periods. When I would read the newspaper accounts that chronicled the number of times the VC broke the truce. The papers would paint the VC as these godless creatures taking advantage of a sacred opportunity to kill Americans. It was this attitude that I carried for several years that manifested itself as a minor PTSD condition.

But, I knew how "real life" worked. I was there during a truce and I knew that soldiers on either side were not going to put their lives in jeopardy based on the political workings of some bureaucrats living "in the world"
It wasn't difficult to realize that this so-called truce was only valid "in the world". In "real life", war doesn't stop. You don't let your guard down - you don't take a chance with your life based on someone else's politics.

LZ Chippewa Artillery Outpost

The next morning we hooked up with the rest of the company and headed for LZ Chippewa, a walk of about 2 or 3 hours away. Chippewa is an artillery outpost located on the top of one of the mountains in our area of operation. We didn't know it at the time, but Chippewa was going to be our Christmas holiday resort.

An artillery outpost is a heavy weapons gun emplacement centrally located out in the boonies on the top of a mountain. Its purpose is to provide heavy cover fire to any unit that requires artillery support. A unit would call Chippewa and they would turn their guns to those map coordinates and begin firing. Normally, the unit would then "walk in" the artillery until it was right on target. I believe there were two or three 155mm howitzers cannons and two 80mm mortars. Chippewa was one such place and it was our destination on Christmas morning.

This walk to Chippewa was fairly uneventful. I wasn't pointman this time, but I do recall having to take cover because someone saw something - I remember the machine gunner, Willie Grissom, being called up to the front of the column to set up- but nothing happened - better safe than sorry.

The valley surrounding Chippewa used to be rice paddies, so consequently it was about one to two feet deep in water. We had to trudge through this mud and leech infested swamp for about 2 hours before we could start up the slope. The day was cold, rainy, and overcast. I was wet clear through to my bones - an all around miserable morning. The kicker was we still had to spend another 2 or 3 hours climbing up the mountain.

At any rate, it was all worth it in the end. Our one or two days on Chippewa turned out to be our Christmas holiday. The afternoon we arrived, Christmas dinner was brought out by helicopter - sliced turkey, mashed potatoes, gravy, and cranberries. It sure was a treat compared to the C rations we normally ate.

Later that afternoon, we were put in pairs and assigned to the bunkers around the perimeter of the mountain for nightly guard duty. Just down from the top, the hilltop was ringed with bunkers every 30 or 40 feet. Each night we would set up our claymore mines and settle in to provide perimeter security. The days were pretty much to ourselves - it's not like we could go to the 7/11 for a slurpee, but we didn't have to work unless we were called to a situation.

As there were no roads leading to the top of the mountain, everything had to be brought in by helicopter. The artillery men had built some elaborate quarters for themselves and for visiting infantry units - we called them "hooches". They must have had a backhoe at one time because the hooches were really neat. They were dug about 10 feet into the ground with sandbags reinforcing the walls and the roofs. You had to walk down several steps to get to the floor. There were dirt floors, and wooden bunk frames mounted against the side walls.

I first saw these bunks and thought how exciting it will be not to have to sleep on the ground. I picked my spot, laid my stuff out, climbed up on the top row and stretched out on the wooden slats, the most uncomfortable thing I had ever laid on in my life. There was no way anyone could be comfortable unless you had a mattress - of course I hadn't seen a real bed and mattress since the Captain Cook Hotel in Anchorage Alaska on Thanksgiving night.

During the day, we filled sandbags, pulled maintenance on our weapons and ammunition and just generally laid around. I remember one day the Red Cross volunteer women (Donut Dollies; look them up on Google, great American women who volunteered to serve in Vietnam) came out by helicopter - not for anything special, but just to visit with the troops. Everybody got real excited to see American women again. We hadn't seen American girls since leaving the United States. Most of these ladies looked pretty good. Before they arrived the Platoon Leader cautioned us all to be respectful, control our language and not use the "piss tubes".

Field sanitation was never a problem in the jungle, you just did your business in the bushes. Everybody always carried a small "roll" of toilet paper because it was provided in each packet of C rations. On Chippewa, the artillery men had dug a latrine. They also had artillery shell casings protruding out of the ground throughout the site and you just walked up and did your business in the open into these "piss tubes".

Looking down from Chippewa into the valley gave you the impression you were looking into the Garden of Eden. Everything was green, peaceful and pristine - how deceiving. We spent two or three days on Chippewa doing essentially nothing - a nice holiday.

After the 2nd day on Chippewa, it was time to stop playing with our Christmas toys and go back to work. We were told that another platoon had been hit and required some help (the actual conversation was something like, "B Company stepped into some deep shit and needed help"). We would be leaving just as soon as the helicopters came to pick us up. So here it was, we were going into the real thing - a helicopter assault and it was only a short flight away. Adrenaline started pumping and the excitement began to build.

I drew my normal 3 day allotment of C rations and made sure that I had a full load of ammo. A basic load consists of 12 magazines each holding 30 rounds apiece and four hand grenades. I took all the rounds out of all the clips and put them back in just to be sure my weapons were not going to jam. In addition to the stuff that I normally carried, I was also given an 80mm mortar round to carry because a mortar platoon was also going out. I strapped the mortar onto my rucksack along with the starlight scope. My rucksack must have weighed about 60 pounds.

We were put into groups of eight and the choppers came in to take us out. I choose to sit in the open doorway behind the co-pilot with my feet hanging outside. I figured last in, first out. I reasoned that once the chopper came into the landing zone (the "LZ"),it would be the main focus of fire if there were any VC in the area and I wanted the first chance of getting away from that big target as quickly as possible.

These helicopters were called "hueys" (I think, because they were made by Hughes Aircraft). They had almost a station wagon appearance - large sliding doors on each side and a good sized cargo bay in the middle. They are manned by a pilot, co-pilot, and 2 door gunners. These transport choppers were armed with an M60 machine gun on each side of the rear doors and a pair of 40 mm grenade launchers out through the nose. Other hueys were fitted out as gunships such that in addition to the machine guns and grenade launchers, they also carried a "six-pack" rocket launchers on each side.

This was to be a Combat Assault into a "hot" LZ. These machines only had door gunners on each side armed with only M60 machine guns. Their cargo bays were always open to the outside (they had sliding doors that generally remained open so the door gunners could shoot their machine guns when necessary and to prepare the LZ for landing.

During the 10 minutes it took to fly there, the pilot informed us that the LZ was "hot". A "hot LZ" means that the incoming choppers are taking hostile fire as they make their runs and drop off troops. Holy cow, talk about a boost in the adrenaline pump. The best thing to do was to get away from this helicopter as soon as it touched down, because it is the biggest target and will draw the most fire.

These pilots fly these choppers like they are driving sports cars. We head towards the landing zone flying at treetop level, the nose of the chopper is down and the tail is up. Just past the LZ, the pilot spins the chopper in the opposite direction and powers into the landing zone, nose down as close to the ground as he can get. At the last instance, he pulls back on the stick and rocks the chopper down towards the ground.

It's a standard practice among the pilots to never completely set their choppers down on the ground, they always hover one to two feet from the ground. As we power into the LZ, I'm straining my eyes and ears to spot any VC around the LZ and I'm concentrating my thoughts on getting away from this chopper as soon as it settles in. As the pilot rocks the helicopter back and begins to settle down, I misjudge the height from the ground and jump out too soon - when we're still too high - about 5 feet from the ground.

Jumping from that height with my 60 pound rucksack, I sink up to my knees in the mud. I thought- ". . . oh crap. . . ". I certainly make an inviting target here, stuck in the mud and unable to get moving. I thought I would hit the ground running, instead I'm planted in the mud like a tree. After what seemed like eons, but in reality was only about 4 or 5 seconds, I pulled my legs out and ran to take up a defensive position on the perimeter of the LZ.

As it turns out, there were no VC firing at our landing. Our platoon joined together, we dropped off the mortar rounds, and started walking and looking for things to do and shoot.

Aerial view of LZ Chippewa. Steep mountain side that we had to walk up on Christmas morning. I believe this is looking south

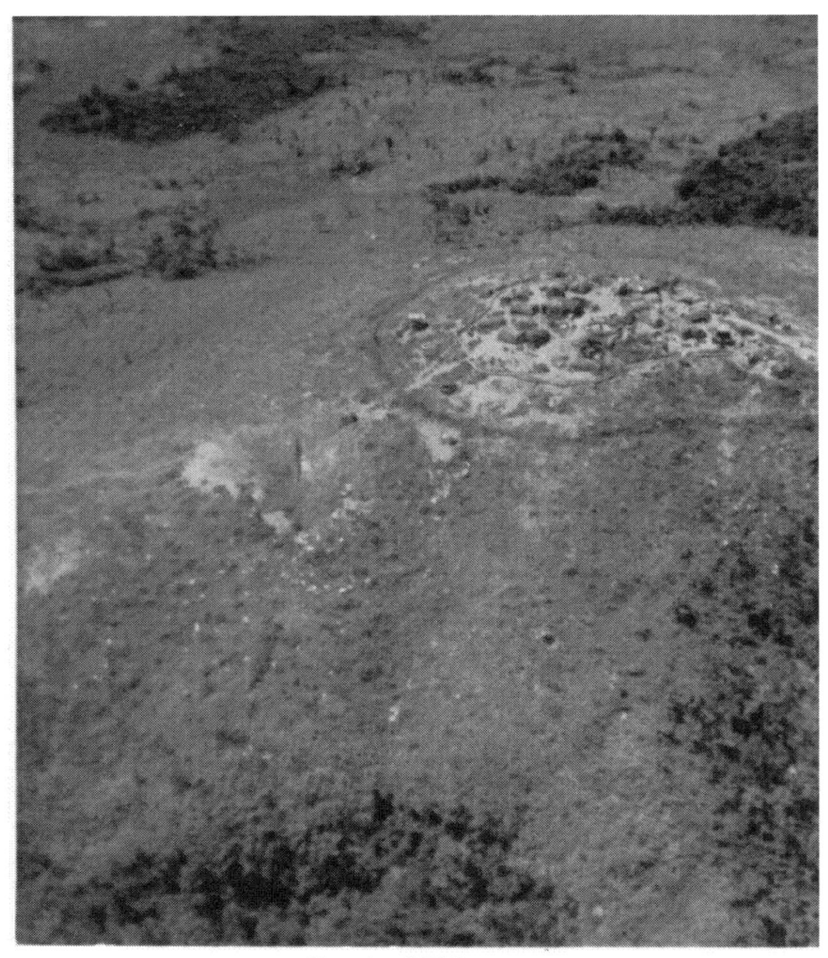

Closer view of LZ Chippewa

This is from the top of LZ Chippewa looking north. The valley below, while looking pristine and beautiful, is sunk about 1 foot underwater infested with bugs and leeches. We walked across it and up the mountain on Christmas morning in 1967

From the top of LZ Chippewa, looking east towards Chu Lai

From the top of LZ Chippewa, looking west

New Years Day Ambush - 1968

31 December 1967, was a wet, cold gray day in Vietnam. We didn't do much walking that day. We pretty much stayed in an area and rested because several squads would be going out that night to set up an ambush. Despite the rain, the day was relatively easy. We were able to lash our ponchos across the bushes to shelter us directly from the rain, but we still had to contend with sitting in the mud. But it was still better than walking around in the rain all day long.

As we usually did, our squad moved out of the company area around 4:00 p.m. to isolate ourselves until dark. We then walked several miles in the dark to another abandoned village and set up behind a hedgerow that lined to the main path around 8:00 p.m. that night.

This hedgerow would have been akin to the front yard fence. To my right, there was an opening of about 6 feet and then the bushes continued until they met the next "lot line" of bushes. As usual, I was with Dennis and Haselbauer, along with the others in our squad, Mouton, Garissom, Picket, and in this incident I remember there was some other guy named Jolly with us. I don't remember Jolly from any other experience except this one.

It had been raining all day long and tonight was not an exception. The rain wasn't continual, but off and on throughout the night. We started our "sit-raps' ' just after dark and we waited for something to happen. Around midnight, we called in one of our "sit-rap negative" reports and rather than the usual ". . Roger" response these guys back at base camp responded with something like ". . . hey you poor bastards, how would you like a beer to celebrate the new year. . ." These guys seemed to be having a really good time. I suppose they had been partying since early afternoon.

I thought, ". . . oh crap, hope we don't need to coordinate support through these guys tonight".

Later that night, Jolly and someone else (I don't remember who) decided they weren't going to let some boring ambush prevent them from celebrating the new year. They threw a poncho over themselves, lit up a joint, and started smoking. Here we were, 5 miles away from the nearest help, in the middle of the jungle, and these guys are smoking dope.

One of the things you learn in basic training is not to show any light at night. We ate cold rations at night because you obviously couldn't build a cooking fire while in the field. Cigarettes were especially noticeable in the dark.

I remember one demonstration back in basic training where one of our ADIs was hidden in the bushes about 100 yards across a field, every time he would take a drag on the cigarette, the glow would encircle his entire face. A perfect target for anybody with basic marksmanship ability.

At least these guys were smart enough to cover up with the poncho. I didn't much care about them getting high, I knew that I was going to do everything to make sure that I wasn't killed or captured, even though these two guys wouldn't be much help. But then, they started coughing and hacking as they would try to keep the smoke in their lungs, it was like they were beating a drum and blowing horns. If there were VC in the area, they certainly knew exactly where we were.

We whispered, "Hey, knock off the noise . . . shut the hell up you guys. . ." But even with only a minute's worth of noise, our location could be easily pinpointed. We were out there to surprise the VC, not to let them know where we were so they could ambush us.

So, a couple of us move about 20 yards away from the main group and took a position behind another part of the hedgerow. If these guys were going to compromise our position, I wasn't going to be a part of the results. They smoked and coughed for a long time.

I think we were lucky that it was raining so hard that night. We didn't see any action. It was one of those nights that you knew you wouldn't be troubled by sleep - I was on the edge all night long. The next morning came quickly. It wasn't raining, but the sky was overcast and gray

As we're getting ourselves ready to walk back to meet the rest of the platoon, I remember smelling the distinct odor of a wood burning fire. We weren't near a village where everyone cooked and warmed themselves with cooking fires. I wondered if it might be some VC or maybe it was just a local farmer cooking his morning rice. I never found out. But that smell always brings me back to that morning in 1967.

It's funny how certain odors bring back certain memories. Whenever I still smell this odor today, I immediately visualize this New Year's morning, of 01 January 1968. I see the gray overcast sky and I see myself and the rest of the squad crouched behind the hedgerow scanning the area for the source of the odor. Every New Year's eve, this experience comes to mind and I think about how fortunate I am that I came out of all this relatively unscathed.

Sketch of the New Years ambush area/site

Sham of the Ambush

By January 1968, I was an experienced veteran of the Vietnam war. I have been out now for about 2 months. As our squad had already received some new replacements, I was no longer considered the FNG. I could read a map and get us from one place to another, if it were necessary; I knew which C rations tasted the best when you had a heat table; which C rations were best when you had to eat them cold; and most importantly, how to act to ensure my own safety as well as the safety of others.

We had been out in the field for about a month since leaving LZ Chippewa working various places within our AO. Some villages in our area of operation were out in the boondocks - farming villages surrounded by rice paddies, populated by farming families. Other villages were located along highway one - commercial villages populated by merchants selling things to the locals and to the GI's. Each was a potential hotbed of VC activity. You couldn't tell a good guy from a bad guy (except at night, if they were out, they were bad guys).

Working the area of operation constituted looking for signs of VC activity. As we would come to a village, we would spread out in a line and sweep across the rice paddies rounding up the people as we went - eventually bringing everyone in the village into the center.

While guarding them, the others would search each hut for signs of VC - guns, tunnels, mines, explosives, etc.. More often than not, we wouldn't find anything, but it kept the VC on their toes. As the Viet Cong generally attacked at night, during the day they were local farmers or merchants and had to store or hide their weapons somewhere.

Those of us in the platoon were becoming a close knit team; Mouton, the squad leader, Dennis, and Hasbrook and I were riflemen, Haselbauer and the red headed guy (I think his name was Bedford) were the grenadiers; Garrison was the machine gunner and Doc was the medic. We recognized the value of taking care of each other. That's why on this occasion we decided to give ourselves a break from the war and treat ourselves to a "campout" night.

Instead of going out to our assigned ambush site, our squad and another squad decided to go out together and set up at one site instead of establishing two separate ambushes This would give us an opportunity relax and rest more as the watch periods could be spread across more people - it's better to be with 12 or 13 guys at night than it is to be with 4 or 5. We used the phrase that we were going to "sham the ambush".

I don't know how this term came to be, but it meant that we were not going to do what we were assigned to do. I'm not even sure how the idea came about - I wasn't involved in the planning. At any rate, I thought it was a good idea because it would give me a chance to get some good sleep for a change. Little did I know that this would not be a restful night, but just the exact opposite.

Each of the two squads left the company area separately and we joined together about 200 meters away. The squad leaders decided on the ambush site and we moved out. There were probably 15 guys in the whole group.

Our squad was last in the column and this time my position was rear security. Douglas Dennis and I were back there together as the last two people in this column. Our job as rear security was to ensure that no one ambushed the column from behind. Specifically, whenever the column stops, we turn and watch the rear. When the column moves forward again, we watch to the rear for another 30 or 40 seconds or so, then get up and catch up to the guy in front of us and continue on. So as the column moves forward, we are responsible for watching our backside

Rear security was one of the good positions in the column because it was also one of the safest. If we walked into an ambush, generally they let the point man pass through in order to get the main body of the column into their primary killing zone. If the main column is in the middle of the ambush, those people in the rear probably haven't made it that far.

To get to the ambush site tonight, we have to walk across an open valley floor. Two small hills are to our left and the river is to our right. Between the hills and the river are what used to be rice paddies that are now overgrown with vegetation about 2 or 3 feet high.

Off in the distance to our front, mortar flares are being fired. These flares, designed to provide sustained light at night, are fired from an 80mm mortar into a particular area. When they reach a prescribed height, a parachute deploys and the flare floats to the ground, illuminating an area for about 30 seconds. Tonight, these flares are close enough that their light spills over and slightly illuminates our column enough that it is not safe to keep moving. Consequently, every time one of these flares are launched, the column stops and we all kneel down so our silhouettes blend with the overgrown vegetation in the rice paddies around us.

The flares are either a blessing or a curse - a blessing if you want to be able to clearly see the area around you and a curse if you don't want to be seen. Tonight, we don't want to be seen. Additionally, whenever the area is illuminated you lose some degree of your night vision. And if you want to stay in the dark, you surely want to be able to see the best you can. When these flares would go off in the distance, we tended to look down or away from the light.

Whenever the column stops, Dennis and I turn to the rear and watch for any activity. When enough light has dissipated, the column moves forward again until the next flare pops up. This goes on for the next thirty minutes or so- we walk a little bit, stop, walk again and stop. Each time Dennis and I turn to the rear, when we hear the column moving again, we get up and catch up with the last guy and move on.

As we always have to wait a little bit after the column begins moving to ensure nobody is coming up on us, we have to hurry to catch up to the column, when I hear the sound of bushes rubbing against pant legs off to my left and I think "oh, the column has turned". But when I catch up, I see that the column has stopped and is still stretched straight ahead. Then I realized that the sound I heard wasn't our guys going through the brush, but it was some VC running through the brush away from us - somehow we must have surprised someone.

All of a sudden it's time to get serious. These guy's sound like they are only about 20 to 30 feet away and I can't see anything. I reach around to my rucksack to grab a parachute flare and can't get hold of it. Then there is silence. Whoever was there is gone now. Dennis and I look at each other and we both know exactly what the other is thinking, "oh crap, there are VC in the area, and they know that we're in the area". Looks like it's going to be a hot time tonight.

The rest of the guys in the column don't seem to be concerned - maybe they didn't hear the movement. Maybe these guys got up and ran when they thought the column had passed them by. – Dennis and I definitely heard something. Tonight was not going to be a campout. Somebody was out there and they knew that we were there also.

We continued walking across this valley, stopping periodically whenever a mortar flare would illuminate our area, until we reached our ambush site. This place was a slightly elevated point at the intersection of two trails - the one we were walking and another one coming from the valley between the hills.. We file into this spot and take our positions in a circular layout. Some to watch the trail we walked in on, some to watch the trail coming from the valley and some to watch our backsides.

As everybody is getting into position, these guys from the other squad are talking - not in whispers, but in low hushed voices. Man, it sounds like they're screaming through bullhorns - their voices pierce the night air. Not only are they talking too loud, but when they remove their rucksacks, they drop them to the ground - as opposed to carefully setting them on the ground. After knowing that they were VC just yards away from me a few minutes ago, I'm getting real concerned about the noise these guys are making because they are giving away our position..

Dennis and I tell them to shut the hell up. We start getting on their case about being quieter, but they just respond with smart remarks and such - acting like a bunch of boys on a campout. I don't understand how anybody can act so stupid. Now, I'm really getting concerned.

As we settle into our positions, I notice that there is a trench running just in front of me. This trench is about 3 feet deep and runs from the valley trail across the front of my position continuing off into the darkness. Now ,I'm really alert. Where does this trench start? Where does it end ? How deep is it? If the VC knows we're in the area (and they certainly do because I heard them just a few minutes ago), this trench would be a good way to sneak up on a large group of guys, lob a hand grenade into their midst and kill them all at once.

Now my stress level has gone ballistic - I'm wound as tight as a cheap watch. We talk to Mouton (our squad leader) about the hazards of staying here in this position with this bunch of idiots, but he decides it's best we stay with the larger body of men. If there are VC in the area, these guys have given away our position because of the noise they made and now this trench is running right under my nose. I don't understand or agree with his decision, but what are you going to do. You can't go out by yourself. The only thing you can do is to do your best to stay alive.

We established a rotation for watch on each of the fronts we were defending. I prop myself up against a tree with my M16 across my lap, a round in the chamber, and my hand on the grip and I catnap off and on waiting my turn. I'm convinced that all hell is going to break loose tonight. When it's my turn for watch, someone whispers "Rick" and I'm awake. Talk about sleeping light. I expect something to happen any minute - all night long. We wait and we watch, minute after minute, all night long. After what seems like an eternity, morning breaks and we all rest a little easier.

It's such a good feeling when morning finally arrives. In the morning, I inspected the trench and saw that it starts close to the valley trail and continues into the woods across the front of our position. This is the worst place in the world to spend the night. We were sure lucky that night.

I can only conclude that the VC must have been setting up an ambush for us or they were waiting to attack the rest of the company later that night. Perhaps, when they realized how many men were in our group, or maybe we literally walked through their staging area, they must have decided they were outnumbered enough that even the element of surprise would not turn the odds in their favor and got up and ran away.

SHAM OF THE AMBUSH

THIS WOULD HAVE BEEN IN JANUARY 68

★★ THIS IS WHERE I HEARD SOMEONE RUNNING THROUGH THE BRUSH WHEN THE COLUMN STOPPED BECAUSE OF AN ARTILLERY FLARE

★ THIS IS WHERE WE SET UP FOR THE NIGHT

OPEN FIELD

★★

TRENCH

★

AMBUSH SITE

XX XXXXXXX X TRAIL

OPEN FIELD

RIVER

TET Offensive - Wounded In-Action

Sometime during the third week in January of 1968, a helicopter came out to the field to pick us up. It was a Chinook type, one of those transport types that had a rotor on each end and an entrance ramp in the back. The platoon piled in and we took seats along the sides - not knowing where we were going. We did know however, that this wouldn't be a combat assault - not in this slow moving chopper - so it was a relaxed trip.

As the pilot cranked up the engine for takeoff, the roar was deafening, that second rotor was right overhead. You couldn't even talk to the guy next to you. The helicopter was totally uninsulated to give it more room inside and to reduce weight so that it could carry more things. We were in the air for about 20 minutes.

We landed just north of the village of An Tan on Highway one at what I thought was a Military Police (MP) facility located on the riverbank, but later learned it was just another position staffed by a rotational infantry group from different groups in the Americal.

The United States had a major air facility at Chu Lai and this village was just outside the facility on Highway One. This station that was located on the north end of An Tan, was on the banks of a river. This facility wasn't anything grand, nothing more than sandbag bunkers, a couple of tents for living quarters, and a command post and a lookout tower. Its mission was to patrol the river looking and searching for VC and weapons and to protect the bridges.

There were two or three boats with outboard motors and they would motor up and down the river throughout the day and night periodically stopping boats and searching for things. I think different platoons would rotate through this assignment to provide support for their activities and security for their facility at night.

The bridge detail was a real cushy assignment. Throughout the day, men were rotated throughout each of the guard posts (about 2 hour shifts). Sometimes, we would go out on their boats. The mission was to prevent arms and explosives from being smuggled on the river. They would patrol the rivers and randomly stop boats for inspections. It was always a time to be alert because you never knew which boats would harbor Viet Cong.

If you weren't on guard duty during the day, we were pretty much on our own, free to swim in the river, lay around in the tent, or to roam through An Tan village, but you always went anywhere with a buddy and with your M16 and ammo. An Tan village was unlike the other villages that I had been throughout in the boondocks. Those were villages established because people had to farm their rice paddies.

An Tan was more of a commercial village. Being on highway one and so close to the Air Base, the GI foot and vehicle traffic was very heavy. There were places to eat, barber shops, souvenir stores, and of course, prostitution was a major source of income. Some of these shops looked like they were stocked by the Post Exchange (i.e., the PX), they sold radios, beer, cigarettes, etc. Of course, everything was contraband.

You have to keep in mind that the local Vietnamese had to make his own living, there were no factories providing jobs for their economy. Either you were a farmer and grew enough food to eat and sell, or you had some business that focused on the GI economy.

At night, we would split into groups of 3 or so and were assigned to the bunkers for security. There were 5 bunkers - 4 around the road next to the bridges and 1 in the rear. As we had a couple of squads on this assignment, not everyone was assigned to the bunkers every night.

On 31 January 1968, someone woke me around 3:30 am for my turn at guard duty in the tower. I walked out of the tent, across the area and climbed the ladder into the tower. I took the starlight scope and scanned the area; around our bunkers; the bridge; towards the mortar platoon and when I didn't see anything I figured it was going to be another uneventful night.

I sat down at the desk, suspended my flashlight so that it was only a few inches away from my paper and started writing a letter home. At 4:00 am I was startled back to reality by several thunderous explosions ". . . . . KABOOM, KABOOM, KABOOM. . . ." followed by small arms fire. I heard small rocks and debris hitting the exposed wood of the tower. I hit the floor then crept over to the side of the tower and looked out.

The whole place erupted with the sounds of war. I could see the rockets hitting and exploding against the sides of our bunkers, I could see enemy tracer rounds going into our bunkers and the tracers coming out of the bunkers as our men fired back. To the south, across the river, I could see the rifle fire coming from An Tan village into our bunkers. I ducked down behind the sandbags and began wondering what I should do next

One option available to me would be to climb to the roof of the tower and open up on them with the fifty caliber machine gun. In a pure situation, that would be the logical step - to open up with the heavy weapons. But, I knew that the NVA knew that I was up here alone. (They must have had their point men in position when I walked out of the tent and up the ladder to start my watch - they must have watched me walk).

Everyone in An Tan village knew we had an operational .50 caliber machine mounted on the roof of this tower, therefore, the VC also knew that the "fifty" was available. I also knew the VC were using RPGs to attack our positions. If I opened up with the "fifty", I'm a prime candidate for a rocket. One rocket directed at this tower, and I'm toast. I figured my best option would be to bail on out of the tower and get into a position where I could offer support with my M16.

This whole thought process only took a couple of seconds. I grabbed the trap door to start down the ladder and then I hesitated again. My mind was racing a mile a minute. If the VC know that I'm up here and I'm not opening up with the "fifty", I wonder if some gook is just waiting for me to show myself on the ladder so that he can pick me off. They knew I was up here, hell, they probably watched me walk from the tent only a couple of minutes ago.

What should I do? Should I go or stay? The alternative of taking a chance of getting shot on the ladder is better than staying up here and taking a rocket in my pants, so I opt to climb down.

I open the trap door and fairly fly down the ladder. I'm not even sure my feet hit the rungs. I land hard on the roof of the CP. and roll off onto the side to begin working my way into a position where I can help.

I was on my hands and knees getting ready to spring across the opening in the sandbag wall and take up a position next to the command post. I could see that one of our bunkers was receiving steady fire directly from the village. I planned to take a position to shoot across the river into the place in the village from where the muzzle flashes were coming.

My thoughts were racing - I tried to imagine where the VC were located. Did one of them focus on me coming down from the tower? Was someone waiting for me to expose myself so they could shoot me? I had to get into position.

Just then, Doc Don Prien, runs by my position coming from the command post and goes into our tent to get his medical bag. I hear him come out of the tent and as he is running back towards the CP I hear the three sharp cracks from a rifle from the direction of the CP, "BAM, BAM, BAM", and Doc is hit. He goes down in a heap in front of my position.

My immediate thought is that Doc was shot by one of our guys standing in the doorway of the command post. The shot came from my immediate right, the only shots from that direction during the entire firefight. The report of the rifle was too close to have been an enemy. My intuition tells me that Doc was shot by friendly fire coming out of the CP.

He says, no he moans, "no, no, no, it me Doc, no, no". I'll never forget his cries of anguish (I can hear him even now as I write these words).. Next, I hear Henry Pickett yell, "Doc, Doc", and he comes running from the CP to help him. Pickett is saying, "no, no, not Doc. Doc, speak to me, Doc. Doc is just moaning "no, no, no".

Henry acted on pure instinct and compassion. This great African American was ready to risk his life for his friend. It didn't matter that Doc was white and Henry was black - both men were soldiers, both recognized their responsibility to every other man in the squad. Years later, I found out Henry was awarded the Silver Star for his actions that morning.

Just then, there is this tremendous explosion where Doc and Pickett are. It's a sound louder than anything I've ever heard. I feel the force of the blast lift me off the ground, lurch me forward and then slam me into the ground. I suppose I yelled, but I don't remember. I see an aura of colors flash into my field of view, red, black, yellow, oranges, I smell the acrid odor of gunpowder.

I feel the impact of something slamming into my foot and leg – it's not a sharp, tearing feeling like you would expect, but it was more like a hard punch - it really felt like someone picked up a sandbag over their head and slammed it down onto my leg and foot. My immediate thought is that the sandbags protected me from the shrapnel and the force of the explosion blew over the sandbag wall. I reasoned that the thud I felt was the sandbags falling on my legs. If I'm hurt, it's probably just broken bones in my foot - no big deal.

Doc and Henry Pickett must have been killed. I can't imagine how they could have survived that explosion out in the open - they must have been right in the center of it. I was about six feet away and I wonder how I survived. This shrapnel I caught in the leg and foot, I just as easily could have caught it in my head.

I still have the presence of mind to realize that the war is still going on around me, and in spite of my situation I had better pay attention if I hope to come out of this alive. So, I drag myself out of the rubble and crawl over against the side of the command post to take stock of my situation.

My plan is that I'll take up a position off the back of the command post and fire across the river at the muzzle flashes that are coming out of An Tan village into our bunkers. But first, I have to make sure I'm not hit too badly. I don't want to bleed to death. I know that I won't be able to walk because of the "broken bones" in my foot, but this position is only 10 or 12 feet away.

I hear Lt Livingston calling for gunship support, but the chopper doesn't show up despite the fact that it was only 10 minutes from the airbase. I remember him calling several times asking where they are, but they don't show. Apparently, they were all busy elsewhere.

I'm sitting up against the side of the CP trying to get myself together and when I notice that the receiver of my M16 is covered with blood. "Oh crap", that can only be my blood, but where is it coming from? I started checking myself over, feeling my chest, arms, neck ,head. If my gun is covered in blood, it can only be coming from me.

Then they thought; "Oh crap, did fragments from that rocket explosion cut a major artery in my neck? Am I going to bleed to death? While moving around, I happen to brush my right shoulder against my neck and chin and now my shoulder is covered with blood. I feel around my neck but can't find anything.

Turns out, that some of the shrapnel cut up my face, my chin on the right side and a small cut just below my right eye. The cut on my chin was the one that resulted in the blood on my M16 and my shoulder. This is a major relief, so I begin to crawl to a position where I can fire across the river.

Just then, all the shooting stops and everything gets real quiet. It was unreal, it was like someone called "time out". This is eerie, one minute all hell was screaming, the next it was quiet as a baby's room.

Then I hear this voice ring out, shouting in Vietnamese. The clarity of it pierces the night air, it sounds like the guy is right in our backyard. Then it's quiet again. I think, "oh crap, are they getting ready to mount a charge?" All the while I'm scrambling to get into a position, to get the magazines out of my ammo pouches and have them handy, and making sure I have adequate cover. I figure the shit is about to hit the fan, big time.

However, within 30 seconds there is this huge explosion - KABOOM - you can feel the concussion sweep the area and water begins coming down like rain.

Now I realize what the voice was saying - he was giving the orders to bring in the boat, set the charges and blow the center span of the bridge. I realize that if they can blow the bridge, then our two bunkers on that side of the road must be in possession of the VC. If they have our bunkers, they must be coming all the way through. I make sure a round is jacked into the chamber of my M16 and my extra ammo pouches are within reach.

This could really get ugly.

I can hear our platoon leader on the radio again calling for helicopter gunship support. This quiet period seemed like it lasted for about one minute, probably more like 30 seconds.

The shooting starts again as the NVA cover themselves to pull back. It's apparent to me that if they were able to bring in a boat and blow the bridge, then they must have overrun and occupied our two bunkers on that side of the road. Our guys were either killed in the bunkers or they had to pull back when they realized they were out gunned. If the VC were able to occupy the bunkers and blow the bridge, they might have a force superior in numbers to ours.

Just then there's another huge explosion from the direction of the air base. I can see a gigantic fireball rolling into the night sky. "Crap, those guys are really on target tonight". That's got to be one of the ammo or fuel storage depots.

But they don't come. After accomplishing their mission, which was to disable the bridge, they pulled out.

It's still dark, it must be about 5:00 a.m.. We hold our positions waiting for more, waiting, waiting....

I remember talking to someone in our platoon (the redheaded guy, I think his name was Bedford) . He was the other grenadier, while waiting for the Medevac choppers to come. He was in the bunker nearest our tents at the north end of camp. He said this big VC started running toward his position. He aimed his 40mm grenade launcher, shot and hit the guy in the chest, but the guy was too close for the round to explode. He said this guy got hit in the chest with this 40 mm projectile and just kept coming. He had to pull out his pistol and finally stopped him about 6 feet from the bunker. He said he was one of the biggest Vietnamese that he had ever seen.

Typically, the Vietnamese are a small race of people. If this guy was so big, I wonder if he wasn't a regular NVA. I wonder if we got hit by regular troops from North Vietnam.

About 7;00 a.m. a medevac chopper was flown in to take out our wounded and dead. This was the first opportunity I had to stand up on my feet and I discovered I couldn't walk - I couldn't put weight on my left leg. This wasn't a total surprise as I already surmised that my foot was broken.

The chopper sat down on the road near our bunkers on the north side of the river. I was helped to the chopper by one of the guys in the squad - he was a black man and I can't remember his name. There were others on the chopper also injured in the fire fight, but I can't remember who they were. I climbed into the chopper and sat up against the bulkhead. I don't remember being in any pain - I suppose the adrenaline was still pumping.

This is the tower on the north side of the An Tan river. You can just make out the two tents at the tower base

Another view of the tower

Building the facilities. I don't know who these guys are. The morning I was hit, I was on the other side of that low sandbag wall on the right side of the picture.

This would be a view from the base of the tower south across the river towards An Tan – obviously, the picture was taken before the sandbags were put into place

Don't know who these guy are but in the background you can see bunker number 1 right along highway 1 heading north

This is a view looking east. The river is on the right

Sitting on the dock between the two bridges. The night we were hit, they brought a boat in and blew the center span on the big bridge.. John Hasbrook was under the bridge on the far side when it blew.

This is the patrol boats we used. Each has an M60 machine on the bow

View from the tower south towards An Tan village and bunker number 4

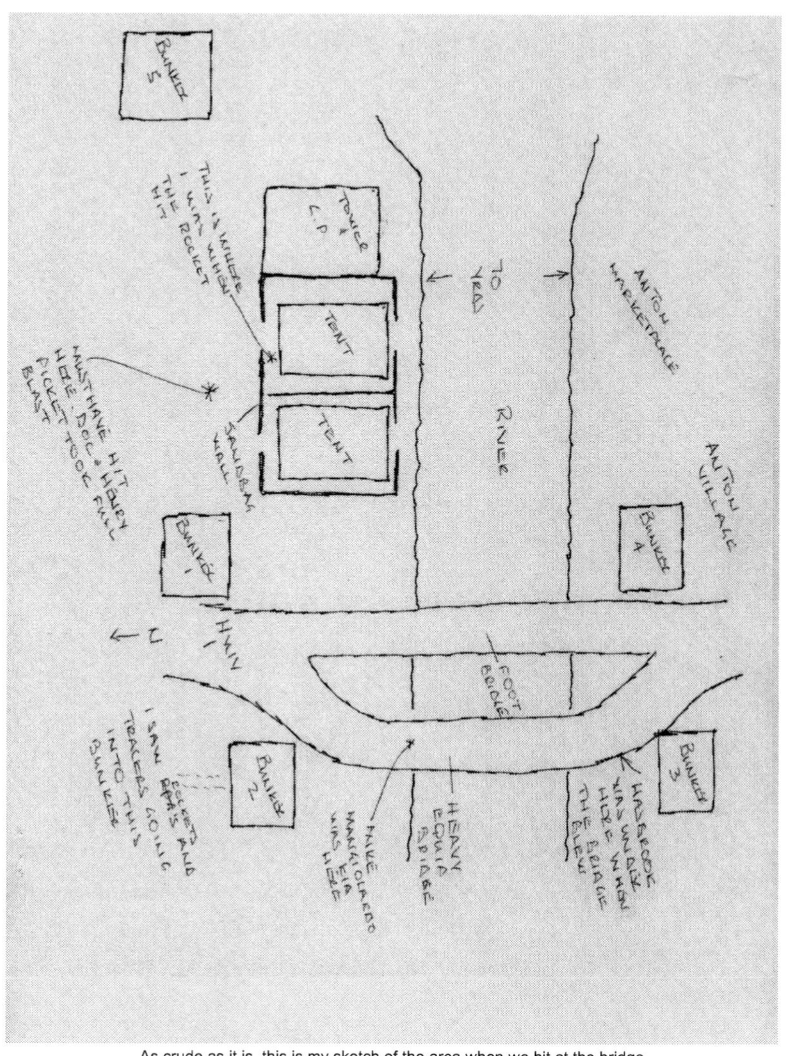

As crude as it is, this is my sketch of the area when we hit at the bridge

AMERICAL DIV TOC CHU LAI RVN 0001 31 Jan 68 2400 31 Jan

CONFIDENTIAL

1	0001	OPENED JOURNAL.
2	0145	LZ Baldy rec'd 15 RR rds.
3	0210	III MAF at 0126H vic BT068514 came under grnd & mtr atk and believed perimeter was penetrated (Duy Xuyen). Arty is supporting.
4	0225	CAP K-4 at 302355H vic BT.49107 PF ptl obs 3 VC in school talking to large group of people. Opened fire on VC and 3 VC ran into trees. 20 VC opened fire on element. Ptl heard many voices and moans. Checked area w/neg res. Apprehended 20 VCS - 4-5 poss KIA.
5	0411	Mtr rds [illegible] knocked out all generator equip in Subsector 6.
6	0412H	Quang Ngai under mtr atk.
7	0413	Bunker 739 rec'd mtrs and SA fire.
8	0415	Reactionary force standing by.
9	0417	Bomb dump hit.
10	0420	23d MP Co reports 85%.
11	0421	G1 reports all personnel on alert status.
12	0425	80th Spt reports 100%.
13	0425	Spt Cmd reports 85%.
14	0427	Large explosion vic MAG-12.
15	0430	AG Classified reports 100%.
16	0430	An Tan Bridge rec'd 30 mtr & SA rds w/some cas.
17	0431	Subsector 1 rec'd 1 mtr rd.
18	0432	Bunker 201 rec'd SA fire.

This is the entry identifying when the bridge was hit at An Ton village

The Tactical Operations Center (TOC) reports is the collection of radio traffic from the field units informing command of occurring events. This is the traffic on 31 January 1968 and the attack on our bridge location at 4:30 in the morning.

AMERICAL DIV TOC CHU LAI, RVN 0001 31 Jan 68 2400 Jan 68

CONFIDENTIAL

Cont Neg contact. SS-4: POI(tank form) intact w/neg damage. SS-7: Neg contact.

40 0635 CLDC, at 0635H Sub sect I, II, VII, Neg casualties or damage.

41 ✓0700 198,3B at 0700H 1/46 A group of demonstrators of approximately 100 persons moving on Hwyl towards Lyn Tin distric Hq. Villagers in vicinity are running away from demonstrators 1/46 has platoon ready for reaction if it is requested. Also Quang Ngai under ground attack.

42 0700 CAP, K-4 at 0415H Vic BT449109 after last contact set in and was surrounded by 1oo VC Chanting various phrases patrol rcv'd SA & AW for 1 hr returned fire called illum and arty H & F called dustoff & completed 1 US KIA, 2 WHA 1 VC KIA 4 WIA

43 0715 1/1 A-B-C at 0709H Approx 1oo VC w/wpns running S to Tam Ky Recv'd fire from indiv Returned the fire unk amount of VC Caus & approx 30 to 40 are moving NW.

44 0705 CAG, CAP K-3 at 0500H Vic BT4[illegible] 3 VC from ambush. Results 1 VC [illegible] CIA, 1 VC believed wounded but [illegible] USMC WHA (minor)

This is the assessment of the damage to the bridge - apparently called in a couple of hours after it exploded.

I was in the hospital in Chu Lai by this time

45 0714 LTC Balmer, Revert to grey alert passed to CLDC.

46 ✓0718 198, Vic BT498067 The AN TAN Bridge center span was blown by a satchel, charge. The town can be passed by using the bridges on the right. Notified Div Engineers

CONFIDENTIAL

At 7:18 a.m. they called in the fact that the center span of the heavy bridge was blown. It actually was blown around 5:00 a.m.

Chu Lai Hospital

The helicopter landed on the helipad outside the 2nd Surgical Hospital at Chu Lai air base, it took only about 3 or 4 minutes to get there - I think it was around 7:00 am. Someone helped me out of the chopper and we hopped until the emergency room personnel met me with a stretcher and took me inside. On the way in, someone took my M16 - I remember seeing it propped up against the wall inside the emergency room. I remember thinking that I hope someone who knows how to handle a weapon takes care of it because there is a round in the chamber and the magazine is full.

I made sure I took it with me when I left my position next to the Command Post bunker and was helped across the area to board the medevac chopper at the bridge, I certainly wasn't going to go anywhere without it. There was no telling what could happen next - maybe the VC were waiting for us to run to the chopper, maybe they were going to shoot down the chopper somewhere along its way. I just knew that I wasn't going to be without my M16. I wasn't going to be defenseless. I wanted to be sure that I could take care of myself.

As soon as the stretcher is inside the building (it's just like you see in the movies), I'm suddenly swarmed by doctors, nurses, and clerks. Some immediately start looking at my leg and my foot, others are cutting off my uniform to look for other injuries. Someone is putting an IV into my left arm.

I remember 3 distinct groups of "information gatherers". These groups are hovering around the head of the stretcher, and they are all talking to me at once.

I turn my head to the right and someone says:

"Who is your next of kin?"	Raymond Ropele.
"What is his relationship to you?"	He's my father.
"What's his address?"	1028 Oak Street.
"What city?"	Santa Ana.
"What state?"	California.

I turn my head to the left and someone else says:.

"What is your name?"	Richard Ropele.
"What is your service number?"	US56707489.
"What unit are you from?"	E Company, 1st Battalion, 6th Infantry, 198th LIB.
"What is your rank?"	PFC, E3.

Someone else says:

"Where are you hurt?"	In my leg and foot.
"When and where were you hit?"	Around 4:30 this morning outside An Tan village.
"When and what did you last eat?"	Last night around 9:00 p.m., I had some beers and corn nuts.
"Are you allergic to any drugs?	No.

With all this conversation going on, I didn't pay much attention to what the doctors were doing or saying. Maybe that was a good thing because I hurt a lot.. The adrenaline rush was beginning to wear off and I suspect that shock was setting in, so I wasn't too aware of the detailed activities that were going on around me. But they are preparing me for surgery and I hope to stop the bleeding.

Suddenly, the next thing I know, John Hasbrook is brought in on a stretcher and put next to me and the information gatherings swarm over him. When I have the chance, I ask him what happened, but I find I have to shout. Hasbrook can't hear me when I speak to him in a normal voice.

Hasbrook and Mike Mangiolardo were in the bunker closest to the heavy equipment bridge on An Tan village side of the river when their bunker was blasted by a series of deafening explosions. Their bunker, like all the others that night, was attacked with rockets and recoilless rifles (i.e., bazookas), only theirs was from point blank range. Their bunker was not more than 25 yards from the nearest hut in the village.

A bunker is made to withstand the force of these kinds of weapons, but the noise of these explosions must have been deafening. When it was apparent to them that they could no longer hold their position, they bailed out of the bunker.

Now, you have to understand that the NVA were firing at them from the village at essentially point blank range - a range of less than 50 feet. That's close and dangerous.

Mike Mangiolardo, who was in the bunker with Hasbrook, ran across the bridge toward our other bunker on the north side of the river, but he was killed on the bridge. He didn't know they had already killed our guys in that bunker, occupied it and were firing on our positions from it. He was killed as he was coming across the bridge.

Months later I found out from Lt Trujillo (my Executive Office in our company at Fort Carson) that his mother had a congressional inquiry started because of this death. On the night he was killed, he should have been on R & R. I guess he must have told his mother he was going. But, the military wouldn't let him leave the country because he had gotten a venereal disease while visiting some of the 'ladies' in An Tan village. It was policy that he wouldn't be allowed to leave until it was cleared up.

Lt. Trujillo said his mother really raised a fuss with the Army about her son dying while he was supposed to be on leave. Sure the Company Commander tried to spare her feelings, but in the end he had to tell the congressman about the VD.

It's too bad he died, it must have been especially hard on his mother. This guy was always getting packages from home with fruit cups, cookies, and the like. He also got a lot of letters from different girls. He told me his mother arranged for different girls to write to him.

When Hasbrook bailed out of the bunker, instead of running across the bridge, he ran down the embankment to the edge of the river and concealed himself in the weeds. He was down there when the VC brought in the boat and blew out the center support span of the bridge.

It's no wonder his hearing was affected. Between the bunker explosions and the bridge explosions, I'm surprised he could hear at all. Hasbrook was only 15 or 20 feet away when the bridge blew.

That's the last time I saw him. I don't know if he had other injuries. I don't know if his hearing was permanently affected. Did he go home also? Did he recover and go back to the unit? I often wonder what happened to him.

In 1989, I saw an article in the outdoor section of the Press Enterprise talking about somebody named Hasbrook (except this guy's name was spelled Hasbrouck). I wrote to an outdoor editor explaining that I would like to get hold of this guy to see if he was related to the Hasbrook that I knew (maybe I spelled his name wrong). I didn't get a response.

According to my medical records, I was rolled into surgery around 7:45 or so and was finished within an hour. After surgery, I was put on a recovery ward and was in a regular bed for the first time in 3 months. My left foot was elevated, I had an IV in my left arm, my right arm was stitched and bandaged and I had several stitches closing small cuts in my face (under the right side of my chin and under my right eye) . Not bad shape for someone who was only 5 or 6 feet away from the explosion of a 122mm rocket. I'm grateful that those fragments didn't enter my head or take out my eye.

Throughout that first night and the next day, I was checked periodically by the nurses and the orderlies. That next day my platoon leader, Lt Livingston came in, talked to me for a while and pinned my purple heart medal on my hospital pajamas. I remember telling him. I would be back to the squad in a couple of weeks - I was under the impression that all I had were broken bones. That was the last time I saw him.

I knew I should write Mom and Dad, but I reasoned that I would be shipped to some other place for recovery and I would write them then when they could correspond back. What I didn't realize was that my buddy, Ted Smith, wrote them first. Turns out that Ted's letter was their first notification that they had that something had happened. I just assumed that the Army would send them something right away. Ted's letter follows:

05 Feb 68

Dear Mr. & Mrs Ropele,

I like to consider myself as being a good friend of Ricks'. He is one of the few men in our platoon.

He is a man to be proud of. I've been with Rick since AIT and he's proven himself over to be a man.

I wasn't with him at the bridge, but from reports he didn't change there.

The medic's told me he was going to be in top shape before long. I know you can't put Rick down for long. He has more fortitude than anyone I know. You truly have a son to be proud of.

Sincerely,

PFC James Smith

Ted is a real good friend and I appreciate his thinking of my folks at a time like this. But he provided just enough information to really worry them. I didn't write until I reached Japan. Several weeks later, Lt. Livingston wrote Mom and Dad. His letter follows:

15 Feb 68

Dear Mr & Mrs Ropele

I'm in from the field for a little break and can sit down to write you. First of all your son is in a hospital but will be all right. I'm sorry you had to find out the round-about way that you did but as you say your son probably did not want to worry you.

Perhaps by now he has written to you about what happened and filled you in as to his immediate condition. I will however, give you what I know happened.

On Jan 29, our bridge was hit by an intense Viet Cong attack. In the battle, which lasted over and hour, Rick was wounded by a mortar round. His wound was in the right leg and foot.

When I got to him, he was conscious and asked that the others men be helped first. He was given first aid and as soon as possible I called in a "Med Evac" helicopter to get the wounded out. The next day, the Col. sent his chopper so I could visit my men in the hospital. I spoke with your son and he was feeling pretty good.

His leg was in a cast or heavy bandage. I did not get a chance to see his doctor but do know he will be okay from reports I received. He was sent to the rear and last word I have received was Japan. This may seem a little vague to you as far as where he is, but once in the hospital, the doctors dictate where the wounded will be sent.

For you information he did an outstanding job. The fight cost us (my platoon) 3 dead and six wounded. The Viet Cong did not take the bridge. That was important.

As I have said before Rick should have written you by now and told you his condition and location. I would appreciate a letter of how he is doing and if I can do anything for you. I will be back in the field soon and will miss him and the others who will not be with me.

Rick did an outstanding job and as I have written you earlier, is an outstanding soldier and man. I'm very proud of him and his actions under fire. You have a fine son.

Sincerely

William Livingston

As Lt Livingston mentioned, we lost 3 men dead and six wounded. The dead were:

Don Prien	Our medic was killed in the same blast that hit me.
Mike Mangiolardo	Mike was in the bunker with Hasbrook and got killed on the bridge while running to the other bunker.
Richard O'Conner	Must have been in the bunker on the north side of the river next to the railroad tracks.

The wounded, besides me, were:

Scott Miller	I don't remember who he was, but he was listed on my Purple Heart Orders.
Henry Pickett	Who was wounded in the same blast that hit me. He was out in the open helping Doc.
Willie Garissom	I don't know where he was, but he was our machine gunner so he and his M60 would have been in the thick of things.
Two others.	

In Lt Livingston's letter to Mom and Dad, he said: "The Vietcong did not take the bridge. That was important." may seem a lot like Army bravado and macho rhetoric, but it is in fact a comment from a Platoon Leader who is concerned about accomplishing his mission and most importantly, the safety of his people. You have to realize that if the Vietcong had taken the bridge, the platoon would have been overrun and wiped out. American lives were preserved by holding and fighting for our position.

I don't remember being in extreme pain, I do remember asking for and getting several injections of pain medication. You know, it wasn't a screaming and yelling kind of pain, I remember real discomfort, a headache, and a constant throbbing in my leg and foot.

My first night in the hospital, the VC was still very active in the area. The explosions of VC mortars were still fairly close as the VC were trying to keep up the momentum of their offensive. Most of us patients are quite concerned about our safety and are also frustrated by our lack of mobility, and most importantly, the fact that we don't have the means to protect ourselves. This was the first time in 3 months that I didn't have my M16 in my hands.

It was only a matter of a few hours ago that you were totally responsible for yourself and your buddies, where control was in your hands. A couple of the male orderlies and night nurses try to reassure us about the mortar attack by laughingly telling us, ". . . don't worry, those guys can't hit anything with those things".

HELLO? WHAT ARE YOU TALKING ABOUT? This whole hospital ward is an example of the VC accuracy with their weapons. There are over 50 men in this ward alone who have proof otherwise, and these dopes say not to worry - where have they been the last couple of months - inside a tin can? I know where I've been the last couple of months and I'm plenty worried.

If the shell starts falling too close, their plan is to move us to the floor under our beds and cover us with our mattresses for protection - oh shit.

This ward I'm on is typical of the hospital complex. It's a long wooden building that holds approximately 50 or 60 patients in single beds along a common center aisle. We didn't socialize much among ourselves - for the most part the men are either drowsy because of the pain medication, or you're only there for a short period of time or people don't feel like talking. Everyone there has suffered some sort of combat related injury. I imagine they are all pretty introspective and quiet because of the associated trauma.

Several beds down from where I was located was this big black guy, evidently hospitalized because of rabies because periodically throughout the day he would get one of the series of rabies shots - I assume he must have been bitten by some animal (dogs were not very common, so it must have been some rodent). I understand that rabies is treated with a series of injections in your stomach which are extremely painful. I remember he would put his arm above his head to grab the headboard rails of the bed and really yell whenever they gave him a shot. I only remember him getting two shots that day.

I was in Chu Lai hospital for the rest of the day and night and then was transferred to Qui Nhon hospital on 02 February 1968. I assumed that I was being sent to some rear area for a few weeks to recover from my "broken bones" and I would be rejoining my unit later.

DEPARTMENT OF THE ARMY
HEADQUARTERS 2D SURGICAL HOSPITAL (MA)
APO SAN FRANCISCO 96374

GENERAL ORDERS
NUMBER 31

1 February 1968

1. TC 320. The fol AWARDS are announced.

Award: Purple Heart
Date of action: As indic in standard name line
Theatre: Republic of Vietnam
Reason: For wounds received in action
Auth: By direction of the President under provisions of AR 672-5-1

ASKREN, DANIEL A. RA67170019 (SSAN UNK) PFC E3 B 6/11 Inf Bde Americal Div
WIA: 31 Jan 68

ROPELE, RICHARD A. US56707489 (SSAN UNK) PFC E3 E 1/6th 198th Inf Bde
WIA: 31 Jan 68

STEWART, GARY US56497943 (SSAN UNK) SGT E5 C 1/6th 198th Inf Bde
WIA: 31 Jan 68

MILLER, SCOTT US51664824 (SSAN UNK) PFC E3 E 1/6th 198th Inf Bde
WIA: 31 Jan 68

GARISSON, WILLIE U. RA11920234 (SSAN UNK) PFC E3 E 1/6th 198th Inf Bde
WIA: 31 Jan 68

LOPEZ, RUFUS A. US56667058 (SSAN UNK) PFC E3 HHC 71st Assult Hel
WIA: 31 Jan 68

PICKETT, HENRY US53426429 (SSAN UNK) SP4 E4 E 1/6th 198th Inf Bde
WIA: 31 Jan 68

SAWYER, GENE R. US56959319 (SSAN UNK) PVT E2 Americal Repl Ctr
WIA: 31 Jan 68

ROSS, DENNIS E. US52678371 (SSAN UNK) SP4 E4 C Trp 1/1 1st Cav Div
WIA: 31 Jan 68

WYANT, RICHARD E. RA15419024 (SSAN UNK) SFC E7 Svc Bty 3/16 Arty Americal Div
WIA: 31 Jan 68

ROSAMBALN, GERALD L. 05336692 (SSAN UNK) 1LT 525th MI (Prov) Group
WIA: 31 Jan 68

WIESS, DENNIS J. US51772740 (SSAN UNK) PFC E3 Hq Bty 3/16 Arty Americal Div
WIA: 31 Jan 68

HARRIS, EDDIE US53701284 (SSAN UNK) SGT E5 A 4/3 11th Inf Bde Americal Div
WIA: 31 Jan 68

KENNETH A. CASS
Major, MC
Commanding

DISTRIBUTION:
"A" PLUS

These are the orders that were cut by the hospital awarding my Purple Heart. I'm amazed that I saved this piece of paper all these years

These are pictures I gathered from the internet – obviously I didn't have my camera with me when I went through this process, but I remember all this. When I went through this facility in 1968, it was called the 2nd Surgical Hospital. In late 1968, the personnel was replaced and it was called the 312th Evac, so when they rotate in another group to man the facilities, the hospital changes names. Obviously, in 1971 it was the 91st Evac

Incoming, 91st Evac
ChuLai, 1971

There were several of us that came into the hospital on the medevac choppers. I don't remember who else there was, I suppose it could have been some of the dead from our unit. The chopper pad was just outside of the trauma ward

91st Evac, ChuLai

I do remember this building. When the chopper landed, they came pouring out of the building with stretchers to get us inside

This is how the room is staged, prepared to treat the casualties. I remember this same layout.

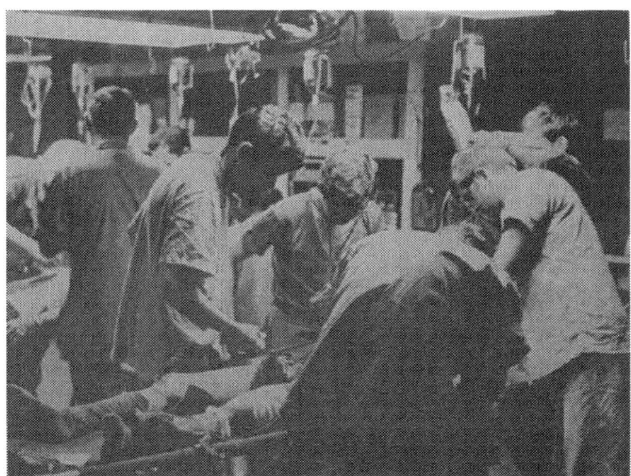
This was the typical scene when I was there. Immediately, I was 'swarmed' by people all ready to do their jobs. Information takers, IV starters, surgeons. How grateful I am for their skills and dedication – just like the men in my platoon, always ready to do their job..

Qui Nhon Hospital

Leaving Chu Lai hospital for the 85th Evacuation Hospital at Qui Nhon should have been my first indication that I was injured worse than I thought. If I wasn't going to recover from this locally, then something more than broken bones must be involved. The possibility that I would ultimately go home because of this injury didn't even enter my thoughts. I figured I would be sent somewhere, recover from the broken bones and then sent back to my unit. After all, I still had 9 months to go before completing my tour of duty.

Qui Nhon was a coastal village located midway between Chu Lai and Saigon and headquarters to the 85th Evacuation Hospital (the 85th EVAC). Regarding the origin of Qui Nhon, I took the following from the book, "Vietnam War Almanac", by Harry G. Summers, Jr.

> A port located in Binh Dinh Province in II Corps, Qui Nhon was developed into a major supply base. Beginning in August 1965, the U.S. Army's First Logistical Command established a support command at Qui Nhon. The command included a transportation terminal, a supply depot, a POL (petroleum, oil and lubricants) depot and an ammunition dump to provide combat service support to the 95.000 U.S. and allied troops in northern II Corps.
>
> Security for the port was provided by South Korea's Capital Division, which was headquartered in Qui Nhon. These facilities were turned over to South Vietnam in April 1972.
>
> Qui Nhon fell to the North Vietnamese in March 1975, when II Corps collapsed in the face of the final offensive.

I can't remember the flight from Chu Lai to Qui Nhon, I suspect the medical staff in Chu Lai must have given us an enhanced dose of painkillers and sedatives to alleviate any pain or discomfort while traveling. One of the first procedures in the Chu Lai emergency room was to put an IV into the vein in my left wrist. By the time I got to Qui Nhon, my hand and arm were so sore that I could hardly use them. As my right arm was cut up from the fragments that penetrated just above and below the elbow, the bandages over the forearm and upper arm to cover the stitches restricted its use. However even with these injuries and bandages on my right arm, it was still easier to use it than my left. They removed the IV on the first day at Qui Nhon and it felt sooooo good.

Now that IV is out, I was given a shot of painkiller and getting ready to fall into a state of ultra relaxation when this nurse walks up to the foot of my bed and says "we can't let those muscles get flabby now can we, we need to start our physical therapy as soon as possible" and she begins wiggling my toes back and forth while encouraging me to provide resistance to the movement. Man, that really hurt. I told her to get the hell away and leave me alone with her physical therapy crap.

Later that day, I found out that my foot was not only broken (the 3rd 4th and 5th metatarsals), but the wounds in my left foot and leg were entry wounds where the shrapnel from the rocket penetrated through a double wall of sand bags and into my foot and lower leg, and purposely not stitched closed in Chu Lai hospital. Leaving the wound open was a medical technique they had learned to allow any subsequent infection to drain. It was a well known fact that the VC would contaminate their rockets and mortars with dirt, urine, feces, or anything else on the premise that the contaminated fragments would cause further complications in the form of a more intense infection. If the explosion didn't kill you, they wanted to make any resultant recovery more complicated.

Once the IV was removed, I got hold of a pair of crutches and was allowed out of bed for short periods of time to move around, although I would tire easily. Just outside the door of my hospital ward was a security compound where wounded prisoners were treated and kept. This was an area sealed off as a security compound, topped by razor wire and guarded by Military Police. The prisoners I saw looked like any other regular Vietnamese only they were wearing hospital pajamas and robes. I remember them smirking as I wandered by on my crutches - I imagine they were thinking how good it is to see injured Americans.

This sure paints a contrast in my mind. Should I hate these guys? After all, they are responsible for my being where I am. But I didn't have any hatred for them or any desire for revenge. I didn't have feelings one way or the other. But here they are getting the best medical care they ever had in their lives out of the goodness of the American government. I just figured they were very fortunate - they could have been left in the bushes to die if some Americans hadn't brought them in.

The intense fighting associated with the TET offensive was still going on while I was hospitalized in Qui Nhon. The American and Korean soldiers are still trying to take back the ground which was gained by the VC. I don't think I'm in any danger, but you never know. The VC proved they cannot be taken lightly. You could hear the sounds of the war off in the distance. Still in some areas of the country the fighting is very intense. Qui Nhon village was one of those areas.

The area of operation surrounding Qui Nhon village was the responsibility of the Republic of Korea (ROK) marines. It was well known among the Americans and the Vietnamese that the ROK marines were a ruthless, no-nonsense group of soldiers. Now this is only 2 or 3 days after the Tet Offensive and the ROK marines were still in the process of reclaiming Qui Nhon village from the VC. I don't suppose that there was any danger for me, but. . . . .

The ROKs method of clearing the village was appropriate for their brutal reputation. They would announce that at a particular time they would be going through a certain section of the village and if anyone were there, they would kill them - man, women, or child, soldier or civilian. At their appointed time, the ROK marines would move out and make good on their promise. They figured that anyone that stayed after their warning must be the enemy. Not a very humanitarian method of operation, but effective in getting the job done.

Qui Nhon was a short stay. I think I was there for maybe 2 days. One day to arrive and one day for them to determine that I was stable enough for further travel and to leave the next day.

I don't remember what time we left Qui Nhon (i.e., in the morning or the evening), I was moved from my bed to a stretcher and loaded on bus for transport to the air base. These buses had most of the seats removed so they could hang the stretchers three high along each side. The second tier of stretchers was the only position where you had a view out the window, the top tier only had a small window portion that gave you a view almost straight down and the bottom tier was too low to see except straight up.

We were then loaded onto special medical evacuated airplanes that were configured similar to the buses (i.e., with stretcher hangers) and were flown to Clark Air Force Base in the Philippines. I thought this would be the place where I would stay and recover and return to my unit.

However, it was just an overnight stop. The next morning we were again loaded onto an airplane and flown to Japan.

249th General Hospital - Japan

We landed in Japan in the evening. Our stretchers were loaded onto the buses and I was put on the bottom tier next to the floor. If I raised myself up on one elbow during the bus ride to the hospital, I could see out of about 3 inches of window. I saw a lot of different colored neon lights, like we were going through a city. The stretcher above me didn't allow me to get my eyes even with the window, so from the angle I had, all I saw of Japan was the tops of buildings and neon signs. I didn't see any Japanese the whole time.

The drive took about 20 minutes. The 249 General Hospital was located in Asaka, just northwest of Tokyo. It was a one-thousand-bed general hospital and they received about one thousand wounded each month and either evacuated or returned to duty slightly less than that number.

Initially, I was put on a surgical floor because of the need to close the wounds in my leg and foot. I thought for sure that this is where I would recuperate, recover from my injuries, then return to Vietnam and my unit. After all, I still had 9 months to go before completing my one year tour of combat duty.

My first day, a Red Cross lady came by with a Polaroid camera and took my picture. I was sitting up in bed without a shirt and had the covers over my legs. I enclosed the picture with the first letter I sent to Mom and Dad telling them the news. I assumed that I would be in Japan for a while and we could correspond easily. In all my letter home I always downplayed the experiences so as not to add to their worries. This letter is indicative of that approach.

6 Feb 68

Dear Folks

If you have already received my Purple Heart certificate, don't worry, if not, I guess I ought to explain.

The gooks hit us at the bridge on the night of the 31st with a mortar attack. I caught some frags in my left foot and leg, not very serious. It broke the 3rd, 4th and 5th metatarsals in my foot. Don can explain to you about that. I got some small frags and scratches on my right forearm also. Right now I am in Japan. It is common to evacuate a patient if recovery is expected to be over 30 days. Right after I got hit, medievac had me to the hospital 30 minutes later.

I drew a map which will help explain as I describe the situation. At 3:00 am I had just gotten up to go on tower guard. At 4:00 am the first mortars started coming down. They hit us with mortars, rockets, and automatic weapons. Well, it took about 2 seconds for me to get down from that tower, and I ran behind some sandbags. The gooks weren't interested in us around the CP and all their fire was directed at the bunkers. Bunkers 2 & 3 received most of the fire because the gooks had to knock those two out in order to blow the bridge (#1). All us around the C.P. were a reaction force. I was crouched in my position and our medic ran by me and into our tent. I guess they must have seen him because a mortar round dropped around there and I got a few frags. The fight was over in an hour, they blew the bridge from a boat that pulled out with 100 lbs of TNT. Wow, what an explosion, water came raining down for 2 minutes. Right after the bridge went, they pulled back. Everything was quiet at 5:00 am, We had 5 wounded and 3 dead.

I am OK and there is no pain. I think this wound is good for about 3 months of loafing. If I do go back to Nam this time counts as part of my time there and believe me I am going to enjoy Japan. This hospital is only 15 miles outside Tokyo and there are trains every 5 minutes.

Well that all up to now. My new address is on the back. Tell me all about the wedding. I am all right.

Love

Rick

PFC Richard Ropele US56707489
249th General Hospital (Patient)
APO San Francisco 96267

I made a conscious effort in this letter to make the news as non-threatening as I could for them - knowing how worried they would be. I knew that I wasn't hurt all that bad - not life threatening anyway. I knew I was going to be OK, I still hurt, you know like a constant throbbing, but not double over and screaming pain. I guess it could have been worse, those fragments could have torn into my head or I could have lost my leg had I been less protected. But fortunately for me, the sandbags absorbed most of the blast and the shrapnel.

The surgery in Japan must have been fairly routine for shrapnel wounds. I didn't realize that my wounds were left open and the surgery in Japan would be to clean out any subsequent infection, I suppose remove any fragments that are still visible and close with stitches. In my case, the wounds in my leg and foot were open for about two weeks

I remember laying on the operating table and this surgical technician was preparing the room - he attached a board to the table and stretched my right arm out on it. I was making small talk and told him that the surgeons could do anything they wanted as long as they knocked me out first.

He looked surprised and said: "they won't knock you out just to put a few stitches in your arm". I thought, ". . . oh crap, I hope this guy not involved in the operation because he doesn't even know why I'm in here". So I pulled up the sheet exposing the cast and bandages on my leg and foot and said, "I think I'm in here so that they can take care of this also".

I had two open wounds on the outside of my left foot, one about 2 inches long running along the side and another about one inch long running across the top of my ankle bone. The other open wound on the outside of my left leg, is about 3 1/2 inches long. My medical records indicated that I retained multiple fragments in both my leg and foot - I assume that the doctors determined that they would cause too much damage if they tried to remove all the fragments - so the ones they figured would not be a problem, they left in. In addition, I also broke the 3rd, 4th, and 5th metatarsals. The doctors had to ensure that all the infection was clear and then they would stitch the wounds closed and put a cast on for the broken bones.

There was also a small cut on my chin from which they removed about 10 or 12 stitches and removed the stitches from the cuts on my right arm. I also had a few stitches on a small cut just below my right eye (I guess I could have lost my eye had those fragments hit about ½ inch higher. How cool would that have been to have to wear an eye patch or maybe have a glass eye like my friend Rusty).

My medical records indicated that I was in surgery for about 30 minutes. They closed my wounds with wire stitches and installed a short leg cast. Later they cut small "windows" in the cast over my stitches so the nurses could clean and change the dressing on my wounds. I was moved off the surgical ward and onto another ward to convalesce.

I wrote another letter to Mom and Dad.

11 Feb. 68

Dear Folks.

I am feeling fine. I have some crutches and can go all over the place. When I got here, the next day I had to go back into surgery. It seems that when they took the frags out in the hospital in Vietnam, they didn't sew me up. They leave the wounds open less chance to get infected. I had to go get them sown up and get a new cast. I have a cast on now that stops just below my knee, so I can bend my leg. There is a snack bar 2 buildings away, a movie house, and a P.X. So I can get whatever I need. We are free to go to these places as long as you sign out.

Did you get my picture? The Red Cross snapped it for valentine's day. You can see my mushtasch, not much to look at yet still real scraggly.

I am saving the good news for last. I am going to be evacuated back to the states. I don't know when but it shouldn't be more than 15 or 20 days. They send you to the closest Army hospital to your home. So I guess it will be Fort Ord. As I said before I don't know when I will leave.

Well time is running short for ole Don. Is he still going through with it or has he skipped out to the High Sierras. I know a lot of nigger girls who are going to be disappointed when he does get married. Tell Pop happy birthday and see you all pretty soon.

Love Rick

There was this one guy 5 or 6 beds away from me that must have had some kind of head injury because his skull was dented above his right eye and into the top of his head. He obviously had some sort of head injury and lost some portion of his skull and brain. There was a sign on the wall above his bed cautioning not to give him any matches or cigarettes. When he would want to smoke, the nurse would light it for him and hold the cigarette while he smoked.

I remember the difficulty this guy had when it was time for him to get a shot of medication. He would initially roll on his side to give the nurse access to his hip and then as if he would suddenly remember that the shot was going to hurt, he would try to roll onto his back and shout, "no, no, no. . .". The nurse would have to hold him on his side and she would try to talk him into calming down and relaxing. When he wouldn't relax, she would just have to give him the shot and he would yell, "OW, OW OW. . " You know how painful a shot can be if you keep your muscles contracted. It's as though he forgot that the hurt would only be for a little while and the medication was for his own good.

Poor guy, what a load to have to carry for the rest of his life.

On Wednesday night, 14 February 1968, I called Mom and Dad to tell them that I would be leaving Japan on a medical evacuation flight in the morning for the United States.. The Government's policy is to transfer a wounded soldier to the Army hospital nearest his home of record - in my case that would be Fort Ord, in Monterey, California.

It was about 8:30 p.m. in Japan when I called home to tell Mom and Dad the news - I didn't even think about the time differential. Japan is 17 hours earlier than California (actually it's the previous day because you have to cross the International Date Line). When it was Wednesday at 8:30 p.m. in Japan, it was Friday, 3:30 a.m. in California.

Obviously, I woke them up. My brother Don answered the phone, he was getting ready to go to work. This was the first time I talked to my family since Thanksgiving in Alaska. I told them I was scheduled to leave Japan the next morning and would be going to Fort Ord and that I would call them from there. We talked for about 10 minutes- what a treat.

I also found out that this was the morning of my brother Don's wedding. Don was going to marry Leslie Crenshaw in just 8 more hours and they would be going on their honeymoon to northern California so they would see me at Fort Ord. So it was a double treat.

This is an excerpt from by brother Don's book of remembrance:

> .I would have had my brother Rick in my wedding, but he was not able to be there as he was in the hospital in Japan. The week before our wedding, Mom and Dad got a communication from the Red Cross that Rick had been wounded in battle (Vietnam) and they did not know his status. Dad immediately came over to Alpha Beta that evening where I was working and told me about the telegram and of course we were just sick. Mom and Dad started communicating with the Red Cross for more information. I think they finally found out that he was alive and was in a Vietnam Army hospital having surgery and soon to be transferred to Japan for another surgery the day before the wedding. Leslie and I were really concerned about my parents. It would be very difficult for them to enjoy the wedding not knowing what Rick's status was. The day before the wedding, the phone rings and Rick calls from a hospital in Japan. He was going to be transferred to a hospital at Fort Ord in central California the next day. That phone call was the best call that we could have ever imagined. During the wedding, Reverend Lestma mentioned to our guests Rick's circumstances and that he was coming home.

The next morning we were prepared and taken to the airfield and loaded onto a C141 Starlifter for the medical evacuation flight back to the United States. The plane was configured like the buses - there were hangers on the sides for all the stretcher cases and some seats near the front for the walking wounded. As I recall, the plane was full. My stretcher was loaded onto the hangers inside the plane and we took off.

How fortunate I was to be going home in one piece. Just 3 short months ago, I was in Japan going the other direction into uncertainty and possible death. Just a mere 2 weeks ago, I was walking around the jungles of Vietnam. I wonder what the guys are doing right now. I sure am a lucky guy. This was the beginning of the 'survivor's guilt' syndrome that I carried with me for a lot of years and still think a lot about it today.

We left Japan on 15 February 1968 (Thursday morning in Japan) and because we crossed the International Date Line and gained a day, we landed at Travis Air Force Base on Friday, 16 February 1968, around 5:00 in the afternoon. Travis AFB is located in the San Francisco area.

I don't remember much of the flight across the Pacific. I was confined to my stretcher, I couldn't see out a window. I'm sure everyone on the flight was heavily sedated?

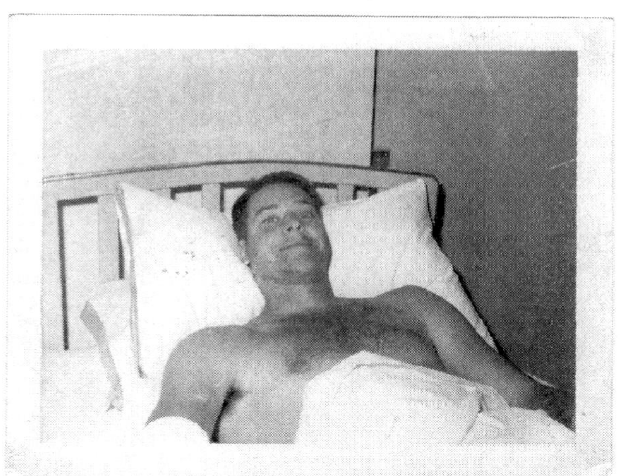

I'm in the 249th General Hospital in Japan in February 1968. One of the nurses took this picture on Valentine's day and I sent it home with the following note: 'Yea, it's me. I'm in my ward now recovering with remarkable success. It must be these Japanese nurses in their mini skirts and mini shirts. Notice on the right side of my face around my mouth and chin. The just took the stitches out. I think it's quite beautiful.'

Travis AFB Hospital

After landing at Travis AFB, we were transported by bus from the flight line to the Air Force Hospital. . Boy, does the Air Force know how to live. This hospital looked exactly like a commercial hospital in the world - very clean and posh.

I shared a room for the night with some Vietnamese officer who said he was injured during pilot training at Travis.

The next morning we were loaded again into an airplane for transport to the hospital at Fort Ord. As Fort Ord didn't have a landing field, the plane landed at the commercial airport in Monterey and bussed into Fort Ord..

Fort Ord Hospital

Back In The World

Fort Ord did not have an airfield, so the military flight from Travis AFB landed at the commercial airport in Monterey on Saturday 17 February 1968 around 9 or 10 in the morning.. The weather was cool, clear, and bright. This time, when my stretcher was loaded onto the bus I was put in the middle set of hangers and had a clear view out the window. We left the airport, drove down the coast highway to the hospital at Fort Ord.

What a treat, I could see everyone and everything. People going about their business, driving their convertibles, the sun in their eyes, the wind in their hair.

How ironic is this? I'm only 10 hours away from my squad. Men I lived with for 3 months, men who are fighting and possibly dying in the jungles of Vietnam right this very moment and here I am, back "in the world" people are going about their everyday business, not thinking or not caring about what is going on in Vietnam. Hell, I still had dirt on me from Vietnam. For all I knew, the men in my squad could be fighting and dying right now (turns out that is exactly what is happening. My company was involved in the Battle of Lo Giang. That's where Haselbauer was KIA and Dennis was WIA.

Guilt is one of those "good news - bad news" emotions that we all experience throughout our lives. Normally, it helps us to recognize that we have committed a wrong and it puts our thoughts and subsequently our actions on the path towards restitution.

But this is a different kind of guilt. I knew I didn't do anything wrong in getting wounded and being evacuated back home. It was not something of my own making that I was here, back in the world. But, I still felt I had somehow let the guys down. Maybe if I was still with the squad, someone else might stay alive because of my participation, but now someone else has to carry my share of the load because I'm not there to do my part. If I'm over here, how can I help them over there?

I know these are not rational thoughts, but this is how I feel, even today. I had a loyalty to the guys in the platoon and I wanted to do my part. We walked the jungle together, they had my back when I walked, and I had theirs. This was the beginning of a major attitude that I developed and I carried this chip on my shoulder for several years. To a lesser degree, I still have it. It's called survivor's guilt and I wonder why I'm alive and someone else is not.

I guess that's one way war changes people.

This is a quote from the book "Inside Delta Force" by CSM Eric L Haney;

> "The military is a profession that brands itself on the soul and causes a person forever after to view the world through a unique mental set of filters. The more profound and intense the experience, the hotter the brand and deeper it is plunged"
>
> (I find this to be very true. Almost dying in Vietnam has set an edge to so many thoughts and actions throughout my life and put me in a position to value my relationship with my Heavenly Father and with my wife and children).

Fort Ord Hospital

Fort Ord hospital was not the classic hospital in the sense of the world – a gleaming multi-storied building with a stylized entrance. It was a series of World War II wood frame buildings, originally built as barracks for the soldiers.

The hospital had taken over this old single story building complex, connected them all with covered boardwalks and created a hospital complex. There must have been some sort of front entrance, but I never saw it.

I was put on an orthopedic ward with some 30 or 40 other guys, all of whom also were in various stages of recovery from wounds received in Vietnam.

Sometime after being admitted, I was examined by a Doctor Loughran. He opened the small windows that were cut in my cast in Japan and noted that some of the stitches had pulled loose on my foot. He said that if it didn't close by itself that he may have to graft some skin in order for the wound to close properly. He said this rather casually to the nurse who was with him, like skin grafts were done all the time - and as I looked around the ward, in fact they were.

There were several guys in various stages of the skin graft process. One guy was having skin from his left thigh grafted around the heel of his right foot. The technique used by these doctors was to open up a three sided "flap" on the top of this guy's left thigh, cross his leg and place his right heel under the flap and then sew three sides of the flap to his heel, leaving the fourth side intact on his thigh.

The premise of this technique was that the skin graft would be more likely to "take" if the skin was still "alive". After they were sure the graft would be successful, they would cut the fourth side of the flap, fold it around his heel, and sew it to the remaining area.

Obviously, this technique severely restricted this guy's mobility, so he was provided with a wheelchair. Whenever he was in his chair, he always looked like he was kicking back - relaxing, sitting there with his legs crossed. But I can imagine how uncomfortable this guy must have been. It must have been tough sleeping. As I recall, he was in that position for one or two weeks.

Another skin graft patient was being treated in the same fashion only they were grafting skin to the back of his right hand. He had his right hand sewn to a flap opened on his stomach. He could walk around and didn't look too bad off. If he would have put on a shirt, he would have looked like Napoleon.

So, these guys were my basis of comparison for skin grafts. When the doctor told me that skin grafts were possible, I got really anxious. If this was their standard procedure, I wondered what position I would be put into. I didn't sleep very well that night because of my anxiety. However, it turned out that my wound began closing by itself and I didn't require a skin graft. That's why the scar on my foot has this round look to it (about the size of a quarter) instead of a straight line look.

Monday or Tuesday (I don't remember exactly what day it was), but here I am sitting in my bed when Don and Leslie walk into the ward. What a neat surprise to see my brother and his new wife. I knew they would be on their honeymoon, but I didn't know that they would be up in this area. I felt really special knowing that they would take time out of their honeymoon to spend time with me.

I still wasn't ambulatory so we couldn't leave the ward. They must have spent a couple hours at my hospital bed with me. I related some of the events of the last couple of weeks to them and the circumstances that brought me home. We called Mom and Dad from a payphone that was wheeled next to my bed. I remember Don saying something like ". . . yea, he looks pretty good, but his foot is still covered with blood."

I can imagine what Mom and Dad must have visualized, but in fact there was only a slight amount of dried blood still visible on the part of my foot that was showing around the cast. One thing you have to remember is that I hadn't had a bath or shower since leaving Vietnam (maybe 19 or 20 days ago - I think we swam in the river that day though. I suppose I could have had a sponge bath somewhere along the way, but I don't remember).

Later that same week, Mom and Dad came to Fort Ord. I don't remember anything specific about their visit or how long they stayed, but I'm sure they wanted to see for themselves what my condition really was. I suspect they must have visualized the worst.

Some years later mom told me that dad almost had a heart attack when they found out I got hit. She said when he read Ted's letter he sank back into his chair, white as a sheet. I can imagine how he felt, especially now that I'm a father.

You have such a feeling of helplessness. The questions that race through your mind are almost incomprehensible because they come and go so quickly. As I said before, I didn't write home right away and tell them about getting hit. My rationale was to wait until I got to Japan, which was three or four days later. I knew they would have lots of questions and I knew that I wasn't going to be at any permanent place for a while. I figured that once I was assigned to a convalescent area I would call them and fill them in.

However, what I didn't realize was that my friend Ted Smith wrote Mom and Dad the day after I got hit and said something to the affect ". . . . although I wasn't with Rick the night he got hit, I understand he conducted himself well and you would be proud of him. . ." or words to that effect. Sounds ominous doesn't it? Imagine what Mom and Dad must have thought.

So that's how they found out. They must have been very anxious for about a week until they got the letter and picture I sent from Japan. I often wonder what thoughts went through their head during that time period. Now that I'm a father, I understand their concern and worry they must have felt. How grateful I am that my Heavenly Father sent me to a family that loved and cared about me.

Sometime during March, my doctor determined that it was time to remove my stitches. I left the ward on a gurney and was wheeled into a treatment room and put on a table next to this other guy who also was getting stitches out of his foot. This guy had his heel crushed in a jeep accident and the doctors had to reconstruct his heel and foot, apparently over a number of surgeries.

This guy must have been in some real pain. As the doctor was working on him, he was calling them every name in the book. He was yelling, ". . . YOU SON OF BITCH, THAT HURTS, WHAT ARE YOU DOING"., ".YOU BASTARD, THAT HURTS. . . ",. I couldn't believe that he would be allowed to talk to an officer like that. But the doctor would just chuckle, reassure him that they were almost done and continue removing his stitches and this guy would continue to yell and curse.

After witnessing this guy's antics, I started to get really nervous. I didn't think removing stitches was such a painful process, but apparently I'm wrong. My doctor arrives, does a quick examination, tells me that I have wire stitches (as opposed to thread) and sends the nurse out for his wire cutting instruments.

I figured If this guy at the next table was having such pain and they were only removing thread stitches, I must be in for a real "treat". The nurse returns with some small wire cutters and needle nose pliers, like you get at the hardware store and the doctor starts. The doctor had me lift my leg so that he would have clearer access to my foot, I was so nervous. My leg shook like I was shivering. The doctor just laughed and said not to worry and started clipping the exposed wires.

As the stitches were wire, the doctor would use small wire cutters to clip the stitch, then he would pull them out with the small pair of pliers. Whenever he would cut a wire, a small burr would be left on the end. I swear I could feel this burr end of the wire being dragged through the muscles and tendons inside my foot whenever he would pull the stitch through the inside of my foot and out the front.. I didn't yell or anything, but it sure was uncomfortable.

They replaced the full cast on my lower left leg with a "splint type" cast and wrapped my leg and foot together in an ace bandage, which I kept for about several weeks.

1st bath since Vietnam

Sometime during that first week at Fort Ord, I got to take a bath. This would have been my first opportunity to clean up since being hit on 31 January. That must be some kind of record, two weeks without bathing. In one of the rooms off the ward floor, was a huge claw foot bathtub. I had to prop my leg up on the side, but it sure was nice to sink into that tub of hot water.

In Vietnam, we had outdoor showers, water was gravity fed from a bag at the top. Obviously, no hot water. Generally, when we were out in the field, you were either rained on or waded through a river – not really a way to get clean, but it was ok.

Convalescent Leave

Often the doctors would authorize a two weeks convalescence leave that wasn't counted against the usual allotment of 30 days a year. During March 1968, I was given my first leave to go home.

I don't remember exactly how I got back to Santa Ana, but I think Rodney Monroy and one of the Keeler boys were coming down from school at Humboldt and he picked me up at Fort Ord in his 67 El Camino and we drove home. I was dressed in my Class A uniform (my dress greens), had my crutches and a bag. I didn't have any civilian clothes.

Moving around on the crutches wasn't really difficult. A lot of people, strangers that is, would open doors for me and such and I appreciated it, but I also resented it. I guess it was the "attitude" coming to the front. I had been responsible for myself for the last 3 months and now that I was not able to function fully, it was difficult to accept help.

Memories of the war were still very fresh in my mind. I felt guilty that I was "back in the world" and men that I fought with and that died beside me were still in the jungle, fighting and dying. I often thought about them. I would try to imagine what they're doing at the very moment while I'm here. This guilt manifested itself into an attitude that I tried to play down whenever I was around my family. I know they wanted to see the "old Rick", but I just couldn't be that guy yet.

Various people came by to see me and I think Mom and Dad had one of their backyard dinners. It was sure good to be home again (even under the 'cloud' of guilt).

I remember sitting in the living room with my foot propped up on something visiting with, I think Mary Ann Hart (Reed), when her little toddler came running by and spotted my foot. Apparently the white sock must have caught his eye - I had the top of a white sweat sock cut in half to cover my toes. This little kid looked at the sweat sock, extended his hand way behind his back, and slammed it forward and snatched the sock clean off my foot. When I saw his arm swing forward, I thought, ". . . oh crap, this is going to hurt a lot." Luckily, he just grabbed the sock.

Returning to Fort Ord was a physically difficult task because of my lack of mobility. I had a late afternoon flight from John Wayne Airport to San Jose, where I would connect with a commuter plane to Monterey. From Monterey Airport, I would take a cab to the hospital. But, my flight out of John Wayne was delayed getting into San Jose causing me to miss my connecting flight to Monterey - which was the last flight out for the night.

Here it is now, the rain is coming down in buckets (remember 'I hate the rain"), I'm in uniform, on crutches carrying a small overnight bag.It's 8:00 p.m. and I'm 90 miles away from Fort Ord on my last day of leave, and all I have in my pocket is $20.00. If I don't check back into Fort Ord by midnight, I'm considered AWOL (absent without leave) - and AWOL is a big deal to the Army.

I found a cab driver who was willing to drive me to Fort Ord for $100, more money than I have - Being a wounded veteran didn't make an impression on him.

Fortunately, the train depot is right in the same building as the airport terminal and for $20.00 I can buy a train ticket. Rather than go all the way to Monterey, the agent tells me that the train stops right across the highway from the main gate to Fort Ord. It's still pouring rain when I get off the train. I have no other choice but to crutch across the tracks and the coast highway and onto the post. The rain is really coming down hard now and I'm soaked through to my skin. Wearing this all wool uniform, I smell like a wet dog.

I show my leave papers to the MPs at the gate, he lets me on Post and I crutch my way to the nearest phone booth. YES, I'm out of the rain. I'll call to get a cab from Monterey to take me from this phone booth to the hospital. The perfect plan.

But, the dispatcher at the cab company tells me that cab service is not allowed on the post. Cabs can only come on the post to pick someone up or drop them off - they can't cruise around to pick up and drop off a fare on the post itself. So my only way to get to the hospital is to crouch along the street for the two miles or so. I'm reluctant to leave the dry refuge of my telephone booth, but I have to get back before midnight. So I start crutching up the road in the rain.

After two blocks or so, someone driving by took pity on me and picked me up and took me to the door of my hospital ward. I got back around 10:30 p.m. It felt so good to get out of the wet uniform and into dry hospital pajamas and a robe

I had two of these convalescence leaves while at Fort Ord and on the second one, I drove my Malibu back up.

Paid twice for February

When it was time to go on this first convalescent leave, I didn't have any money. As a matter of fact, I don't even remember having a wallet or ID. If I had a wallet with me when I got hit, then it must have been taken in the emergency room in Chu Lai and I suppose it traveled with me to Fort Ord, but I don't remember.

At any rate, the Army created temporary financial records so that I would get paid. I remember getting $100.00 – a lot of money in 1968. Later on in February, my records arrived from Vietnam and I got paid again.

Death on the Ward

As I stated earlier, I was assigned to a bed on the orthopedic ward where we had some guys recovering from some of the most traumatic injuries that you could ever imagine. Men who had their bodies ripped apart by explosions, by bullets, scarred by fire, etc.. There were guys without limbs, guys undergoing skin grafts, guys having reconstructive surgery because their bones have been crushed.

Surprisingly the morale on the floor was always up. We realized that we had passed through the "great test". We all knew guys that died and we were among the living. We had made it, we were back in the world. There would be no more ambush patrols, no more walking points, and no more worrying whether you would be alive tomorrow.

Now, it's just living and getting better.

One day, the medics brought in a young man around 16 or 17 years old. He was unconscious and wrapped in bandages from head to foot. They said he was the son of an officer and that he had an accident while riding his motorcycle. They said he had been drinking. He was in really bad shape.

I don't think he ever regained consciousness. He was on the ward for two days, then one morning we awoke and his bed was empty. The nurse said he died during the night and as was a common practice, they moved his body out quickly.

What a waste! In our ward there were 50 other guys, all of us around the same age (early 20's). We experienced the horrors of death and destruction in Vietnam. We were back home, we were going to make it, we just had to get through both the physical and mental healing process.

And then, to have someone die, again, in our midst was tough. It was so avoidable. For one moment of "pleasure", this kid chose to run on the edge, and then stepped over the line. What a terrible experience for his parents. A motorcycle accident! How sad.

One of the lessons you bring back with you from Vietnam is that staying alive is not a guarantee. At any point in time, a step in the wrong place, being in the wrong place at the wrong time, and your history. I'm reminded of the saying, "If it's to be, it's up to me". I'm responsible for my future.

Moved to the Convalescence Ward

During my convalescence at the hospital, those of us that were in a "healing mode", that is, those that didn't require any direct medical care, but were just using time to heal our physical difficulties were moved off the surgical ward into a convalesce ward.

There was one guy in our convalescence ward that had had his right leg amputated about 4 inches above the knee. I don't know if it was intentional or what, but this guy was assigned to a top bunk. He would walk into the ward, pop off his artificial leg, and hop right up on his bunk, hardly without a thought or effort. In the mornings, he would jump down to the floor, pop on his leg and after dressing would walk with hardly a trace of a limp.

In this convalescence ward, we were assigned to various "no brainer" jobs around the hospital to keep us busy.

Day Pass

I don't remember the specific date, but one day several of us hospital patients got a day pass and we left the hospital and I drove us down to the beach in Monterey- I think we were somewhere on '17 Mile Drive', which is scenic route along the beach, a place of high end houses., lots of trees, everything looking out over the ocean.

All of us being wounded veterans of Vietnam, fresh from Vietnam, home for only a matter of month, we determined that it was necessary to have some beer in order to enhance our enjoyment of the day's activities. There were three of us. One of the guys was named Riley, from the 9th Division. We went to some parking lot along the coast and parked and drank a little – nothing where we got sloppy, but just a good buzz.

While there, we met some local guys, and they started drinking with us. I don't remember what went on, but eventually we got into a fight with them. I remember Riley swinging his crutches, breaking one across this one guys back.

Eventually, these other guys left and the police showed up. I thought we were really busted, here we were, a little drunk, fighting in some public parking lot in the middle of 17 Mile Drive. We told the cop we were wounded vets from Fort Ord hospital and these guys started calling us baby killers and crap like that. We had to take it to them. The cop believed us and told us to get back to the post.

Field Jackets for Dad and Don

My job was a weekend responsibility to work in the clothing storage room in which the hospital would store the clothing of new people checking in. While in the hospital, all the patients would be issued pajamas and robes. I would take their clothes, usually army clothes, put them on hangers, cover them in plastic, tag them with the patient's identity, and hang them on one of the racks. I had an index card filing system on the desk that would track the location of the clothing for every patient.

One Saturday afternoon, I was working in the clothing room around 6:00 p.m.. Suddenly, there was a tremendous explosion, KABOOM. The building shook and my adrenaline level shot through the ceiling. I dove to the floor and my thoughts flashed back to An Tan (not more than five weeks earlier). Then I realized where I was and got up rather sheepishly, luckily there was no one else there to see me freak out like this.

When my heart rate returned to normal, I started to investigate the source of this explosion. It turned out that the clothing room was right next to the Division Headquarters building. At 6:00 p.m. every evening, when it's time to retire the colors (i.e., to take down the flag), they always fire the cannon just before lowering the colors and the playing of "retreat".

Man, this incident scared the crap out of me - I thought I was back in the war. The last time I heard an explosion like that, people got killed. To this day, I can't stand being startled.

This was my job on Saturday and Sunday nights, starting around 5:00 p.m. until 6:00 a.m. The next morning During this work assignment, I stole two army field jackets and took them home Dad and Don. I thought they would get lots of use out of them.

Fort Carson

Assigned to Fort Carson, Colorado

My next duty station couldn't have been more perfect. I was assigned to Fort Carson, Colorado, home of the 5th Mechanized Infantry Division and located just outside of Colorado Springs. Colorado Springs was my "home away from home", both my Mom and Dad grew up in Colorado Springs and I had been going back and forth to visit my grandparents since I was a baby. Assignment to Fort Carson was like going home. It wasn't a great cultural shock.

Fort Carson had been built prior to World War II and a lot of buildings still reflected that wood frame design that I saw at the reception center at Fort Ord. I was assigned to B Company, 2nd Battalion, 11th Infantry. Our barracks was one of the fairly new concrete buildings similar to that at Fort Ord, except the squad bays were 8 man rooms, no bunk beds. My MOS was still infantry.

Our Company was made up of senior NCOs and Vietnam returnees. Most of the troops in the unit had 6 months or so left and they were just marking time waiting to get out (6 months in Basic and AIT training, 12 months in Vietnam, leaving only 6 months on a 24 month term of service). Everyone, including the officers and NCOs were easy going and willing to mark their time together.

Life in this unit was like any other job in the world - up at 5:00 am, morning formation, breakfast, lunch, and dinner, and finish work around 5:00 p.m. then you were off until the next day. If you lived off post, you would go home, if you lived in the barracks, you had the run of the post and its facilities. Regular Army life, outside of the training units, wasn't so difficult.

When I left Fort Ord, the doctors restricted my physical activities until my wounds were fully recovered. They called this a Physical Profile and I had to keep a copy of it with me at all times. A physical profile is a soldier's dream, it relieved me from having to do any running, jumping, extended marching, etc., for the first 3 or 4 months while I was stationed at Fort Carson.

Maintenance on the Vehicles

Every day after lunch, the platoon sergeant would march us over to the motor pool to pull maintenance on the Armored Personnel Carriers (an APC or also known just as the "tracks"). As our small company (about 50 guys) was composed entirely of Vietnam returnees, most having 6 months or less of their service, we were not really interested in doing real Army things.

So our brand of maintenance consisted of removing the pin from one of the APC, driving the track in reverse to allow the track to peel off onto the ground, then we would all sit in the back and talk for the rest of the afternoon. Maybe we'd replace one or two of the track pads. About 4:00 p. m., we'd drive the APC back on its track, put the pin back in and go back to the barracks for evening formation.

Despite this "non-maintenance" effort, every day the platoon sergeant would ask to see my profile. The conversation would go something like this:

"Ropele, you got that profile?'

"Yes Sergeant, here it is".

He would take my profile and read it, EVERYDAY, then send me back to the barracks to clean up while the rest of the platoon would tend to their tracks. This went on everyday until about September.

Riot Control Training

The summer of 1968 began a volatile time in the history of the United States. President Johnson is escalating the war in Vietnam and is increasing the troop commitment of the United States. Protests against the United States involvement in the Vietnam war were being held across the nation, from college campuses to downtown rallies.

It seemed that every time you turned on the news, there was newsreel footage of the war direct from the front lines. Can you imagine the impact this had on people in the United States, seeing the fighting first hand, almost in real time? What if you were a parent and saw your son in one of the news footage? How shocking! Newspapers reported on every negative aspect of the war and every negative comment from anybody who was anybody.

This controversy was not lost on us. However, as most of us had "already done our time" and knew we wouldn't be going back, we were only concerned about the direct effect these demonstrations and riots had on our everyday activities. As it turned out, the effects could be most dramatic.

In a lot of cases, the active military was used as support to local law enforcement units and to National Guard units around the United States to control the demonstrators and to protect federal properties. Fort Carson was one such support base and as such, we spent a lot of time that summer learning the techniques of crowd control and dispersal.

On a regular basis during the summer, we drew our weapons and bayonets (not ammo) from the Armory and would go out to one of the fields to practice crowd control movement and techniques. This technique was to divide and conquer. It was a control process.

We would deploy in a long single line along the "front of the crowd", at the command of the Platoon Sergeant, we would fix our bayonets to our M16s, hold your M16 against your hip with the bayonet pointing into the crowd, then again on command, the guy in the center of the line would begin "half-stepping" forward, each guy following a half step behind, turning the single line into a wedge as it moves forward into the crowd.

We were required to have a duffel bag packed and ready so that if the command came to move out, all we had to do was "grab and run". There were a couple of instances when we were put on preliminary alert, but the actual orders to deploy never came about. The rumor said we would be going to Washington D.C.

New Job as Company Clerk

One afternoon I was upstairs in the barracks buffing the floors while the rest of the platoon was in the motor pool pulling maintenance when the First Sergeant (I can't remember his name) came down the hallway. Lucky for me that I was actually working this time. Most of the time, I would prop the buffer up against a corner of the room and just let it run and kick back on someone's bunk until the rest of the company returned from the Motor Pool.

The First Sergeant says:

> "Ropele, you have any college?"

"Yea, Top, I've had two years" (you always called the First Sergeant "Top" because he was the top enlisted man in the company, that is, he is the "Top Sergeant").

"You know how to type?"

"Yea Top, I've done a lot of typing, used to type all my papers in college".

"In two weeks, Swerdlo (that's the current Company Clerk), goes on TDY (temporary duty) and I need another clerk in the orderly room, are you interested?"

"Yea Top, I'd like to try that." I answer in a calm, measured voice. But on the inside, I'm screaming (AM I INTERESTED, AM I INTERESTED? DOES A BEAR EAT BUCKWHEAT IN THE WOODS? DO DUCKS FLY SOUTH IN THE WINTER? HELL YES, I'M INTERESTED.)

Working in the Orderly room is one of the best assignments I could ever fall into. Orderly room clerks are considered part of the Company staff, they are not required to pull duty like the rest of the troops and they have private rooms. What a deal.

I didn't bank on the fact that this First Sergeant was a real square shooter. The weekend before I moved into the Orderly Room, the First Sergeant pulled me ahead on the weekend duty roster so that I could complete my duty assignments. That Saturday I pulled KP from 4:00 am to 6:00 p.m. On Sunday, I pulled guard duty from 6:00 p.m. Sunday night until 6:00 am Monday.

Monday morning I moved into my desk in the Orderly Room. I was the junior clerk, Weaver (I can't remember his first name, he was from Ohio) was the senior clerk.. I moved out of the eight man squad bay and into the two man room with Weaver. I was pulled off the duty roster. Once I became part of the company staff, life became a breeze. I became part of the "privileged few". The staff took care of each other.

I worked for this First Sergeant for about 3 months, then he received orders for Vietnam. His replacement was a real loser - but more about him later.

Our primary duty was to account for all the men in the company. Every morning, we would turn in the roster information on the "Morning Report" accounting for the whereabouts of every man in the company. People were either on leave, in the hospital, on loan to another unit, etc. Whenever one of the staff (that is the "privileged few") would go on leave, we would carry him present at the company for a couple of extra days, so he would have some extra time. It was, you scratch my back, and I'll scratch yours.

This relationship worked out well, especially with the Armor. The Armor is the guy who stores and keeps track of all the weapons and the qualification status of everyone in the company. Every quarter everyone had to qualify again with the M16 rifle. During the months of November and December when the snow was on the ground and the sky was gray and cloudy, going out to the range in the back of a truck could be an ugly afternoon.

So in exchange for a couple of extra days leave, the Armor would update our weapons records, post our "requalification scores" and pass us on weapons inspections.

I remember one cold snowy November day in 1968 when everyone in the Battalion had to requalify with the M16. It was one of those edicts from the Division Commander because in prior years, the percentage of those that requalified was real low. So this year, he says that EVERYBODY has to requalify. So our First Sergeant's hands were tied, the "good ole boy network" was short circuited by a direct order.

The main portion of the Company checked out their weapons from the Armory and left the company area somewhere around 7:00 am. However, at the range the atmosphere was like all military activities, there was a lot of hurry up and wait. As I recall, the sky was gray and it was cold, wind was blowing and there was no chance for the sun to come out. Not a pleasant day to be in the mountains, just standing around.

Around 10:00 am, the Company Commander's driver came in to pick up the Orderly Room staff and take us back out to the range. When we arrived, we "talked" to Sgt Lanahan (the senior NCO) and made a "deal"(the usual deal, "how would you like a few extra days the next time you take leave?").

He put us in the next group that went up to the firing line and we blew off a magazine of shells. Even before we got our scores, we hopped back in the truck and went back to the Post. We were only at the range for about 15 minutes. The rest of the Company didn't get back until well after lunch.

Division Field Training Exercise

Sometime in the fall of 1968 the annual Division Field Training Exercise (Division FTX) was scheduled. This is an annual event to demonstrate the Divisions readiness in manpower and equipment, but it took on even a greater importance since the 5th Division was preparing for full deployment to Vietnam.

Typically, whenever there was a major training exercise, the sick call rolls on the morning we were to leave always increased as the troops tried every excuse to get out of the exercise. This time the Division Commander was adamant, everyone including clerks, where to participate in the exercise.

During the spring training exercise, I had already proven myself "vital to the everyday activities" of the Company. I did this by locking all the important papers, especially everyone's leave authorizations, in my desk and taking the key with me to the field. I was out only a couple of hours, when I had to come back in and process the papers for those that remained in the barracks. This time I convinced Lt. Costanza (the Company Commander) that I had better stay in with Sgt. Lanahan to help him manage the affairs here.

However our new First Sergeant was not as fortunate. This was a new guy that was just waiting for retirement. His philosophy was, "the less I have to do , the better I like it". That made for an increased workload on me and McClure (my Jr. Clerk). He was a real "scrud".

This FTX rocked him back on his heels and he had to resort to all these tricks to get out of the activity.

On the day before the Company was to leave, the First Sergeant tells us that he has an appointment the next morning to interview for an NCO position in the ROTC unit at Colorado College in Colorado Springs. He said that he would be finished by mid-morning and to have a truck ready to take him out into the field at 10:00 a.m. The conversation went something like this:

At 10:00 am, the First Sergeant calls in:

> "Ropele, tell the CO (the Commanding Officer) that I'm still tied up in this interview here. Have the truck back there at 2:00 p.m. to take me out to the field".
>
> OK, Top, Good Luck.

I wrote a note to Lt Costanza, gave it to the driver and told him to come back at 2:00 p.m.

At 2:00 p.m., the First Sergeant calls in, again:

"Ropele, tell the CO that I'm still tied up in this interview here. Have the truck back there at 7:00 a.m. tomorrow morning to take me out to the field".

OK, Top, Good Luck.

I sent a second note to Lt. Costanza and told the driver to come back tomorrow at 7:00 am

The next morning, the First Sergeant calls in, again. This time Sgt. Lanahan answers the phone (I'm listening on the extension. We both know this guy is just blowing smoke).

The First Sergeant says: "Sgt. Lanahan, I won't be there this morning. I went up to the mountains last night and we got snowed, but I couldn't get out until this afternoon. (In the background, I can hear muffled voices, the sounds of jukebox music, laughter, you know, barroom noises).

Sgt. Lanahan says: "Snowed in? Snowden? Snowed in with what Top, crushed ice?

The First Sergeant says: "Have the truck there tomorrow morning at 10:00 am to take me to the field.

Well, this guy never did show up for the FTX. As a matter of fact, he didn't even show up the day the company returned from the entire exercise. Lt. Costanza was really mad. The CO had him brought up on charges of AWOL (serious stuff for a man of his experience and rank). He sure was an idiot. I suppose that he was an alcoholic and just couldn't cope any longer.

He was never court martialed. I'm sure they worked out an agreement that possibly allowed him to retire at a lesser rank. At any rate he never came back to the unit - another First Sergeant was assigned to our unit within the week.

Winter Driving

One afternoon, Terry Haro, Jim Esposito, and I left the Post heading down the main highway towards Colorado Springs for home. The three of us were living off Post in a cabin in a Motor Court in Manitou Springs (just below the Cog Rail Line that takes you to the top of Pikes Peak).

Like most afternoons in Colorado, it had just started raining. I'm driving my Malibu, slightly worried because all four tires are real bad, bald in fact. But I intend to replace them soon and it's not likely anything will happen anyway (little did I know). Haro is sitting in the front seat, on his hip talking, Esposito is in the back. and like everybody else who just got off work, we're trying to figure out what we're going to do that night.

I going about 45 mph, having just shifted into third gear, when the car hit a slick spot on the highway. All of a sudden, the car is sliding sideways down the highway, the back end has come around almost even with the front end and, crap, we're going into a spin.

Instinctively, I jerk the steering wheel to the right, and the car pops back straight.

All this happened quicker than you could say ". . . oh crap!. Haro never saw anything. As a matter of fact, he didn't even skip a beat in his conversation.

But Esposito, he was as white as a sheet, his mouth was open to the floor. He yells, ". . . did you see that ? What happened. .? He's stuttering, "We, we, we. .. . . .

Haro says, "What? See what? What the matter with you, man?

I couldn't believe it. One minute we're driving down the highway, the next second, we're sideways, and a second later, we're driving down the highway again. We laughed about it all the way home. Needless to say, later that week I replaced all four tires.

What a sobering experience. How ironic would that be, to survive Vietnam and then get killed in an automobile accident in Colorado.

The 5th Division Prepares for Deployment to Vietnam

Somewhere around November of 1968, Fort Carson started getting replacements direct from AIT as the 5th Division was preparing to deploy to Vietnam. Our little Company grew virtually overnight from about 25 guys to a full unit of about 200 people. We didn't have the room to house all the people and their stuff, so we put about 40 sets of bunk beds in the day room and turned it into a squad bay

As there was no longer a day room, the Supply Sergeant stored the pool table in the supply building, but before he could store the television set, Weaver and I grabbed it and took it into our room. This was a nice big 25 inch color console TV set. We rigged up an antenna out of metal coat hangers in a bottle. Everyone really ragged on us, but we told them to shove it.

We started getting new officers directly out of school (either just out of Officers Candidate School (OCS) or those who just completed basic training after graduating from ROTC from college). These new guys looked 21 or 22 years with virtually no military experience. Some of these guys were so young, it seemed as though their voices hadn't changed yet.

This buildup in personnel and the accompanying training was very stressful on the veterans. They had already done their time and were just waiting to get back to real life. Now they have to put up not only with the new troops, but with all these young officers who are just itching to put their warfare theories into practice. It was almost like going back to basic training again.

I was a little worried as I had about 9 months to go and I thought that it was a real possibility that I could be sent back to Vietnam. The stress and worry on all the veterans increased dramatically and it was inevitable that there would be some problems.

I remember a specific instance when one of the new 2nd Lieutenants (a 2nd Lieutenant is the lowest rank in the officer ranks and is typically a Platoon Leader position) came running into the Orderly Room. This guy was frothing at the mouth. He yelling at the First Sergeant to schedule a court martial because he wanted to prosecute one of the veterans for insubordination.

Well, the first thing, nobody orders the First Sergeant to do anything (except maybe the Company Commander, and especially, not a 2nd Lieutenant). Fortunately, this First Sergeant was a real laid back kind of guy (I don't remember his name). He told the Lieutenant to relax, to calm down, and to tell him what happened.

Seems this Lieutenant, while conducting a morning inspection of the barracks and the troops, started harassing one of the Vietnam veterans about the fact that his bunk was not made good enough - the blankets were not pulled tight enough, I think. This soldier, who had served a full combat tour in Vietnam, and only had about 5 months to go on his enlistment, told the Lieutenant, in very graphic terms, to have sexual intercourse with himself' (you can imagine the language he used). I think the other troops even had to restrain the veteran from jumping this guy.

The new officer took offense at the lack of respect for his rank and came unglued. The Lieutenant came charging into the Orderly Room, screaming that the First Sergeant called the Military Police (MPs) and scheduled a court martial.

The First Sergeant was really cool. He realized the difference in priorities of these two soldiers (one guy was an experienced combat veteran that was just trying to go home and the other guy was so new to the regular Army that his uniform hadn't even faded yet). He calmed the Lieutenant down and told him that he would handle the situation.

Immediately, the First Sergeant called the soldier into the office and reamed him royally. He told this guy he had better control his mouth and show respect for the officer, or he would process the court martial and send him to the stockade for the next 5 months. He disciplined the soldier with extra duty.

But the neat part was that the First Sergeant also met with the Lieutenant and taught him that the men in his platoon were men, and to treat them with the respect they had earned.

There were many instances like these over the next 6 months. Sometimes the guys would get so stressed with this "stateside" military that they would volunteer to go back to Vietnam. Even guys with less than 6 months would ask me to prepare papers for them to reenlist and go back to Vietnam, just to get away from the bullshit that was going on.

The Sandwich Man

The Sandwich Man showed up during the spring of 1969. He was a man who recognized opportunity and made a buck or two in the process.

As a member of the U.S. Army, the Government took care of all my needs. My job in the U.S. Army was to be ready to go to wherever the Government deemed my presence was necessary, any place at any time. In exchange for my 24 hour availability and service, I was paid a living wage, I was furnished with a place to live, I was issued a basic supply of work clothes, and all my meals every day were furnished, "three squares a day".

It was like eating in a restaurant, except the choices were not as broad and it was like eating in the same restaurant every day. Breakfast usually consisted of your choice of eggs (fried or scrambled), bacon, sausage, toast, or hot cereal, or sometimes pancakes or waffles. Lunch and dinner were similar in the sense that hot meals were made available, a meat dish, potatoes or rice, salad. The food was always pretty good. But there was always something lacking.

What you didn't have is the freedom to just go into the kitchen and "graze". You know, open the refrigerator or the pantry and look until something appeals to you. Hence, the success of the Sandwich Man.

The Sandwich Man would walk through the barracks with one of those styrofoam type camping coolers strapped around his neck, much like the vendors at the ballpark, selling sandwiches that he had made at home. Nothing fancy, just your basic bologna, or ham and cheese on two pieces of white bread, a little mayonnaise and mustard.

He would sell them for about $1.00 each, more if you wanted one with cheese. He would walk through our barracks hawking his wares, then on to the next building, and so forth.

Granted, we're not talking about anything big here. It's just a plain ole sandwich you might say. But when you don't have these basic kinds of comforts available to you, they take on a new level of meaning. Somehow, you still had to feed your passion for junk food.

Moved off Post to Manitou Springs

In the early part of 1969, Terry Haro, Jim Esposito, and I decided that it was appropriate that we move off post and get ourselves a place in town. We were a "permanent party" at Fort Carson, we were out of the training mode of Army life, being in the Army was just like an everyday job in the real world.

We would have to be at work at 5:00 am for morning formation and we were essentially done working at 5:00 pm at night. So between 5:00 pm and 5:00 am, we were "off duty". There were no restrictions going on or off the post, you didn't have to show a pass to the guard. So why stay in the barracks?

Because you had to have special permission to live off post, that's why. Off-post living was usually restricted to married soldiers with families, who couldn't get on-post housing. But we decided to move off anyway, what were they going to do about it, send us to Vietnam? As long as we kept our bunks in the barracks, who would be the wiser?

Right at the base of the Pikes Peak Cog Railroad in Manitou Springs was a group of cabins, like those little motor courts that you would see in the 1940's movies. Most of these cabin units were little two or three room affairs, essentially built for overnight lodging.

We rented one of the larger ones from the widow women who owned the place and rotated between the couches and the bed in the bedroom

Now that we off post, we would get up at 4:30 am to dress and get to the Fort in time for breakfast. In my case, I would then report to the orderly room and be waiting for the First Sergeant when he arrived at 5:30 am. At the end of the day, usually, 5:00 pm, we would get in the car and take off for home.

Just like the real world.

The Corvette

Sometime in the early part of 1969, I was driving by a used car lot in Colorado Springs and this burgundy red 1967 Corvette threw itself in front of me and said "Buy Me, Buy Me". It was "lust" at first sight, I had to have it. I knew we were meant for each other. I traded in my 1965 Malibu, gave them an additional 500 dollars and financed the rest. It was all done within a week. I think the total price was $3200.00.

The "Vette" was a convertible. It had a removable hard top and a soft top that folded into the rear boot. It was 427 cu .in. V8, 4 bbl carburetor, and 4 speed transmission. This car was fast. I would downshift into second gear, stomp the accelerator to the floor, the front end would lift up and this machine would scream forward.

I bought an 8 track stereo tape deck and mounted two speakers in boxes behind the front seats. I would put the top down, turn up the stereo, and cruise. I was hot. Even when it was cold outside, I could still cruise with the top down because I would turn the heater up full blast.

I recall driving home from Colorado and going across the Utah desert between Green River Colorado and Richfield Utah on highway 70 running at over 100 mph and this car just cruised along.

This is not my corvette, but it's just like it. Mine was a burgundy red and gray hood scoop. Why would anyone want to get rid of car like this?

Separation from the Army

Veterans Administration (VA) Compensation

During my time in the service, I never thought of myself as "disabled". I knew that I had retained fragments from the explosion in my foot and leg and possibly in my arm and that I wasn't 100%. I felt somewhat "hobbled" in the sense that my ankle and foot felt. What's a good word to use here, "squishy"? Sure, when I first got to Fort Carson, I had the profile that limited my physical involvement in certain activities, but the Profile was only good for the first 3 months there, then I was considered "back to normal".

As I got closer to my End of Term of Service (ETS) date and as I talked with others in the platoon who were leaving the service, I became more aware of the details of the activities associated with "clearing the post". Clearing the post is the process of checking out through various organizations to ensure that all your "accounts" have been settled. For instance, when you turned in all your field gear, the Supply Sergeant would sign-off his block on the checkout sheet certifying that you returned all the things the Army had issued you to use. You would process through all the Post organizations in a similar fashion.

During my process of checking out of the medical division, they gave me my medical records to turn in at final checkout. I thought, "hot dog", now I see exactly the extent of my injuries and what treatments I received. I figured that would give me a leg up in dealing with the VA once I got home.

I eagerly opened the packet and to my dismay, they were the original records the Army created when I got drafted. There were no injuries in Vietnam. As it turned out, the medical record set that began at the 2nd Surgical Hospital in Chu Lai and that followed me through my treatment at Fort Ord hospital was still at Fort Ord. Evidently, Fort Ord pulled and sent the wrong set of records when I transferred to Fort Carson.

Certainly, these wouldn't support a VA claim of my injuries. I figured that it would be really difficult to obtain the proper record once I left active duty. I had this vision of a warehouse building, crammed from the floor to the ceiling with filing cabinets and the end of the building disappearing into a bank of fog. The type of place where it would take years to find something. The "elephant burial ground" for military records. I was really concerned that the VA might not have the appropriate records available to them to rule on my claim.

So, exploiting the capabilities of my office, as the company clerk and my relationship with the Company Commander, I composed a letter to the Fort Ord Hospital Administrator requesting that the proper records be forwarded to the commanding officer of the Company. I had Lt. Trujillo, the Company Commander, sign it.

To my surprise, the records came within two weeks directly to the Orderly Room – I expected they would go directly to the records branch. So, taking advantage of the situation of having them in my possession, I went to the Battalion Headquarters and copied everything and then I turned them over to the records branch.

When I processed through the Finance Branch, I obtained the VA Claim notification and sent it in. I was pretty sure that I would be classified as disabled because of the retention of the fragments.

Some weeks after leaving the Army, I was notified and examined by doctors at the Veterans Administration Hospital in Long Beach. They took x-rays of my leg and foot to verify the fragment retention, x-rays of my right arm and I made them give me a hearing test. I'm convinced that I have a hearing loss on my left side due to my proximity to the explosion.

In November of 1969, I was notified by the Veterans Administration that I was classified as 20% disabled because of the retention of fragments in my leg and foot. There were no fragments in my right arm and apparently my hearing wasn't impacted.

They began by sending me $43.00 per month. Disability compensation is non-declarable income, that is, it's tax free. With the cost of living increasing over the years, the monthly amount has increased to $245.00 today.

Today, the leg and foot don't give me much trouble. I do get a little tightness sometimes in my ankle that causes me to limp when I first get out of a chair or out of bed in the morning. Sometimes, there's an ache that seems to last for several days, but there is nothing major. I can still run, I play a little basketball, and my physical activities are not really inhibited.

DEPARTMENT OF THE ARMY
BRAVO COMPANY 2D BATTALION (MECH) 11TH INFANTRY
5TH INFANTRY DIVISION (MECH) FORT CARSON COLORADO 80913

8 May 1969

SUBJECT: Medical Records of SP4 Richard A Ropele US 56 707 489

Commanding Officer
US Army Hospital
Fort Ord California

1. I have a member of my command, SP4 Richard A Ropele, US 56 707 489 who was a patient in your hospital from 18 February 1968 to 27 May 1968. He was a medi-evac from Viet Nam and was on ward D-15 and his doctor was Dr. Loughran.

2. When SP4 Ropele first came to your hospital temporary medical records were being used because his original medical were still in transit from Viet Nam. When he was clearing the hospital to come to Fort Carson his temporary records could not be located at that time so he only had his original records to bring with him.

3. SP4 Ropele is going to ETS on the 20th of June 1969 and in order to qualify for VA Benefits he is going to have to have his temporary records that show that he was in the hospital from wounds suffered in Viet Nam. Inclosed is a copy of his profile signed by Dr. Loughran and also his X-Ray card. Any answer you could give me would be greatly appreciated.

4. SP4 Ropele goes for his ETS interview on 28 May 1969 and he has to have some proof of his hospitalization to put in a claim for VA Benefits.

1 Incl
as

DAVID A TRUJILLO
1LT, Inf
Commanding

Letter I composed and had the Company Commander sign so that I could get my proper medical records in place before I left the Army

VETERANS ADMINISTRATION

VETERAN'S APPLICATION FOR COMPENSATION OR PENSION AT SEPARATION FROM SERVICE

FOR VA USE ONLY

2A. LAST NAME—FIRST NAME—MIDDLE NAME OF VETERAN (Type or print)	2B. SERVICE NUMBER	2C. SOCIAL SECURITY NUMBER
ROPELE, Richard Anthony	US 56 707 489	546-66-1648

NOTE: Items 3A through 5B to be completed if you had prior service in the Army, Navy, Air Force, Marine Corps or Coast Guard.

ENTERED SERVICE 3A. DATE	3B. PLACE	3C. SERVICE NO.	SEPARATED FROM SERVICE 3D. DATE	3E. PLACE	3F. GRADE AND ORGANIZATION	3G. BRANCH OF SERVICE
21 Jun 67	Los Angeles Calif	US 56707489	20 Jun 69	Ft Carson Colo	E-4 Co B 2d 11th Inf	Army

4A. IF YOU SERVED UNDER ANOTHER NAME, GIVE NAME UNDER WHICH YOU SERVED: NA

4B. PERIOD DURING WHICH YOU SERVED: NA

5A. IF RESERVIST OR NATIONAL GUARDSMAN, GIVE PERIODS OF ACTIVE DUTY: NA

5B. BRANCH OF SERVICE: NA

6. NATURE OF SICKNESS, DISEASES OR INJURIES FOR WHICH CLAIM IS MADE AND DATE EACH BEGAN: Suffered fragment wounds in the Republic of Viet Nam, 31 Jan 68. Some frags are still remaining.

NOTE: Items 7A through 7C to be completed if you received any treatment while in service.

7A. NAME, NUMBER OR LOCATION OF HOSPITAL, FIRST AID STATION, DRESSING STATION OR INFIRMARY	7B. DATES OF TREATMENT	7C. NATURE OF SICKNESS, DISEASE OR INJURY
2d Sergical Hospital RVN	31 Jan-4Feb	Frag wounds
85th Evac RVN	4Feb-10Feb68	Frag wounds
249 General Hospital Japan	10Feb68-18Feb	Frag wounds
USAH Ft Ord Calif	18Feb-29May	Frag wounds

NOTE: Items 8A through 8D to be completed if you had treatment by civilian physicians for any disease or injury prior to or during your service.

8A. NAME OF CIVILIAN PHYSICIAN	8B. PRESENT ADDRESS	8C. DISABILITY	8D. DATE

NOTE: Items 9A through 9D to be completed showing persons who know any facts concerning any sickness, disease or injury which you had prior to or during your service.

9A. NAME	9B. PRESENT ADDRESS	9C. DISABILITY	9D. DATE

10A. HAVE YOU EVER HAD A MEDICAL EXAMINATION FROM ANY U. S. GOVERNMENT CIVILIAN AGENCY? [X] YES [ ] NO (If "Yes," complete 10B and 10C)

10B. DATE EXAMINED: 3 Jun 69

10C. NAME AND LOCATION OF AGENCY: USAH Ft ØCarson Colo

11A. HAVE YOU EVER FILED A CLAIM FOR COMPENSATION FROM THE U. S. BUREAU OF EMPLOYEES' COMPENSATION? (Formerly the U. S. Employees' Compensation Commission) [X] YES [ ] NO

11B. UPON DISCHARGE, ARE YOU TO BE FURNISHED HOSPITALIZATION BY THE VETERANS ADMINISTRATION? (If "Yes," fill in 11C) [ ] YES [X] NO

11C. NAME AND ADDRESS OF HOSPITAL

12A. HAVE YOU EVER APPLIED FOR OR RECEIVED DISABILITY SEVERANCE PAY FROM THE ARMED FORCES? [ ] YES [X] NO (If "Yes," fill in 12B)

12B. AMOUNT NA $

13A. HAVE YOU EVER RECEIVED A LUMP SUM READJUSTMENT PAYMENT FROM THE ARMED FORCES? [ ] YES [X] NO (If "Yes," fill in 13B and 13C)

13B. DATE RECEIVED NA

13C. BRANCH OF SERVICE NA

14A. HAVE YOU EVER APPLIED FOR BENEFITS FROM THE VETERANS ADMINISTRATION? [ ] YES [X] NO (If "Yes," fill in 14B, 14C, and 14D)

14B. NAME THE BENEFIT NA

14C. VETERANS ADMINISTRATION OFFICE WHERE APPLICATION WAS FILED: NA

14D. CLAIM NO. ASSIGNED (If known) NA C-

VA FORM JUN 1968 **21-526e** EXISTING STOCKS OF VA FORM 21-526e, JUN 1967, WILL BE USED.

Application for VA compensation

VETERANS ADMINISTRATION

Regional Office
Federal Building
11000 Wilshire Boulevard
Los Angeles, Calif. 90024

NOV 2 5 1969

File Number
024979838 00 344

This is to certify that

RAROPEL

Richard A Ropele
1028 Oak St
Santa Ana CA 92701

Veterans Benefits Award

is awarded Veterans Administration benefits payable in the amount and beginning with the date shown below.

Monthly Amount	Beginning Date
$ 0043.00	06-21-69

It is MOST IMPORTANT that you note the contents of the attachments which may affect your right to continue to receive these payments.

Encl.
VA Form 6752, 339, 1900
Copy CIVA APPEARED ON YOUR BEHALF

VETERANS ADMINISTRATION

Show veteran's full name and VA file number on all correspondence. If VA number is unknown, show service number.
VA FORM 20-822, APR 1969 VETERAN OR BENEFICIARY - 2

The award of $43.00 per month, tax free, for the rest of my life

ORIGINAL DISABILITY COMPENSATION

A check covering the initial amount due under your award of disability compensation will be mailed soon. Thereafter, checks will be issued at the end of the month. Payments will be made subject to the conditions explained below.

This award has been made to you for the following service-connected condition(s): Residuals shell fragment left leg with retained foreign bodies rated 10% disabling from 6-21-69; Residuals shell fragment wound, left foot with fracture 4th and 5th meteresl and cuboid and retained *

Your disabilities listed below are service-connected but they are less than 10% disabling and compensation is not payable. Residuals, shell fragment wound, right elbow rated 0% from 6-21-69; residuals shell fragment wound, face rated 0% from 6-21-69.

The evidence does not establish service-connection for:

Any new evidence which you believe would justify a different decision should be sent to us promptly. If you have no further evidence but believe this decision is not correct, you may initiate an appeal to the Board of Veterans Appeals by filing a notice of disagreement at any time within one year from the date of this letter. A notice of disagreement is simply a written communication which makes clear your intention to initiate an appeal and the specific part of our decision with which you disagree. It should be sent to this office. In the absence of timely appeal, this decision will become final.

Veterans rated 50% or more disabled may be granted additional compensation for a wife, children or dependent parents. For wife and children, submit a certified copy of your marriage certificate, birth certificate of each minor child, and Declaration of Marital Status. For dependent parents, submit a certified copy of your own birth certificate together with Statement of Dependency completed by your parent or parents. In order that additional benefits may be payable from the earliest possible date, this evidence should be submitted within one year from the date of this notice.

You are entitled to necessary treatment by the VA for the service-connected conditions referred to above. This letter will help to establish your entitlement and should be presented to the nearest VA office when you feel treatment may be necessary. This is not an authorization for treatment. Under certain circumstances you may qualify for hospital treatment or domiciliary care, for a condition not due to military service. To determine your eligibility for such treatment or care, if the occasion arises, you should apply at the nearest VA field station.

Compensation payments are exempt from taxation; the payments are not assignable, are exempt from claims of creditors, are not subject to attachment, levy or seizure except as to claims of the U. S.

Please notify this office immediately, in writing over your signature, of any change of address.

CONDITIONS AFFECTING RIGHT TO PAYMENTS

1. Your award of disability compensation is subject to future adjustment upon receipt of evidence showing any chang in the degree of your disability.

2. Your payments may also be affected by any of the following circumstances which you should promptly call to our attention.

   a. Re-entrance into active military or naval service.
   b. Receipt of armed forces service retirement pay, unless your retirement pay has been reduced because of award of disability compensation.
   c. Receipt of benefits from the Bureau of Employees Compensation.
   d. Receipt of active duty or drill pay as a reservist or member of the Federally recognized National Guard.

Monthly payments of your award may be stopped, if you fail to furnish evidence as requested; fail to cooperate or submit to a Veterans Administration examination when requested; or if you furnish the Veterans Administration, or cause to be furnished any false or fraudulent evidence.

The law provides severe penalties which include fine or imprisonment, or both, for the fraudulent acceptance of any payment to which you are not entitled.

If you are paying premiums on Government life insurance (GI insurance) and are unable to work, you may be entitled to certain benefits as provided for in your policy. For complete information contact the Veterans Administration office where you pay premiums.

* foreign bodies rated 10% disabling from 6-21-69 combined 20%.

VA FORM MAR 1966 **21-6782** EXISTING STOCK OF VA FORM 21-6782, FEB 1965, WILL BE USED.

U.S. GOVERNMENT PRINTING OFFICE : 1966 O - [illegible]

VETERANS ADMINISTRATION
REGIONAL OFFICE
FEDERAL BUILDING 11000 WILSHIRE BOULEVARD
LOS ANGELES, CALIFORNIA 90024
November 25, 1969

IN REPLY REFER TO: 344-211
C 24 979 808

Mr. Richard A. Ropele
1028 Oak St.
Santa A na, Ca. 92701

Dear Mr. Ropele:,

As a veteran with a service-connected disability, you may be eligible for vocational rehabilitation training in addition to any compensation or retirement benefits which you now receive. The purpose of such training is to help you obtain suitable employment.

We will be glad to arrange time for you with a counselor who will assist you in the selection of a suitable vocational or educational objective if you are interested in such service and are eligible for training. We will arrange an interview at the VA office nearest to you.

If you are interested in this program, or desire additional information, complete the enclosed application form and return it to us in the enclosed postage free, pre-addressed envelope.

Your interest in vocational rehabilitation will not obligate you in any way nor affect your present rate of compensation or pay.

Sincerely yours,

M. C. Holland

M. C. Holland
Adjudication Officer

Encls:

FL 21E-389
SEP 1966 (R)

Show veteran's full name and VA file number on all correspondence. If VA number is unknown, show service number.

This is a letter I received some years after from the VA notifying me that vocational training was available. I never considered myself as being handicapped so I never took advantage of it

DEPARTMENT OF THE ARMY
OFFICE OF THE ADJUTANT GENERAL
U. S. ARMY ADMINISTRATION CENTER
ST. LOUIS, MISSOURI 63132

IN REPLY REFER TO:

AGUZ-PAD-M

24 May 71

SUBJECT: Physical Condition

SP4 Richard A Repeto, USAR SSAN: 546-66-1648
1028 Oak St
Santa Ana, CA 92701

1. Your claim to a medical condition which may limit your ability to serve on active duty has been received. A claim of this nature must be supported by a written evaluation prepared by a health care specialist as indicated below:

a. Doctor of Medicine or Osteopathy.

b. Doctor of Optometry.

c. Doctor of Chiropody or Podiatry.

d. Doctor of Clinical Psychology.

2. The statement submitted by the health care specialist should be detailed and include the following:

a. Diagnosis.

b. Treatment.

c. Prognosis for complete recovery.

d. Physical activity limitations in detail to include special diets, geographical residence restrictions, etc.

3. This letter may be presented to your health care specialist so that he may know exactly what is required. Remember, any professional or administrative fees involved in securing examinations or medical reports from civilian health care specialists to support your claim must be borne by you. The Army cannot assume this responsibility.

4. Attach the statement from your health care specialist to this letter and return it to this Center. Upon receipt, the statement will be incorporated with your medical records and a determination of your medical fitness status will be accomplished. Until additional evidence is received, your medical fitness status for military service will remain as currently documented in your file.

5. VA Compensation examination and VA Form 21-6732 will suffice

FOR THE COMMANDER:

1 Incl
Rtn Envelope

NORMAN L. DAVIS, JR
Captain, AGC
Asst Adjutant

USAAC Form
1 Nov 68 375

This is the only time I heard from the VA where I thought they were looking for me to come in for a reexamination. I thought maybe they were trying to reduce my compensation. But I just resubmitted the form they asked for and everything went on as normal

Time to Draw this Memory to a Conclusion

For years now, I have been wrestling with the way to draw this manuscript to a conclusion. I started this back in the 1980s, printed out various proof copies, for editing purposes, but I've always been reluctant to get back into it because of having to 'relive' each of the experiences. It's not that these are so painful, but it puts me back in the moment, where I can 'see' the environment, 'smell' the humid air, 'feel' the intense heat or constant rain and the wet uniform sticking to my back..

I thought it important to get these experiences down on paper, not to purge them from my memory, but that others in my family would know about this major experience in my life, how I conducted myself in the war and how it led me into being the person that they know today. You don't 'purge' these memories, you put them into a 'protected' space where they are only as close to the surface as you allow them to be.

Sometimes, I don't know how close they are, until something causes me to look into that space opens and I 'flash on one of those instances; it could be a song on the radio, it could be that smell of burning firewood, it could be a particular date in time, that puts me back in the environment, always juxtaposed against the present..

.

I came back from Vietnam physically scarred, and somewhat emotionally scarred. I'm not a classic PTSD driven type of person, where I use these experiences as an excuse to avoid life events, but I do use them to frame my concerns/responses. and the degree in which I'll allow myself to be involved in an activity/conversation. January 31, 1968, when my life changed dramatically and I was no longer just a carefree young buck, but a fully committed Vietnam soldier fighting for my life and the lives of the men in my squad. It was a turning point when I knew it would be difficult being that guy that I once was.

I often wonder why I didn't get killed that TET morning of January 31, 1968 when that 122mm rocket impacted and exploded no more than 6 feet away from me – shrapnel in my leg and foot instead of in my head and upper body – was it a stroked of luck or was it the hand of God, saving me for some other mission in this life? How would I find out?

What I now believe is that my life was spared by the hand of God as I was in a position where the full force of that explosion was absorbed by the sandbag wall – why was I blessed when others weren't so fortunate that morning? I searched for the answer for several years – not overtly searching, but living life and always being aware of the extra gift of time/life with which I was blessed. My Mom and Dad raised my brother Don and me as Christians – although we didn't attend a particular church, Mom led us in the Lords' Prayer every night before bed.

It wasn't until I met Cathy Harrison while working at Ford Aerospace in Newport Beach in 1971 that things in my life started to come into focus. We started dating and I felt an immediate attraction to her and enjoyed being with her. I eventually found out she was an active member of the Church of Jesus Christ of Latter-Day Saints (the Morman's).

It wasn't long before she invited me to meet some of her friends and to attend a Regional Devotional meeting one Sunday evening at the Anaheim Stake Center. I remember we walked in the back doors of the building and I saw this full size basketball ball floor connected to Chapel; I thought that any Church that coupled basketball with their religion was something I wanted to pay close attention to. I had played basketball every year since the 6th grade, sometimes on school teams, in industrial leagues and in open leagues. Basketball was something I enjoyed.

It wasn't long after dating for a couple of months that I started taking the missionary lessons in the restoration of the Gospel through the Prophet Joseph Smith and reading and praying about the Book of Mormon, I freely chose baptism. Into the Church of Jesus Christ of Latter-Day Saints and began my discovery as to why I wasn't KIA that morning of TET, but was WIA – to develop a relationship with God and Jesus Christ and begin my journey with Cathy and our eventual family into eternal life.

Cathy and I were married in the Saint George Temple on November 17th 1972. We have been blessed with 5 children and 8 grandchildren. This manuscript is a small part of my life about me and why I act.

them to know exactly what was going on. They could watch the news and see, but I didn't want them to hear any gory details from me.

Can you imagine how worried they would have been if I had told them about walking to a night ambush spot? I was in the midst of death and destruction, I didn't want them to know details.

Here they are:

Fort Ord

This is the postcard that I filled out upon arriving at Fort Ord on 22 June 1967 to notify my folks that I had arrived safely

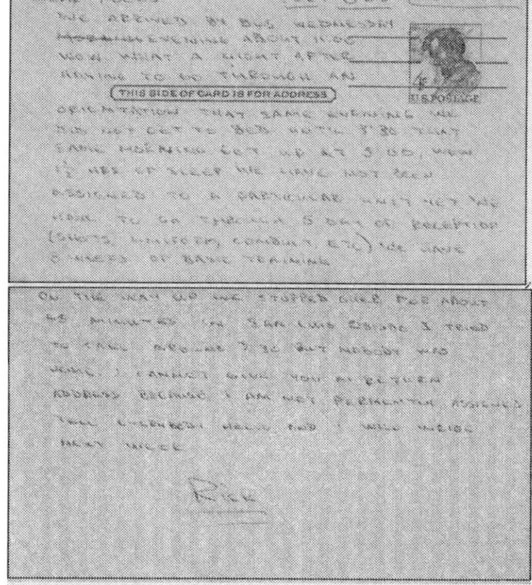

U.S. POSTAGE

THIS SIDE OF CARD IS FOR ADDRESS

This is a 'fold out' postcard that I addressed that first morning at Fort Ord that was also sent home

Dear Parents, Guardians and Wives,

A member of your family has just arrived safely at the US Army Reception Station, Ft Ord, California. He will be with us for about four working days, during which time we will process him into the US Army. The purpose of this card is not only to assure you that he arrived safely, but to furnish you with some information about the Reception Station.

During the time that the receptees are in the Reception Station, THEY ARE NOT ALLOWED TO LEAVE THE RECEPTION STATION AREA. They may receive visitors, however, in our visitors lounge. The visitors lounge is open Saturday, 1:00 - 8:00 PM Sunday and holidays, 10:00 to 6:00 PM. Due to medical precautions taken with all receptees, we can only allow PARENTS, LEGAL GUARDIANS, AND WIVES to visit receptees. Brothers, sisters, friends, children etc., will not be allowed to visit receptees. We would appreciate your cooperation in observing this restriction.

Since a receptee is with us only four days, sending mail to him here will only slow down its delivery. We therefore recommend that families do not write a receptee using the Reception Station as an address. A receptee is given a post card and the name of the training unit to which he will be sent soon after he arrives in the Reception Station so that he may forward that address to his family. Using the address of a receptee's training unit will facilitate the delivery of his mail. In addition, if you write me about a receptee, by the time your letter reaches me he will have left my authority. Write "COMMANDING OFFICER" at the address he gives you.

Should a situation arise which you feel requires the presence of the receptee at home, contact your local Red Cross for assistance. This will aid us in getting him home as quickly as possible, should it prove to be an emergency.

We fully understand the natural concern that families have when one of their men enters the Armed Forces. You may rest assured, however, that our receptees are well cared for.

Edward F. Fiora Jr

EDWARD F. FIORA JR
Major, Infantry
Commanding

This is the first letter I sent home from Fort Ord. As it's dated 01 July 67, I was then out of the Reception Station and assigned to my basic training company.

1 JULY, 67

DEAR FOLKS

I HAVEN'T HAD A CHANCE TO GET A LINE OFF EARLIER, WE HAVE BEEN SO BUSY EVERYDAY. TODAY WE STARTED OUR BASIC TRAINING. WE WENT OUT AND RAN THE MILE (WITH ALL OUR CLOTHES ON.) HOLY COW, I RAN IT IN 8:19, NOT THE FASTEST BUT NOT THE SLOWEST EITHER. WE HAVE FIVE EXERCISES TO DO WITH A MAXIMUM POINT TOTAL OF 100 POINTS EACH, THEY ARE 1) MILE RUN, UNDER 6:00 MINUTES FOR A HUNDRED POINTS 2) HORIZONTAL LADDER, 76 RUNGS UNDER 60 SECONDS 3) GRENADE THROW, 4) RUN DODGE & JUMP AND 5) 40 YARD CRAWL UNDER 30 SECONDS. THE REALLY HARD TRAINING HAS NOT STARTED YET, BUT I DON'T THINK IT WILL BE TOO BAD.

I AM DOING REAL FINE. WE GET 3 GOOD MEALS A DAY, EVERYDAY, AND 8 HOURS OF SLEEP A NIGHT. THE ONLY BAD PART IS HAVING TO GET UP AT 5:30 EVERYMORNING, BOY HOW I WOULD LOVE TO SLEEP IN. WE ARE ON THE SECOND FLOOR OF THE BARRACKS, AND THEY GIVE US 1/2 HOUR TO RISE DRESS, MAKE YOUR BED AND CLEAN THE FLOORS, AND ON TOP OF THAT ONLY 2 MINUTES TO FALL OUTSIDE OF THE BUILDING AND IN FORMATION, NOW THAT IS HURRYING.

JUST ABOUT ALL THE KIDS UP HERE ARE FROM ORANGE COUNTY, SO I GUESS THEY REALLY HIT IT LAST MONTH. MOST OF THE KIDS ARE FROM, SANTA ANA, ORANGE, ANAHEIM, ETC, REAL CLOSE TOGETHER.

I HAVE BEEN MADE A SQUAD LEADER, IN CHARGE OF 11 MEN, WE HAVE 4 SQUAD LEADERS, 1 PLATOON SARGENT, AND 1 PLATOON GUIDE, HERE IN THE BARRACKS

WE HAVE OUR OWN ROOM AWAY FROM THE REST OF THE MEN, WE DO NOT HAVE TO PULL DETAILS. WE JUST BOSS THE OTHER GUYS AROUND, IT IS REALLY GOOD. WE CAN MAKE THEM DO PUSH-UP, ETC TO KEEP THEM IN LINE, AND THEY CANNOT TALK BACK. THE BEST PART IS NOT HAVING TO DO ANY DETAILS, SOME GUYS ARE IN THE KITCHEN FOR 14 HOURS AT A CRACK.

THIS IS ACTUALLY THE FIRST CHANCE I HAVE HAD TO REALLY SIT DOWN. WITH TOMORROW BEING SUNDAY WE GET TO SLEEP IN UNTIL 6:30, THEN WHAT A TREAT. IT IS NOW 7:30 PM AND BEFORE 9:00 I HAVE TO POLISH MY 2 PAIR OF BOOTS, TAKE A SHOWER, AND HAVE SOMEBODY SWEEP OUT MY ROOM.

EVERY NIGHT AFTER LIGHTS OUT A DRILL SARGENT COMES THROUGH AND CHECKS EVERYBODIES LOCKS ON THEIR WALL LOCKER, AND FOOT LOCKER, ALSO CHECKS TO SEE IF EVERYBODIES FOOTGEAR IS IN THE PROPER ORDER, IF IT IS NOT HE HAS ALL THE PEOPLE GET OUT OF BED (LIKE JACK WEBB DOES IN "THE D.I.") HE THROWS THE TRASH CAN DOWN THE AISLE, AND MAKES THEM DO 25 PUSH-UPS. BUT SINCE I AM IN A ROOM WITH ONLY ONE OTHER MAN IT IS EASY FOR US TO GET SQUARED AWAY AT NIGHT, SO NO PUSHUPS.

HOW IS THE WEATHER DOWN THERE? HOT AND SUNNY I'LL BET. EVERY MORNING HERE IT IS FOGGY, THEN BY 11:00 IT CLEARS UP UNTIL ABOUT 5:00 AND THEN IT ROLLS IN AGAIN. HAS ROD AND DAN BEEN GOING TO THE BEACH A LOT? THAT IS THE MOST PART I MISS, WELL NOT REALLY THE MOST PART IS JUST PLAIN

RELAXING. THE FUNNIEST THING TODAY, I WAS CRAWLING THROUGH THIS DIRT AND HAD THE STRONGEST TASTE FOR A LEMON PIE.

MY ADDRESS HERE IS:

PVT. RICHARD A. ROPELE
US56707489
CO. D 1ST BN. 1ST BDE (BCT)
PLATOON 1
FT. ORD CALIFORNIA 93941

I AM TRYING TO WRITE TO EVERYONE IF I CAN FIND THE TIME. IT IS IMPORTANT THAT THE ADDRESS IS EXACTLY RIGHT, OR YOU KNOW WHO IS GOING TO BE PUSHING FT. ORD DOWN 6 INCHES. I TRY TO GET ANOTHER LETTER OFF NEXT WEEK, I SURE MISS YOU ALL

LOVE
RICK.

P.S.
I HOPE TO SEE YOU ALL IN ABOUT 8 WEEKS. WE WILL NOT GET LEAVE TIME WHILE IN BASIC, BUT UPON GRADUATION DAY YOU ALL CAN COME ON UP. I WILL WRITE MORE ON THIS WHEN I KNOW MORE ABOUT IT

RICK

Fort Polk

Vietnam

This is the 2nd note I wrote to my folks after arriving in Japan

This is the note that my Company Commander, Lt Livingston wrote to my parents on the 15th of February. After I got hit, the company was heavily involved in the TET offensive in the Tam Ky area. That was when John Haselbauer was killed and Douglas Dennis was wounded. I'm sure he had too much to worry about to get to writing them sooner.

Feb 15.

Dear Mr & Mrs Rofele

I'm in from the field for a little break and can sit down to write you.

First of all your son is in a hospital but will be all right. I'm sorry you had to find out the round-about way that you did but as you can see, your son probably did not want to worry you.

Perhaps by now he has written to you about what happened and filled you in as to his immediate condition. I will however, give you what I know happened.

On Jan 24 our bridge was hit by an intense Viet Cong attack. In the battle, which lasted over an hour, Rick was wounded by a mortar round. His wound was in the right leg and foot.

When I got to him he was conscious and asked that the other men be helped first. He was giving first aid and as soon as possible I called in a "Red Cross" helicopter to get the wounded out.

The next day the Col sent his chopper so I could visit my men in the hospital. I spoke with your son and he was feeling pretty good.

His leg was in a cast or heavy bandage. I did not get a chance to see his doctor but I know he will be okay from reports I have received.

He was then sent to the rear and last word I have received was Japan. This may seem a little vague to you as far as where he is, but once in the hospital, the doctors dictate where the individual will be sent.

For your information he did an outstanding job. The fight cost us (my platoon) 3 dead and six wounded. The Viet Cong did not take the bridge that was most important.

As I have said before Rich should have written you by now and told you his condition and location. I would appreciate a letter of how he is doing and if I can do anything for you. I will be back in the field soon and will miss him and the others who will not be with me.

Rich did an outstanding job and as I have written you earlier, is an outstanding soldier and man. I'm very proud of him and his actions under fire. You have a fine son.

Sincerely,
William [illegible]

This is a note that Ted Smith wrote to my parents after everything settled down after TET.

19-Feb-68

Dear Mr. & Mrs. Rupeli,

I'm sorry to have upset you so. I was sure Rick had written you. He may have wanted to keep it quiet. I'm sorry if I messed things up for him.

I'm sure he has told you by now that he got his foot injured at Chu Lai Bridge. I really don't know the extent of it. I'm sure it wasn't very bad because the Army is required to notify the parents if it is serious. Only optional if not serious.

Don't worry about Rick!!

Sincerely
Ted Smith

I'm not sure that I have anything left inside me that I haven't already discussed, so I'm not exactly sure how this closing section is going to work out, so here goes:

When I came back from Vietnam and got out of the Army, I had a chip on my shoulder for about three or four years. as I would follow the war coverage in the news. The government would point out the number of times the enemy violated the Christmas truce

1. Wondered why my life was spared
   a. Discuss those aspects of Survivors Guilt
2. How have these experiences shaped my character
   a.

You know, we all go through life you never know why certain things happen in your life

Years later I found out

Member of the Church

Holder of the priesthood

Foreordained to that office in the pre-existence

I guess I go back to that defining morning on 31 January 1968 and wonder why I didn't die. Those shrapnel fragments could have just as easily gone into my head instead of into my foot and leg. As it was, I got some small cuts under my chin and just below my right eye. One inch higher and I could have lost my eye.\

I've asked myself many times in my life; why was I saved, why didn't I die, what's in store for me after this, what am I supposed to do to pay this back? That's the basis of survivors guilt That fragment ust as easily could have just a

ound that there are good people everywhere in life

Cacy family

Greatest experiences of my life:
Being born and raised by Ray and Anne Ropele

Going to Vietnam and almost dying

Finding and marrying Cathy Harrison

Joining and being active in the Church of Jesus Christ of Latter Day Saints

against the numbers of dead versus

My mom and dad
Ted Smith
Doug Dennis and John Haselbauer

How do you put these things behind you?

You don't – you put them in perspective and go on
You live better because of what you learned and pass on the good lessons to your family
By word and deed
Took several years before I lost the chip on my shoulder
There was a certain inequity that I had to work through
Some people I lived with are dead and I'm alive.
Right now, my buddies are in the midst of the war, are they dying right now while I'm home and safe?
There's no glory in knowing that you have killed another human being.
To the contrary, there's guilt, and the memory of that . . .
Post Traumatic Stress Syndrome is an overused "ailment" since the war
Used as an excuse to avoid accountability.
Something we all live with
Some choose to control it better than others

Summarize Ted Smith's account of what happened to Dennis and Haselbauer.

Appendix I - People/Names

Fort Ord

Charles Anderson Was in my squad in basic training.

John Armstrong Was in my platoon in basic training. John was one of the other trainee squad leaders.

Bruce Collins Military records indicate that Sgt Bruce Collins was killed on 02 June 1968 in Binh Duong Province. I'm sure this is the same guy I was with in Basic Training. Our service numbers are only 47 digits apart. His is US56707447 and mine is US56707489.

Paul Corr Paul was one of the other trainee squad leaders. Military records indicate that Sgt Paul Corr was KIA on 11 June 1969 in Quang Tin Province. This was almost 2 years after our basic training. Paul must have been on his second tour or he had extended. I'm sure this is the same guy I was with in basic training. Our service numbers are only 49 digits apart. His is US56707440 and mine is US56707489. Paul was with D Co. 1/6th 198th LIB – the same company I was with – what a coincidence. Paul is on the wall at panel W22, line 19.

Frederick Esber Was in my platoon in basic training.

Harold Flowers Was in my platoon in basic training.

Sgt Abrey Henley Sgt Henley was my drill instruction (the "DI") during basic training. He was a tall slim black man. He was KIA on 19 August 1968 with the 25th Infantry Division. Sgt Henley is on the wall at panel 48W, line 55.

John Herrold John was one of the nice guys in basic training. We went through basic training together and hooked up again at Fort Lewis when we shipped out to Vietnam. John was with me during the Thanksgiving experience in Anchorage Alaska.

Del Holland Was in my platoon in basic training. Del was one of the other trainee squad leaders

Thomas Johnson Was in my platoon in basic training.

Les Kalil Les Kalil was designated our "Trainee Platoon Sergeant" because he told them he once spent some time in a Military school and he was in a band that toured for the DoD. Les was a hippie type from Laguna Beach.

Ronald Lutz Was in my platoon in basic training. I was acquainted with Ron from Jr high school. He always had a basketball and would shoot around anytime the opportunity was there. He wasn't very aggressive in basic training, kept a low key and just did what he was told.

Dwight Mumm Dwight was the ultimate hippie, the make love not war kind of guy. He couldn't, or wouldn't do anything right in basic training. I don't know if it was because his brain was so whacked out because of drug use, or just because he didn't want to.

He smuggled in a joint that was wrapped in foil and rolled inside his toothpaste tube. I remember he and Les smoking it in the bathrooms after midnight one night. After basic training, Dwight was sent to Fort Sill Oklahoma to Artillery School. I saw him again in Japan on the way to Vietnam, his foot was in a cast.

Fred Phelps Was in my platoon in basic training.

Gary Peters Was in my platoon in basic training.

Wayne Persall Was in my platoon in basic training. Wayne was one of the other trainee squad leaders. He and I shared a room.

James Riseling Was in my platoon in basic training.

Larry Rosean Was in my platoon in basic training.

Don Shepherd Was in my platoon in basic training. Nice guy.

James Strasser Was in my platoon in basic training.

Thomas Utter Utter was the guy during basic that wouldn't perform. He was the guy Anderson was kicking along the way to the rifle range so he would keep up running with the platoon.. When we left for Fort Polk, Utter was mowing the lawn in front of the barracks laughing about how he was getting out of the Army and we were going to get our butts shot off.

I saw him in a car stereo shop in Santa Ana during 1970 and he was talking about how he was going to go back in the Army and "kill me some gooks" because he had a brother killed in Vietnam. Blowhards and cowards are everywhere you look.

Robert Weddendorf Cpl Weddendorf was our ADI in Basic Training. He was one of those guys that was held over after his AIT to work with new troops. I thought it would be a good job in that it would keep you out of Vietnam – but sad to say it didn't. He was KIA on 05 May 1968 in Quang Tin province. What a coincidence, CPL Weddendorf was assigned to E Co. 1/6th Inf, 198th LIB on 01 January 1968 in the same platoon as me, but I don't remember seeing or meeting up with him. He is on the wall at panel 55, line 35.

Several years later in Corona, I met a Sister Weddendorf, in the Corona Stake Women's Presidency who was related to him. She said he was her cousin, having been adopted by her uncle. I showed her his picture from my Fort Ord graduation book and she recognized him.

Appendix I - People/Names

Fort Polk

Bodey

Bodey was our "trainee platoon sergeant" while we were at Fort Polk. He was selected because he said he had prior military service. He was just another guy with a big mouth and no backbone.

I remember once when he tried to rust Tom Jordan out of bed one morning by picking up the bunk and dropping it and yelling in his face. Tom was on the top bunk, opened his eyes, and told him if he didn't leave he was going to get out of the bunk and wipe up the floor of the barracks with him. After that, every time Bodey would say, "come on Tom, get up, ... in a whiny voice. We all considered him a loser - if he was prior military, what was he doing in the service again - did he want to get his butt shot off in Vietnam?

Ed Cahill

Cahill and Tom Jordan were friends from home - both were from Oklahoma City. Cahill was one of the nice guys. I remember seeing him in Vietnam. He was walking down Highway 1 when I was at the bridge outside of An Tan village. He had been assigned to the 196th Light Infantry Brigade - which was located north of An Tan.

Tom Jordan

Tom was a "good ole boy" from Tulsa Oklahoma. I hooked up with him and Cahill while at Fort Polk. Tom slept on the bunk above mine. Tom was a nice guy, but he had the attitude of a fighter. Wouldn't be afraid to start or step into a fight.

After AIT, Tom was recommended for "Jump School" at Fort Benning Georgia, so I lost track of him.

Ted Smith

James T. (Ted) Smith was from Oklahoma. Ted and I hit it off well while we were in AIT at Fort Polk. We hooked up again at Fort Lewis Washington and were together during my time in Vietnam. He was also assigned to E Company, but was in the third squad with Sergeant Yamani. Ted was the guy who wrote to Mom and Dad telling them that I got hit and not to worry. Ted is one of the good guys.

Robert Cacy Family This is the family from Anchorage Alaska that took me into their home for Thanksgiving dinner in November 1967.. Robert Cacy, 4811 Kupreanof, Anchorage Alaska 99502.

Douglas Dennis Dennis and Haselbuaer were the guys I hung around with. These guys came over with the unit from Fort Hood Texas a couple of months before I arrived. I understood from Lt Trujillo (my executive officer when I was stationed at Fort Carson) that Dennis was wounded the week after I was hit, in the friendly fire episode that killed Haselbauer in the battle of Lo Giang during the TET offensive.

That must have been the announcements I found in the Stars and Stripes newspaper where it mentioned that my company was awarded the Meritorious Unit citation for action during the first week in February of 1967. I was still in the hospital in Chu Lai at that time.

Dennis was from Orange, New Jersey. I looked up his name in the telephone books at the library and saw a number of Douglas Dennis's.

Willie Garissom Tall black man carried the M60 machine gun. . His name is on the same listing as mine for the award of the Purple Heart so he must have gotten wounded the same night I did. I never saw him in the hospital.

John Hasbrook Hasbrook was another guy Haselbauer, Dennis and I hung around with. He was in one of the bunkers the night we got hit. I last saw him in the emergency room in Chu Lai hospital. They brought him in on a stretcher and put him next to me. He couldn't hear very well, so I had to almost shout to talk with him. He said the VC hit his bunker continually with recoilless rifle fire from point blank range. The noise was so deafening, they had to bail out of the bunker. Mike Mangiolardo bailed out and ran across the bridge towards the other bunker, but got killed on the bridge because the VC had already occupied the bunker. Hasbrook bailed from the bunker and hid in the bushes under the bridge. He was there when the bridge was blown.

John Haselbauer Haselbauer and Dennis were the guys I hung around with. John was from somewhere in the east - I suspect from the New Jersey area like Dennis. Haselbauer was next to me the night of my first ambush. His was the 40mm grenade launcher that misfired when the VC were walking right in front of me - about 6 feet away I understood from someone later, that Haselbauer got killed the week from friendly fire during the battle of Lo Giang.. He is on the wall at panel 38E, line 29.

Jolly The only thing about this guy I remember is the night of the New Years ambush he was under a blanket smoking dope and coughing his head off - really scared me and several others - we moved about 20 feet away from him and the others.

William Livingston Lt. Livingston was my platoon leader. I don't remember any direct contact with him except in the hospital in Chu Lai. He did send two nice letters to Mom and Dad, one as an introductory letter when I first arrived in his platoon and another when I got hit at the bridge.

Mike Mangiolardo Mike was killed crossing the bridge running to the other bunker after he and Hasbrook bailed out of their bunker. Couldn't remember his name until I sorted the casualty list I got from the Internet for those killed on 31 January 1968.

Scott Miller This guy's name was on my Purple Heart award, listed as being in our company, but I can't put a face to his name.

Appendix I - People/Names
Vietnam

Bedford He was the red-headed guy in 1st squad that carried the M79 grenade launcher. I last spoke with him while waiting for the medi-evac chopper at the bridge. I remember him telling me that he shot a VC running towards his bunker with the M79 but the guy was too close and the grenade didn't go off, so he had to shoot him with his sidearm.

Fred Brown He was the Radio Telephone Operator (RTO) for Lt. Livingston. I think he came over as a replacement shortly after I arrived.

Charlie Denning Sgt Denning was the Platoon Sergeant. I remember him as a tall slim guy (I think we were all slim guys back in those days). My main recollection of him is that he was in charge the night I walked point on my first ambush. I corresponded with his daughter sometime in 2005 and he had passed away from the cancer due to exposure to agent orange,. He's buried at the Fort Bliss National Cemetery.

Henry Pickett This was the black guy that ran out to Doc after he got shot. He got caught in the same 122 mm rocket explosion as I did. I didn't see him after the bridge explosion at An Tan. I assumed he got killed because he was out in the open with Doc when the explosion hit. I was glad to see his name on the same set of orders as mine for the purple heart award because it meant he was still alive.

Mouton Sgt Mouton (I don't think this is the correct spelling) was my squad leader. He was an average size black guy. I once found his name on a replica of the Vietnam Memorial once during its display at Knotts Berry Farm as killed in action, but I can't find it in the Churches genealogy records or on the Internet index of Vietnam deaths. I must have the spelling wrong. Could it have been "Moutoon" or "Mooton", **or "Moulton", or "Mootoun"?**

Richard O'Conner Another guy in the platoon, killed that night during TET. Couldn't remember his name until I sorted the casualty list I got from the Internet for those killed on 31 January 1968. He's on the wall at panel 36E, line 32.

Don Prien This was our medic - Doc was shot the same night I got hit. It was right in front of me. I think he got shot by Radar, who was in the doorway of the command bunker. Doc was running from the tents, after getting his medical bag back to the command bunker when three shots rang out. Doc went down and began to say "No. No. It's me, Doc, it's me, no no".

Benjamin Yamani Sgt Yamani was the squad leader for the 2nd squad.

Appendix I - People/Names

Fort Carson

Westbrook Westbrook was one of the new guys that came into the unit as the 5th Division was ramping up for deployment to Vietnam. He got busted by the MPs for smoking dope in the parking lot of the barracks. He and some other guy were smoking catnip, thinking if it got a cat high, it would do something to them. As there is no law against smoking catnip, they thought they were safe - however the MPs scraped the pipe bowl and stem and found traces of marijuana - busted for stupidity.

Jim Woodley Jim was the main guy I hung around with at Fort Carson. He originally lived in Aspen Colorado. He was a also returnee from Vietnam. I think he was with the 9th Division. Jim's parents were divorced and when Jim's father died (before I knew him), Jim and his brother inherited all his dad's estate. We went back and forth to Aspen a couple of times during my year in Colorado Springs.

Jim Esposito Jim Esposito , Terry Haro and I had a cabin in Manitou Springs when I was stationed at Fort Carson. Our place was at the base of the Cog Railroad to Pikes Peak.

McClure McClure was a black guy that came in as a junior clerk in the Orderly Room when I was the company clerk at Fort Carson. McClure and I shared a room in the barracks. I think he was married. He came into the company when the 5th Division was getting ready to deploy to Vietnam.

Terry Haro Haro was from Detroit. He was the driver for the Battalion commander.

Gene Shipley Shipley was a friend of Weavers. They were from the same town in Ohio

Tim Weaver Tim was the company clerk when I came into the Orderly Room as the trainee clerk. He was from Ohio.

Appendix II

C Rations

There's an old adage that "an army travels on its stomach". I guess that's true, because without field rations, you lose your focus and edge pretty quickly. Without adequate food service, the soldier in the field is vulnerable to fatigue and mistakes. The food service I remember in Vietnam was neither especially good nor especially bad. Because of the environment under which we worked, physical and mental alertness was imperative to success of the mission and you couldn't afford to compromise that success because of hunger.

During the three months I was in Vietnam, I only spent about 10 days total in base camp. If you were in base camp, you ate your "3 squares a-day" in the mess tent, which provided the regular Army menu, servings and portions. I don't remember eating in the mess hall at base camp. The other 50 days I spent in Vietnam were in the field

When you were in the field, you mainly ate C Rations, commonly referred to as 'Cs'.. Occasionally, a hot meal was brought out in the evening by a resupply helicopter, but mostly you ate the C's you carried in your rucksack.

This is the official Quartermaster's description of C-Rations used in Vietnam

> The Meal, Combat, Individual, is designed for issue as the tactical situation dictates, either in individual units as a meal or in multiples of three as a complete ration. Its characteristics emphasize utility, flexibility of use, and more variety of food components than were included in the Ration, Combat, Individual (C Ration) which it replaces. Twelve different menus are included in the specification.
>
> Each menu contains: one canned meat item; one canned fruit, bread or dessert item; one B unit; an accessory packet containing cigarettes, matches, chewing gum, toilet paper, coffee, cream, sugar, and salt; and a spoon. Four can openers are provided in each case of 12 meals. Although the meat item can be eaten cold, it is more palatable when heated.
>
> Each complete meal contains approximately 1200 calories. The daily ration of 3 meals provides approximately 3600 calories."

B-1 Units	B-2 Units	B-3 Units
Meat Choices (in small cans): Beef Steak Ham and Eggs, Chopped Ham Slices Turkey Loaf Fruit: Applesauce Fruit Cocktail Peaches Pears Crackers (7) Peanut Butter Candy Disc, Chocolate Solid Chocolate Cream Coconut Accessory Pack*	Meat Choices (in larger cans): Beans and Wieners Spaghetti and Meatballs Beefsteak, Potatoes and Gravy Ham and Lima Beans Meatballs and Beans Crackers (4) Cheese Spread, Processed Caraway Pimento Fruit Cake Pecan Roll Pound Cake Accessory Pack*	Meat Choices (in small cans): Boned Chicken Chicken and Noodles Meat Loaf Spiced Beef Bread, White Cookies (4) Cocoa Beverage Powder Jam Apple Berry Grape Mixed Fruit Strawberry Accessory Pack*

C Rations are prepackaged, canned food products. We would load up with a three day supply (9 boxes) before going into the field. Generally while getting ready for the field, you:

Packed your rucksack with your "comfort things" (poncho, poncho liner, camera, writing paper and pens, matches, candy, etc.).

Load your web gear with your basic load of M16 ammo, hand grenades, claymore mines, hand flares, and anything else that you were assigned to carry for the squad (maybe, extra machine gun bandoleers, or mortar rounds).

Usually, you drew 3 days worth of C's. They were divided equally so that everyone got some of the best. You would trade with others to get the ones you liked best. Because of the added weight, you would not take the ones you normally wouldn't eat. The c-rations we would take with us, we would put in our extra socks and hang them off the back of our rucksacks. Generally, contributing to the load of about 60 pounds.

I remember that C's came in three classes, B1A units, B1 units and B Units. It quickly became obvious that the basis for the classification system was the desirability of the main entree. B1A units had the best, B1 units were second, and B units were the worst.

Each box consisted of the following items:

An 8 ounce can containing the entrée.

I remember Franks and Beans (beanies and weenies), Spaghetti and Meatballs, Ham and Lima Beans (obviously a B Unit, ugh). Even today, whenever I look at lima beans, this mental picture forms in my mind. I can see myself sitting in the jungle, plastic fork in one hand, this can of Ham and Lima Beans with a big hunk of ham fat in the other. I can smell the odor, I can still feel the hesitation of not wanting to eat it because I know it's going to taste awful, but having to eat because that's all there is, and I'm hungry.

Two "half size" cans.

One containing something like white bread or crackers. The other contains a dessert like pound cake or fruit cake.

Plastic utensils

A package of cocoa powder.

A packet of sugar.

A packet of cream powder.

A "Four Pack" pack of cigarettes.

Winston and Marlboro were the most desirable cigarettes, but were the least available. Mostly Kent or Pall Mall, a lot of Lucky Strike or Camels

A small toilet paper roll.

A can opener.

Known as a "P38" – one of the most valuable items you could have in your possession. If you didn't have one, you could still open the can with your knife, but what a hassle. Usually, you carried one on the chain around your neck with your dog tags.

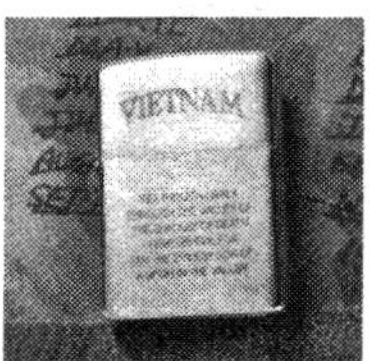

Matches must have been provided.. Many people carried Zippo lighters, which were readily available in the PX or from local Vietnamese merchants. A lot of the time these Vietnamese lighters were engraved with dirty sayings. One of the most common was: "If I die, bury me face down so the world can kiss my ass". It was funny in the context of the war, but sounds rather crude now.

Meals were on an irregular basis. If something was going on, you would eat cold, whenever you could. C Rations were only tolerable when eaten cold - it's just the same as eating any canned food product cold from your cupboard. Not very appetizing, but it won't kill you. Try it – go into the kitchen and take out a can of Pork and Beans, or worse a can of lima beans, open it and eat. It's not as good as when it's warm, but it's also not going to kill you.

What could kill you or someone else was the improper disposal of the C Ration cans. As it was common practice for the Viet Cong to set booby traps, one of the most convenient would be to place a hand grenade inside of a tin can and set it on the trail somewhere. An unsuspecting GI coming along could kick the can, thereby freeing the handle on the grenade and a subsequent explosion.

Cooking a Meal requires a Stove

Eating warm required a little more preparation and made a world of difference in the taste of C Rations.

Some of the time we had heat tablets for warming the entree. Heat tablets were round, blue objects about the size of a fifty cent piece and twice as thick. In order to use the heat table properly, you had to have a "stove". You just couldn't put the heat table on the ground and set the can on top of it because it would get smothered from lack of air.

A stove was made from one of the small cans provided in the box, like the bread can or the fruit cup can, Using your P38, you would completely remove the top, then using a wedge shaped can opener (i.e., a "church key"), open three or four holes around the sides and two or three holes in the top. These holes provided sufficient air so the heat tablet could burn and the stove provided a platform for the main meal.

How to make a C-Ration Stove

The small cans included in the meal were ideal for making a stove. Using a church key, pierce a series of closely spaced holes around the top and bottom rims of the can. This stove was satisfactory, but did not allow enough oxygen to enter which caused incomplete burning of the blue Trioxin heat tablet, causing fumes which irritated the eyes and respiratory tract. A whole heat tab had to be used.

A better stove was created by simply using the can opener end of a "church key" (a flat metal device designed to open soft drink and beer containers with a bottle opener on one end and can opener on the other commonly used before the invention of the pull tab and screw-off bottle top) to puncture triangular holes around the top and bottom rims of the can which resulted in a hotter fire and much less fumes. With this type of stove only half a Trioxin heat tab was needed to heat the meal and then the other half could be used to heat water for coffee or cocoa. A small chunk of C-4 explosive could also be substituted for the Trioxin tablet for faster heating. It would burn hotter and was much better for heating water.

A stove was usually carried in the back pack or cargo pocket and used repeatedly until the metal began to fail.

Set the heat tablet on the ground, light it, and place the stove over the top of it. Place the open entree can on top of the stove and stir the entree during the heating process. The heat tablet lasted about 30 seconds, enough time to heat the meal. Eating C's warm was a real treat.

A lot of times heat tablets were not provided, so you had to learn to be creative. Obviously, we weren't going to build a campfire (in a combat zone?), so you had to acquire other means to cook your meals.

The most common alternative fuel source was C4 explosive. C4 was the plastic explosive inside of a claymore mine. Claymores were fired electrically through a fuse attached to a hand held electrical generator. But the explosive material was combustible if you put a match to it. If you didn't have heat tablets for cooking, you could take a "pinch" of C4 from the back of a claymore mine. The claymores were never ravaged such that they were inoperable or ineffective. We just took enough C4 to heat the meal.

The procedure was the same as with a heat tablet, you'd lit the C4 or the heat tab, put the stove over the top of it, put the can on the stove, and stirred. As C4 burns much hotter than a heat tablet, you had to stir the meal constantly in order to distribute the heat and keep it from burning

One of the treats I learned was how to make chocolate pudding. In the large can, you add the cocoa powder, the sugar packet, the cream packet and fill with water. Put the mixture over a heat tablet and stir constantly until the heat table is extinguished - instant pudding.

.Generally we ate about 2 times a day - sometimes they would fly out a hot meal, but mostly we at C's.

Like everything else in Vietnam, the unusual would become the norm. What would normally be distasteful in the world would become an acceptable standard - so it was with C-Rations

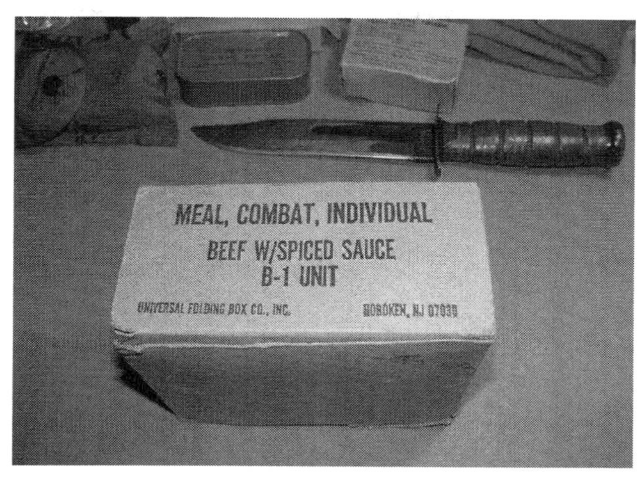
MEAL, COMBAT, INDIVIDUAL
BEEF W/SPICED SAUCE
B-1 UNIT
UNIVERSAL FOLDING BOX CO., INC.
HOBOKEN, NJ 07030

Appendix III – Awards/Decorations and Documents

In 2006 I wanted to apply for VA health care benefits so that I could participate in the Agent Orange testing/screening program to see if I was affected. Knowing that my Purple Heart (PH) award would move me up in the priority process, and that submission of a copy of my DD214 would be necessary, I got out my archives and saw that my PH award was not listed. Fortunately, I still had a copy of the General Order issued by the 2nd Surgical Hospital those 39 years earlier (I marvel at how I kept this documentation over the years), so I started to research the process to get my DD214 modified.

The Army Review Board Agency (ARBA) Application and Case Tracking System (ACTS) online is the capability I found that was able to repair my DD214. Their criteria that my case qualified under was 'an error or an injustice occurred'. My justification was:

> Correction to my DD214 to show the award of the Purple Heart medal for WIA on 31 January 1968 in the RVN. Correction to my DD214 to show the award of the Combat Infantryman Badge (CIB) for hostile action in the RVN from my time in the country from 11/67 until being medevaced back to the US in 02/68.
>
> I believe it was just a clerical error in my records as at the time I was to ETS from Fort Carson Colorado in 06/69, I had to obtain my medical records showing my hospitalization and treatment for WIA injuries which were still at Fort Ord, California. I have a copy of orders from the Americal Division awarding my Purple Heart. I don't have orders awarding my CIB because I believe it was just an oversight because of the medievac situation during the 68 TET offensive.

I don't remember how I came across this capability, but it is what I used to get my DD214 modified (https://secureweb.hqda.pentagon.mil/ACTS_Online).

The process was simple and satisfactory. I was pleasantly surprised at the depth and detail this review board went to on my behalf

During my two years in the Army, I was awarded and authorized to wear the below listed decorations. These awards were worn over the left pocket of my Class A uniforms (i.e., the "dress greens" or the summer khaki uniform). However, when I initially processed out at Fort Carson, I didn't really pay attention to my DD214 (Report of Transfer or Discharge) and noticed years later that it didn't contain all the things to which I was entitled.

I knew I was awarded the Purple Heart because it was pinned on my pillow while I was still in the hospital at Chu Lai and I also kept the copy of the Orders from the Hospital awarding it

So in 2007, I set out to rectify this seemingly small inconsistency and created an account on ACTS On-Line so I've included the detailed criteria for each on the following pages.

Purple Heart

The Purple Heart medal is probably the one decoration that I am most proud to wear. I like to think that I pulled my share of the load in working with the men in the squad/platoon. A Purple Heart indicates a level of commitment that develops when you are living a life and death existence with the other men in the squad. It's not something you try to earn, but it's something that is awarded based on commitment.

General Order #31 awarding my Purple Heart medal was cut by the hospital unit after determining that my injuries were received in the line of duty.. I don't remember if it was the first or second day I was in the hospital and I don't remember if this is the original medal, but I do remember Lt. Livingston coming by my bed and pinning it on my pillow.

All the other men listed on the order from E Company were from my squad. They were injured in the same attack that morning at the bridge in An Tan.

Garissom: Willie Garissom carried the M60 machine gun. I don't remember which bunker he was in, but you have to assume that the machine gun would have been located where we would anticipate the most contact. I would guess he must have been in one of the bunkers on the north side of Highway One.

Pickett: Henry Pickett was the guy who ran out from the Command bunker to help Doc after he got shot. The same explosion that got him also got me. I'm glad to see that he didn't get killed. Subsequently, Henry was awarded the Silver Star for his actions that morning.

Miller Scott Miller - I don't remember who he was.

See Army Regulation 600-8-22, paragraph 2-8 for the criteria for the award.

Combat Infantryman Badge (CIB)

The CIB award is also one that I am most proud to own. It is awarded to individuals that have both given and received hostile enemy fire. I'm proud that I was an infantry soldier, that I was able to fulfill my small part in providing for the safety and success of the men in my squad, and that I was able to fullfill an honorable role for my country.

See Army Regulation 600-8-22, paragraph 2-6 for the criteria for the award.

National Defense Ribbon

The National Defense Ribbon is awarded to everyone who is an active member of the Armed Forces. It is given to each soldier upon graduation from basic training. I received mine at Fort Ord.

Sharpshooters Badge with Machine Gun Bar

I qualified as 'Sharpshooter' with both the M14 during Basic Training and with the M16 during AIT. The three levels indicating proficiency are 'Marksman', 'Sharpshooter' and 'Expert'. I don't know where my badge is.

Experts Badge with Rifle Gun Bar

I qualified as 'Expert' with the M16 while at Fort Carson.

Vietnam Service Ribbon

The Vietnam Service ribbon is awarded to everyone who served in Vietnam.

Army Regulation 600-8-22, paragraph 2-13 follows with the criteria for the Vietnam Service Ribbon.
Vietnam Campaign Ribbon

Vietnam Campaign Ribbon

The Vietnam Campaign ribbon is awarded to everyone who served in Vietnam

I could find any documentation on this award.

DEPARTMENT OF THE ARMY
HEADQUARTERS 2D SURGICAL HOSPITAL (MA)
APO SAN FRANCISCO 96374

GENERAL ORDERS
NUMBER 31

1 February 1968

1. TC 320. The fol AWARDS are announced.

Award: Purple Heart
Date of action: As indic in standard name line
Theatre: Republic of Vietnam
Reason: For wounds received in action
Auth: By direction of the President under provisions of AR 672-5-1

ASKREN, DANISC A. RA67170019 (SSAN UNK) PFC E3 B 6/11 Inf Bde Americal Div
WIA: 31 Jan 68

ROPELE, RICHARD A. US56707489 (SSAN UNK) PFC E3 E 1/6th 198th Inf Bde
WIA: 31 Jan 68

STEWART, GARY US56497943 (SSAN UNK) SGT E5 C 1/6th 198th Inf Bde
WIA: 31 Jan 68

MILLER,SCOTT US51664824 (SSAN UNK) PFC E3 E 1/6th 198th Inf Bde
WIA: 31 Jan 68

GARISSOM, WILLIE W. RA11920234 (SSAN UNK) PFC E3 E 1/6th 198th Inf Bde
WIA: 31 Jan 68

LOPEZ, RUFUS A. US56667058 (SSAN UNK) PFC E3 HHC 71st Assult Hel
WIA: 31 Jan 68

PICKETT, HENRY US53426429 (SSAN UNK) SP4 E4 E 1/6th 198th Inf Bde
WIA: 31 Jan 68

SAWYER, GENE R. US56959319 (SSAN UNK) PVT E2 Americal Repl Ctr
WIA: 31 Jan 68

ROSS, DENNIS E. US52678371 (SSAN UNK) SP4 E4 C Trp 1/1 1st Cav Div
WIA: 31 Jan 68

WYANT, RICHARD E. RA15419024 (SSAN UNK) SFC E7 Svc Bty 3/16 Arty Americal Div
WIA: 31 Jan 68

ROSANBALM, GERALD L. 05336692 (SSAN UNK) 1LT 525th MI (Prov) Group
WIA: 31 Jan 68

WIESS, DENNIS J. US51772740 (SSAN UNK) PFC E3 Hq Bty 3/16 Arty Americal Div
WIA: 31 Jan 68

HARRIS, EDDIE US53701284 (SSAN UNK) SGT E5 A 4/3 11th Inf Bde Americal Div
WIA: 31 Jan 68

KENNETH A. CASS
Major, MC
Commanding

DISTRIBUTION:
"A" PLUS

Appendix IV – TOC Reports

Tactical Operations Center (TOC) Reports

Reports from the Tactical Operations Center (TOC) are minute by minute situational reports (SITRAPS) that are reported from the field and logged by clerks so that those in the command center have visibility to the situations going on in the area of operation.

The images that follow are specific report pages that affect the action when we were hit at the bridge during the TET offensive of 1968.

AMERICAL DIV TOC CHU LAI RVN 0001 31 Jan 68 2400 31 Jan

CONFIDENTIAL

1	0001	OPENED JOURNAL.
2	0145	LZ Baldy rec'd 15 HR rds.
3	0240	III MAF at 0126H vic BT068514 came under grnd & mtr atk and believed perimeter was penetrated (Duy Xuyen). Arty is supporting.
4	0225	CAP K-4 at 302315H vic BT.49107 FP ptl obs 3 VC in school talking to large group of people. Opened fire on VC and 3 VC ran into trees. 20 VC opened fire on element. Ptl heard many voices and moans. Checked area w/neg res. Apprehended 20 VCS - 4-5 poss KIA.
5	0411	Mtr rds ~~xxxxxxxx~~ knocked out all generator equip in Subsector 6.
6	0412H	Quang Ngai under mtr atk.
7	0413	Bunker 739 rec'd mtrs and SA fire.
8	0415	Reactionary force standing by.
9	0417	Bomb dump hit.
10	0420	23d MP Co reports 85%.
11	0421	G1 reports all personnel on alert status.
12	0425	80th Spt reports 100%.
13	0425	Spt Cmd reports 85%.
14	0427	Large explosion vic MAG-12.
15	0430	AG Classified reports 100%.
16	0430	An Ton Bridge rec'd 30 mtr & SA rds w/some cas.
17	0431	Subsector 1 rec'd 1 mtr rd.
18	0432	Bunker 201 rec'd SA fire.

This is the entry identifying when the bridge was hit at An Ton village

0430 is when we were hit at the bridge

AMERICAL DIV TOC CHU LAI, RVN

0001 31 Jan 68 2400 Jan 68

CONFIDENTIAL

Cont Neg contact. SS-4: POI(tank form) intact w/neg damage. SS-7: Neg contact.

40 0635 CLDC, at 0635H Sub sect I, II, VII, Neg casualties or damage.

41 0700 198,3B at 0700H 1/46 A group of demonstrators of approximately 100 persons moving on Hwy1 towards lyn Tin distric Hq. Villagers in vicinity are running away from demonstrators 1/46 has platoon ready for reaction if it is requested. Also Quang Ngai under ground attack.

42 0700 CAP, K-4 at 0415H Vic BTAA9109 after last contact set in and was surrounded by loo VC Chanting various phrases patrol rcv'd SA & AW for 1 hr returned fire called illum and arty H & F called dustoff & completed 1 US KIA, 2 WHA 1 VC KIA 4 WIA

43 0715 1/1 A-B-C at 0709H Approx loo VC w/wpns running S to Tam K, Recv'd fire from indiv Returned the fire Unk amount of VC Caus & approx 30 to 40 are moving NW.

44 0705 CAG, CAP K-3 at 0500H Vic BTA8[illegible] 3 VC from ambush. Results 1 VC [illegible] CIA, 1 VC believed wounded but [illegible] USMC WHA (minor)

This is the assessment of the damage to the bridge - apparently called in a couple of hours after it exploded.

I was in the hospital in Chu Lai by this time

45 0714 LTC Balmer, Revert to grey alert passed to CLDC.

46 0718 198, Vic BT490067 The AN TAN Bridge center span was blown by a satchel. charge. The town can be passed by using the bridge on the right. Notified Div Engineers.

CONFIDENTIAL

0718 was the time the bridge was reported destroyed. By that time, I was in the hospital at Chu Lai

Appendix V –Hospitalization Timeline

Reviewing my hospital records, I put together this timeline of my hospital stays since being wounded on 31 January 1968. One of the highlights of that time period was calling home in February from Japan telling my Mom and Dad that I was being medevaced back to the U.S. for further recovery. It was such a neat coincidence that when I called home it was the day that my brother Don was getting married that same evening.

I believe I called about 8:00 p.m. on a Wednesday night, Japan time and awoke my folks about 3:00 a.m. on Friday morning (time change crosses the International Date Line and gains a day). This is what my hospital timeline looks like:

1/28/1968 - 2/17/1968

Sunday	Monday	Tuesday	Wednesday	Thursday	Friday	Saturday
January 28	29	30	31	February 1	2	3
			WIA at the bridge outside of the village of An Ton, near Chu Lai airbase around 5:30 a.m., At about 0700, medievaced to the 2nd Surgical Hospital at Chu Lai	Saw Lt. Livingston in the Hospital. He pinned my Purple Heart medal to my hospital pillow. Last time I saw anyone from my Vietnam unit	Transferred from 2nd Surgical Hospital at Chu Lai to the 85th Evac Hospital at Qui Nhon	
4	5	6	7	8	9	10
		Transferred from the 85th Evac Hospital at Qui Nhon to the 249th General Hospital in Japan	Spent the night in the hospital at Clark Air Force Base in the Philippines	Arrived at the 249 General Hospital, Japan. First time I notified Mom and Dad by letter about being wounded, included a picture of me in the hospital bed		
11	12	13	14	15	16	17
			About 8:00 p.m. called Mom and Dad from Japan telling them I was coming back to Fort Ord the next day. It was Friday. 3:00 a.m. in California, Don's wedding day	Transferred from 249th General Hospital in Japan to U.S. Army Hospital at Fort Ord.	Back in California. Spent the night at Travis AFB before being moved to Fort Ord Don's wedding day	Arrived at Fort Ord I was a patient there until 20 May 1968 then released for active duty then assigned to a mechanized infantry company at Fort Carson Colorado.

Appendix VIII – The Tower

Where I was on 31 January 1968

This is the enclosure I prepared a couple of years ago for my Mom and Dad so that they could have a more detailed explanation of the circumstances of my situation that morning of 31 January 1968.

These are the first set of pictures that I've been able to find of the area where I was wounded on that first morning of the TET Offensive on 31 January 1968. These were posted on the web site of the 1st Battalion 46th Infantry (1/46, 198 LIB) (http://www.1stof46.com/) who evidently were the builders of the tower and the bunkers and I suppose assigned the responsibility for the river patrol (I always assumed it was an MP group, which was obviously wrong).

Before getting to the actual pictures of the site, this is an aerial map that shows the location of the area where we were located relative to Chu Lai air base and gives you a broad perspective of where we were actually located in I Corp.

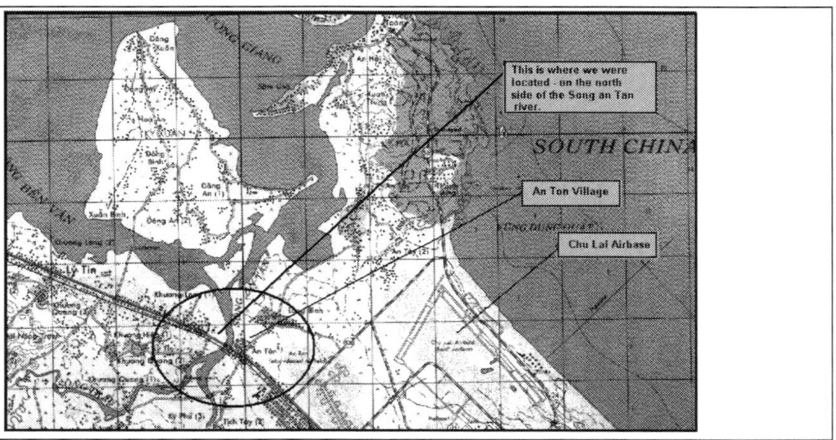

This 'encampment' was on the north riverbank of the Song An Tan river. The village of An Tan was on the south bank. The U. S. air station at Chu Lai was a major base and just southeast of our position, about 2000 meters away.

Two squads from our platoon were assigned here about the second week in January 1968 along with our Company Commander (CO) Lt. Livingston. We were housed in one of the tents and would go out on river patrol with the regular troops of the 1/46. Mostly though, we were there to pull tower and bunker guard at night.

I had a nice 35 mm camera that I bought at Fort Polk and always carried in my rucksack whenever we were in the field. I had taken a number of pictures of this area along the river, but as I didn't finish the roll, I never sent them back home for development. Consequently, after I got hit and was medevaced to the hospital in Chu Lai, I never saw the guys again, never saw my camera again, and until I found these pictures, this place only existed in my memory.

It holds a very special meaning, as this was the place where I almost bought the farm.

This is a view looking northeast from bunker #4 from the south side of the Song An Tan river.

The tower is on the north side of the river. You can just make out the two tents to the left of the tower base. We 'lived' in the leftmost tent and the permanent party guys lived in the one closest to the tower. Directly under the tower was the Command Post (CP) bunker.

At 4:00 a.m. I climbed the ladder to go on guard duty in the tower. I spent that first half hour scanning the area visually and with the Starlight scope (a night vision apparatus). Seeing nothing, I sat down to begin writing a letter home. I had a small flashlight suspended a few inches from the paper.

We were hit about 4:30 a.m. on 31 January 1968 by elements of the 2nd NVA Division. They must have been in place and watched me walk from the tent to the tower – as we were hit about 20 minutes after I got into position.

Almost immediately, I heard the initial explosions and small arms file as we were attacked. I jumped up and looked out the west side and could see tracers and rocket propelled grenades (RPGs) coming in to Bunker #2 from the north side the railroad berm. I could also see tracers and RPGs coming into bunkers #3 and #4 from the village.

I think this guy is looking to the west.

I remember in the morning when we were hit by the thought process of 'should I bail out of this tower, or should I climb up on the roof and open up with the .50 caliber machine gun'. It's amazing how quickly the human mind processes information.

I knew, that they knew, that we had a .50 caliber machine gun on the roof of the tower. I knew also that we were being hit with RPGs, rockets and automatic weapons. If I were to open up with the .50, I could bring some real heat on their positions.

But I also realized that the .50 on the roof of the tower was completely exposed. All it would take to silence the gun would be one well placed RPG or quick burst from an AK to blow me out of there. I figured I would be a sitting duck and shortly a dead duck if I lit up the .50. All it would take would be one RPG to hit the box and I would be floating face down in the river.

Once I made the decision to bail out of there, I had to go through the rationale of exposing myself on the ladder on the way down. I knew that they knew that I was up there. I even think they must have been in their positions and must have watched me walk from the tent and up the ladder at 4:00 a.m.

When I made the decision to bail out of there, I don't think my feet even touched the rungs of the ladder on the way down. I hit the top of the CP and rolled to the ground next to the tent.

I included this view to give you a perspective of the bridges to our living area. The river is about 75 yards wide.

This is the '2nd tent' that is located directly adjacent to the tower, but obviously before the sandbag wall was erected. This view is looking southwest towards bunker #4. The An Tan market square would be located to the left.

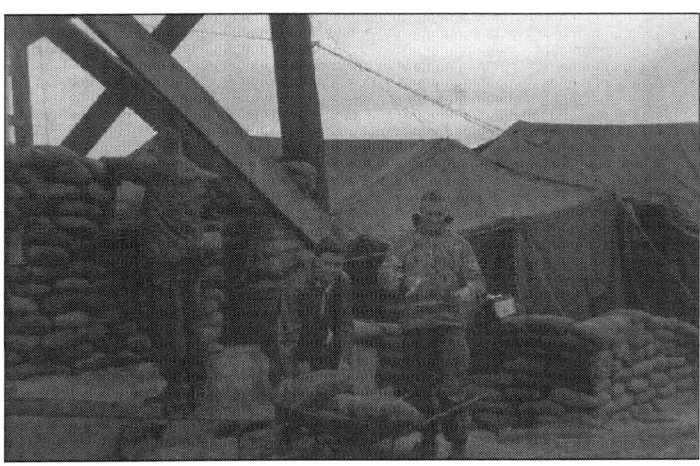

These guys are building the CP in the base of the tower. The river is on the opposite side of the CP.

When I got hit, I was located behind the lower portion of the sandbag wall near the doorway of the tent nearest the CP. The explosion killed Doc (Don Prien) and wounded Henry Pickett and I.

The force of the explosion caused the wall to topple and fall. I remember yelling as the force of the explosion lifted me off the ground and the 'thud' of the shrapnel dug into my leg and foot. It wasn't a sharp piercing blow, it really was like a 'thud'. I don't remember feeling pain. I thought it was the sandbag wall falling and a heavy sandbag was dropped on my foot and leg.

I suppose without the wall being there, I would have been killed. As it was, the shrapnel from the rocket blew through the sandbags (through 1 foot of compressed sand) and tore into my left leg, foot, right arm and scratched my face on my chin and under my right eye.

Several days later when Lt. Livingston came by the hospital to give me my Purple Heart, he told me that we were hit by regular NVA with 122 mm rockets, among other things. We had 3 KIA and 5 WIA.

Behind these guys is Highway 1, which runs north and south through Vietnam, and bunker #1. Across the road, and not in view is bunker #2. When we were hit, I could see the RPGs and tracers coming directly into bunker #2.

After the firefight and before the medievac choppers came in, Bedford (he was armed with a M79 Grenade Launcher and carried a .45 caliber sidearm) told me that he shot this guy who was charging their position in bunker #1 directly in the chest with a round from the grenade launcher. But as the guy was too close, the grenade didn't explode. He said he had to use his sidearm to stop him.

I suppose had they killed everyone and occupied bunker #1, we would have been overrun all through the camp.

This is the dock on the north side of the river where the boats would tie up for the night. Bunker #3 is over the rise on the road coming off the heavy equipment bridge. Sometimes during the day, we would throw hand grenades in the water from the bridge and the kids from the village would get the fish that floated to the surface.

The night we were hit, John Hasbrook and Michael Mangialardo were driven out of bunker #3. Mangialardo ran across the bridge toward bunker #2, and not knowing that the NVA had already killed the men there and occupied the bunker, and was killed on the bridge. Richard O'Conner was in bunker #2. Hasbrook ran under the bridge and hid in the weeds and was there when they brought in the boat and blew the center span.

Later that morning, I saw Hasbrook in the emergency room at Chu Lai. As they were working on me, they brought him in on another gurney. He couldn't hear, I had to shout at him to be heard. He said that between the explosions of the RPGs hitting the bunker and the sound and concussion of the explosion as he was under the bridge his eardrums blew out. That was the last time I ever saw him so I don't know how well he recovered.

This is another view towards bunker #4. Must have been taken from the tower. You can see how close An Tan village is to our positions. The NVA infiltrated the village and we were hit at point blank range as they were in the dwellings throughout the village.

I'm sure the locals knew several days in advance of TET that they were there.

This picture is looking south across the river at An Tan village showing the river patrol boats. Aluminum hulled, flat-bottomed boats driven by a 50 hp outboard motor. Each had an M60 machine gun mounted in the bow and generally carried three men.

On the occasions when we would go out with these guys, they would select and stop a Vietnamese boat and search for contraband, weapons, ammo, etc. I remember some incident where they shot up a Vietnamese boat while on a night patrol and afterwards didn't find anything to justify the killings.

The night we were hit, I saw tracers and RPGs coming from the Market Square across the river in to bunker # 4.

This is the back-end of the camp, looking west. I don't remember this outhouse being there, I thought we had a bunker there.

This is the bridge after the explosion. I understand that the Engineers had it back up again in two days.

This is how I looked in 1967 – 1968. This picture was taken in December 1967, the day after the first night that I "Walked Point" to the ambush site and the first ambush where I had contact with the enemy. A couple of us were sent out that next morning to be perimeter security for the rest of the squad. The ambush site and the river is about 50 yards behind me on the trail

Appendix IX – Articles I wrote for the Americal Journal

A Visit to Angel Fire - Vietnam Veteran Memorial

This is the third article I wrote that was published in my veterans magazine, the Americal Journal. I received a number of emails from other veterans who had read Cathy's poem and were so impressed that they wanted to share it to others. I told them it was okay as long as they gave Cathy the authorship credit.

It was an awe inspiring sight to drop down into the valley and come around the bend to see that gleaming white chapel emboldened against the hillside. Ever since I knew that Cathy and I would be on vacation through this area of New Mexico, I knew I had to visit, to experience I knew not what, but I knew there was something there for us.

I haven't had a chance to go to Washington D.C. to visit The Wall, so Angel Fire was my first opportunity to experience a memorial dedicated to the sacrifice of those men and women we served with in Vietnam. It was an emotional afternoon, but more importantly, it was an eye opening, visionary experience, for Cathy. Let me explain.

Cathy and I have been married for 31 years. I got out of the Army in 1969 and took a job in the Aerospace industry here in California and pretty much tried to put Vietnam behind me as I got on with my life. Cathy and I married in 1973 and we set about having and raising our family. In those busy years of furthering education, earning a living, attending our Church and raising our 5 children, my memories of Vietnam were never in the forefront of my thoughts, but it never ceased to amaze me just how close to the surface those emotions and experiences always were. It could be something as innocent as an odor (that smell of burning wood that the people used when cooking), or it could be a song on the radio ('The Letter' by the Boxtops, '. . . lonely days are gone, I'm a going home, my baby wrote me a letter. . .) that would pop an incident into my conscious mind.

As I grew in maturity and became more and more involved in Church activities, I began to appreciate more and more how those Vietnam experiences had contributed in shaping my character in providing a value basis for living my life and in shaping my outlook in many associations with my fellow men and women. I began to realize that my Heavenly Father must have had a larger life plan in mind for me as I just as easily could have been KIA instead of WIA that morning of the TET Offensive in 1968 at the bridge outside of An Tan.

Cathy knew somewhat of my time in Vietnam. She knew I was only over there a short time before being wounded and medevaced back to the U.S.. She knew of retained fragments and some of the discomfort that I occasionally experienced, but those combat experiences are so intensely personal you don't let them surface unless the situation is comfortable. These are not something that you would just bring up in day-to-day conversation. How can someone who hasn't been in those situations relate to what it's like to walk, point to a night ambush position, or to pull the trigger when you have another man in your sights?

During my time in Vietnam, I was associated with a different kind of 'family' and we had to develop a different kind of code of conduct in order to deal with the various situations that arose. It wasn't difficult to develop a 'hard edge' that is not appropriate 'back in the world'.To her credit, she certainly didn't have perspective to understand the depth in which these experiences changed our lives. She never said it in so many words, but her perception was, 'hey, the past is in the past, don't dwell on it, move on'.

Now, I'm not a PTSD type person, where these processes are cranked up every day, or where they drive daily thoughts and actions, but the memories are always there and their trigger is something of which I'm not always aware. So, it was with this basic background, we made a visit to Angel Fire part of our vacation.

When we first arrived at Angel Fire, we went into the Chapel. Featured across the back wall were 10 photographs and biographies of soldiers who had lost their lives in the war. These photos are changed out regularly so that whoever visits in the Chapel is reminded of its purpose, its significance, and the people who made the ultimate sacrifice for their fellow man. It was plain in its simplicity, but its poignancy wasn't apparent until after we went through the exhibits in the other structure.

In the main building there were the usual things on display, a diorama of a patrol in the jungle, helmets, web gear, photographs, newsreel footage, etc. However, what was most appealing was Dr. Wesphall's efforts to personalize the experience.

Do you remember going into the auto parts store several years ago where they had their parts catalogs in these racks spread across the counter and the clerk would move along the rack as he looked through the catalogs for the stocking number of your part? Angel Fire also had this same kind of a display rack, except the rack was filled with picture after picture of the men and women who died in the war. Each one was accompanied by a small biography that Dr. Westphall had prepared. It is here that the experience becomes personal to everyone.

The black and white photo of the person on a page took on the persona of the real individual. You could look into the smiling faces and easily relate to each of them. Most of the pictures were those 8 x 10's they gave us all after graduation from Basic Training. As you looked into their faces and read their biographies, you knew them. These men and women who answered the call to serve, they were us. They had hopes and dreams of a bright future, they had parents, brothers, sisters, and friends who can still feel of their loss today, 40 years later.

We looked at faces, read biographies and became acquainted with real people, not just names on a wall or in a book. It was a very personal experience. I didn't realize how deeply Cathy had been affected.

As we walked back through the Chapel just before leaving, she went down the steps to the front, knelt and lit a candle in honor of all those men and women who have served and who are serving in the Military today. That evening, she composed the following poem:

ANGEL FIRE

Today I knelt at Angel Fire
and in compassion, lit a candle there.
As I turned and looked up those stairs,
It was then, with a grateful heart, I said a prayer.

We walked this memorial for the first time today
and viewed countless photos of those now gone.
That era of protest left heroes unspoken, till now...
those unappreciated warriors of Viet Nam.

When I knelt today at Angel Fire,
and looked up at that top step....
you were standing by the photos there.
You...one who lived...a VietNam vet.

Only those like you can feel so awakened
when kneeling here, or by The Wall....
and seeing the names of your comrades who fell...
those who died to answer that wartime call.

Survivor's guilt, somehow it just grows
out of a sense not well understood.
It compels its keepers to speak out often
of those heroes whose intentions were good.

When I knelt at Angel Fire today,
I realized the calling of VietNam vets.
God brought them back to tell of heroes,
and to ensure this nation never forgets.

In the candle's glow at Angel Fire,
I gave thanks to God in humble prayer
that you are here with me today,
and not in one of the photos posted there.

Dedicated to Rick Ropele
by
Cathy Ropele

I'm thankful that I am one of the lucky ones who came back from the war unscathed. I'm thankful that I was led to this compassionate and understanding woman with whom I have been able to spend 31 great years. I'm thankful that I got to serve my country and associate with some of the finest men and women of my generation. There are countless millions of people alive today throughout the world because of the sacrifice and dedication of the men and women of the United States Military. I'm proud to have been a part of that great cause of preservation.

The United States has been preserved as a great country due to the sacrifices and dedication of the great men and women who answer the call to serve - honorable and great are they that wears the colors of the United States of America

Richard Ropele
E. Co. 1/6th 198 LIB
Nov 67 – Feb 68
RRopele@earthlink.net

The Chapel at Angel Fire

Memorial Day Thoughts

This is the first article I wrote that was published in my veterans magazine, the Americal Journal.

There are several versions regarding the origins of the Memorial Day observance, initially designated as 'Decoration Day'. Based on my research, I chose this version to begin my remarks:

In 1865, Henry C. Welles, a druggist in the village of Waterloo, NY, mentioned at a social gathering that honor should be shown to the patriotic dead of the Civil War by decorating their graves. In the spring of 1866, he again mentioned this subject to General John B. Murray, Seneca County Clerk. General Murray embraced the idea and a committee was formulated to plan a day devoted to honoring the dead.

Townspeople adopted the idea wholeheartedly. Wreaths, crosses and bouquets were made for each veteran's grave. The village was decorated with flags at half-mast and draped with evergreen boughs and mourning black streamers. On May 5, 1866, civic societies joined the procession to the three existing cemeteries and were led by veterans marching to martial music. At each cemetery there were impressive and lengthy services including speeches by General Murray and a local clergyman. The ceremonies were repeated on May 5, 1867.

The first official recognition of Memorial Day as such was issued by General John A. Logan, first commander of the Grand Army of the Republic. This was General Order No. 11 establishing "Decoration Day", as it was then known. The date of the order was May 5, 1868, exactly two years after Waterloo's first observance. That year Waterloo joined other communities in the nation by having their ceremony on May 30.

What do you think about Memorial Day? Hopefully, you don't just look at it as another holiday, a day off, to catch up on things to do around the house.

I think about men like Jack Lucas, Henry Pickett and Don Prien. Ordinary men who, when the opportunity presented itself, did extraordinary things in behalf of their fellow man.

Jack Lucas was born in Plymouth, North Carolina in 1928. Shortly after the Japanese sneak attack on Pearl Harbor on December 7th, 1941, he joined the United States Marine Corp in 1942. If you're doing the math now, you'll see that this young man was only 14 years of age.

Now you have to ask yourself, what would prompt a boy to want to do a man's job, to put himself in harms way at such a tender young age? The answer to that question is the essence of Memorial Day. I suppose one thought might be that like all Americans of that time, Jack Lucas had a heightened sense of patriotism. He must have felt the need to pull his share of the load that was placed upon the country when it was forced to fight these two enemies in the Pacific and in Europe.

The strengths of the words 'patriotism' and 'sacrifice' have to enter into your thought process, to put your life, ambitions, and dreams on hold in order to aid your country and your fellow man. A different time and a different culture of people than what we are used to today.

I believe that the men and women of this World War II era were a special generation of valiant souls, which were saved and sent to this earth by our Heavenly Father at that time to be available for these particular circumstances.

Obviously too young to join the service, but just as obvious, Jack Lucas must have successfully lied about his age. Because at that tender age of 17 years, Jack Lucas was awarded the Congressional Medal of Honor for service to his country and service to his fellow man for his actions during the battle of Iwo Jima.

Jack was initially assigned a non-combat MOS and stationed in Hawaii. This is where he met up with the men of the 5th Marine Division who were in training for the assault on Iwo Jima. Many of these men were already veterans of previous military campaigns in the Pacific, Tarawa, Guadalcanal, etc. Jack Lucas was not.

The 5th Marines shipped out in February 1945 for the invasion, Jack Lucas shipped out also, by stowing away on one of the troop transport ships.

When it came time to climb down the cargo nets into the Higgins boats to assault the island, Jack Lucas was right there again. Because he had been a stowaway, he didn't have any of the standard equipment, a steel pot, a gun, ammunition, food rations, or even a life vest. Secondary issues to a man who wanted to do his part. He did have the courage of his convictions that a job needed to be done, that he joined the Marine Corp to serve his country and his fellow man. Jack Lucas stepped up to the bar, and by his actions told everyone, 'I'm ready, I'm willing, and I'm able'.

When the landing craft hit the beach, Jack picked up a rifle, web gear and ammo, and a steel pot from a dead Marine and joined himself up with a squad of Marines who subsequently fought their way off the beach into the cover of the jungle. Several days later while on a patrol, his squad was ambushed by the Japanese. Two grenades were thrown into the middle of the patrol. Jack knew that the explosion would kill every man in the squad, unless someone did something.

Without hesitation, he threw himself on top of those two hand grenades and absorbed the full impact of the explosion with his 17-year-old body. The explosion threw him six feet into the air, tore apart his insides and riddled him with shrapnel. Miraculously, he didn't die and neither did the others in the patrol, thanks to his selfless act.

Jack Lucas was awarded the Congressional Medal of Honor, at the young age of 17 for his actions that day. The youngest man to be awarded the nation's highest military award for valor. He was the only Medal of Honor winner that enrolled as a freshman in high school after the war.

Jack Lucas always comes to my mind on Memorial Day. He was one of those ordinary men who, when the opportunity presented itself, did an extraordinary thing on behalf of his fellow man, irrespective of the consequences. A lot of men and their posterity are alive today because of the actions of Jack Lucas.

Closer to home for me, I think about Henry Pickett and Don Prien.

We were hit on the morning of January 31st, 1968, the infamous TET offensive, just outside of the village of An Tan by elements of the 2nd NVA Division. Their objective was to destroy a bridge and kill as many of us soldiers as they could. Our objective was the opposite. They started to work at 4:30 a.m. with mortars, rockets and automatic weapons. In some cases, from almost point blank range because they had previously infiltrated into the village directly adjacent to our positions.

We began taking casualties almost immediately. Don Prien (Doc) was the platoon medic; he left the protection of the command bunker to sprint across 30 yards of open ground to get his medical gear. I saw him as he ran across the front of my position. The NVA were so close you could hear their voices. Doc was hit by 3 rifle rounds as he was returning to his covered position. I remember the instance as if it were yesterday; I can see it all in my minds eye. Doc went down immediately. I can still hear the surprise in his voice and every word he spoke.

Then I heard another voice yell, 'DOC! NO! NOT DOC!' That voice belonged to Henry Pickett. Henry, without hesitation, immediately ran from the command bunker, across this same 30 yards of open ground to assist Doc. Henry acted on pure compassion and instinct, just like Jack Lucas did 23 years earlier. Henry certainly didn't think about race. This great African-American man was ready to make the ultimate sacrifice to aid a friend. It didn't matter that Doc was white and Henry was black. Both men were soldiers. Both recognized their responsibilities to every other man in the squad.

Someone needed to help Doc and Henry Pickett stepped up to the bar.

Almost immediately after Henry got to Doc' side and cradled him in his arms, there was a tremendous explosion. I can still see the reds, the yellows, and the blackness of that blast that killed Doc, showered Henry and I with multiple hot and sharp rocket fragments. I can still smell the acrid odor of the explosion and I can still see and hear every word and sound from that morning.

Don Prien died that morning at 22 years of age because he did a soldier's job. He was a medic, trained to help and heal. He exposed himself to danger because the men in his unit needed his help, because he was a soldier. Henry was wounded, and almost killed that morning because a friend needed his help.

These are some of the kinds of things I ponder on Memorial Day. Jack Lucas, Henry Pickett and Don Prien always come to my mind. All three men stepped up to the task and by their actions said 'I'm ready, I'm willing, and I'm able' to make the ultimate sacrifice. And when the opportunity presented itself, all men did an extraordinary thing in behalf of their fellow man.

I also think about men like Hugh Thompson, Mike Andreotti, and Lawrence Colburn and women like Sharon Lane. I challenge you to find out about them and put them in your Memorial Day thoughts.

Now today, in light of the September 11 2001 mass murders, a lot of us are again stirred up to a patriotic fervor. We want to participate in holding the perpetrators accountable for their actions. If I could, I would go in again. But in reality, I'm not what is needed today. War, and the preservation of freedom have always fallen into the hands of the younger generation, who are led by experienced and compassionate officers. Are you willing to encourage your sons or daughters to step up to the task?

You should be! The cause is just. It's time to stand up for our country, for our fellow man, and say 'I'm ready, I'm willing, and I'm able'.

Too often in life, there are groups of individuals that stand in the back and report on the efforts of those who put themselves on the cutting edge. These are people that some have placed on pedestals, people that they look to for opinions and answers because they don't have the courage to step forward on their own.

The individuals on the ground, making split second decisions based on immediate circumstances that few of us can ever put into perspective will win this struggle against terrorism. Often, these decisions involve life and death.

Read the following passage from Theodore Roosevelt, and think of it when you listen to the news. Having Dan Rather (or someone like him) reporting from the 'field' on the decisions and actions of others doesn't compare to the insight that the man on the front line has.

Theodore Roosevelt said:

> "It is not the critic who counts, not the man who points out how the strongman stumbled or where the doer of deeds should have done better. The credit belongs to the man who is actually in the arena, whose face is marred by the dust and sweat and blood; who strives valiantly, who errs and comes short again and again; who knows the great enthusiasms, the great devotions and spends himself in a worthy cause; who at best, knows in the end the triumph of high achievement, and who, at worst, if he fails, at least fails while daring greatly; so that his place shall never be with those cold and timid souls who know neither victory or defeat." (Theodore Roosevelt, Paris-Sorbonne 1910).

We've heard the expression numerous times; 'Freedom is not free'. Someone had to pay the price for it. We're fortunate to live in the greatest country in the world and there are countless millions of people alive today throughout the world because of the sacrifice and dedication of the men and women of the United States Military. I'm proud to have been a part of that great cause of preservation. I'm proud of those men and women today who wear the colors of the United States of America.

The pure essence of Memorial Day is to honor those that gave their life for their country and for their fellow man, men and women who laid their lives on freedoms' doorstep that other men, women, and children would be free to live their lives without tyranny, without fear, and without encumbrances on their religious beliefs.

We enjoy the freedoms we have today because our fathers, neighbors, and family answered the call to serve.

Richard A. Ropele
E. Co. 1/6, 198th LIB
1967 - 1968
RRopele@earthlink.net

My Thanksgiving Day 1967

This is the second article I wrote that was published in my veteran magazine.

We left Fort Lewis Washington on the morning of the 23rd of November 1967. I was one of some 200 – 300 servicemen aboard a Northwest Orient 727 flight to Vietnam. I was 22 years old and this was the beginning of the 'biggest adventure' of my life. What did the next year hold in store? Where would I be 365 days from now?

Our plane stopped in Anchorage Alaska about 2:30 in the afternoon before crossing the Pacific for Japan. I assume for refueling, as we had to disembark and go into the terminal. As you all know, airports are such depressing places to wait, and this one was no exception. It was practically empty. I think they must have had a minimum staff working because of the holiday.

While waiting, I took the opportunity to call home. I knew my family would be celebrating Thanksgiving, as usual with the Monroy family at Nana and Grandpa's house.

Nana and Grandpa are the Monroy's grandparents. They lived in Tustin California and I had known them all my life. We were one big family and we always spent Thanksgiving at Nana and Grandpa's.

My Mom and Dad had established traditions in our family just for events like today. I knew where my family was and what they were doing and I wanted them to know where I was and what I was doing.

I talked to everybody, Mom and Dad, Don, Jeff, Rod, and Linda, everybody. It was so good to hear the voices of my parents, my brother, and my friends. When I hung up the phone, I had that warm feeling that comes over you when you know there are people that are concerned about you. Yet, it was that classic good news/bad news scenario.

The good news was that I got to reconnect with family on this holiday, and the bad new was that I realized again just how far away I was. With the future so uncertain, it was going to be a lonely holiday. But, that's the situation that all of us on the plane bought into when we answered our countries call to service. So, this was just one of those circumstances that you just take in stride and move forward.

During this refueling process, a snowstorm blew in and closed the airport preventing us from continuing our flight until the next day. The military made arrangements for us to spend the night at the American West Hotel in downtown Anchorage and leave again the following day.

John Harrold and I shared a room. John and I went through basic training at Fort Ord and AIT at Fort Polk. It was after 5:00 p.m., by the time we were settled into our rooms.

Because it was the holiday, the hotel notified us that a full Thanksgiving dinner was being served in the dining room and we were all welcome to eat our fill. John and I and my most of the others on the plane readily accepted the invitation. When you remember that we anticipated Thanksgiving dinner on the airplane (imagine, airplane food for Thanksgiving, holy cow), this was quite a pleasant surprise.

We feasted on turkey, mashed potatoes, and all the trimmings, pumpkin pie. You name it and the hotel served it. We ate and we talked and we relaxed. Those anxious feeling about our futures were temporarily put in the background.

It was after this dinner that I was privileged to be on the receiving end of one of the most extraordinary acts of compassionate service that I have ever experienced.

You know, some life changing experiences happen boldly and noisily and you realize at the time that you won't be the same person after it's over. This was one of those experiences that comes along simply and quietly. It's only later, when you have time to reflect, that you understand the deep and immense impact that has taken place in your soul.

John and I were leaving the dining room, walking down a corridor leading from the dining room to the lobby. We were going back to our room, watching a little television and then going to bed, when I felt the touch of a child's hand in mine. I looked down into the eyes of a young boy, 5 or 6 years old, he grasped my hand tightly in his and began pulling me across the lobby while calling, "Daddy, Daddy, I got one, I got one".

It was then that I became more aware of our surroundings. The hotel lobby was filled with people, with families, children, people were everywhere. These were local residents of Anchorage.

Unbeknownst to us, a local radio station had broadcast the news that a planeload of soldiers, bound for Vietnam, had been stranded for the night because of the storm. This station suggested that it would be a nice gesture if the residents of Anchorage would invite these soldiers into their homes for Thanksgiving dinner. And boy, did these good people respond.

John and I had the good fortune to be "captured" by the Robert Cacy family. Like all the other local residents that gathered in the hotel that night, the Cacy family interrupted their Thanksgiving celebration to drive downtown, in a snowstorm, to share their time, their homes, their meal and most importantly, their family with us.

They drove us to their home where we sat down and had a real family style Thanksgiving dinner, turkey, potatoes, dressing, gravy, just like the one my family was having at home. We didn't tell them we had just eaten at the hotel. The enjoyment of the evening was not in the food, but in the company and in their compassion for us. We ate, we talked, we laughed, we watched football - we did those things that families do when they are together during the holidays.

The evening was magical. Thoughts of our present circumstances and our immediate future were temporarily put into the background as we enjoyed the sacrifice and the graciousness of this good family. I felt like I was at home.

After dinner, they drove us around to see some of the sites of Anchorage and then returned us to our hotel about 9:00 p.m. After wishing us well, they left. Just as quietly as they came into our lives, they were gone, without fanfare. The next day we left Anchorage to continue our journey.

Each time I sit down to a Thanksgiving dinner, I ALWAYS remember this experience. Even to this day, even now when I'm writing these words, I can still feel that little child's hand squeezing mine and I can still hear those words that made me feel so at home, ". . . Daddy, Daddy, I got one, I got one . . .".

The Cacy family wrote the following letter to Mom and Dad.

> To the Ropele family.
>
> You don't know us, however we had the pleasure of meeting your son on Thanksgiving day. The plane he was on going to VietNam was grounded here in Anchorage at about 2:30 pm. There was a general appeal on the radio to invite the boys from the plane home for dinner. We were happy to have your Rick as one of our guests.
>
> He is certainly a fine young man. We were very pleased by his whole outlook with regard to going overseas. We have a boy on his way over there also. He is in the Navy. His ship is the USS Manley, a destroyer – He has been in the Navy a year. Rick said he had been in five months.

Our prayers will be with Rick and the many others who are in Viet Nam.

Sincerely,

The Robert Cacy family.

I didn't realize until years later what an impact these people and their compassion would have on my life. I can't help but think how that scripture in Matthew 25: 35 – 40 applies:

41. For I was an hungered, and ye gave me meat: I was thirsty, and ye gave me drink: I was a stranger, and ye took me in:
42. Naked, and ye clothed me: I was sick, and ye visited me: I was in prison and ye came unto me.
43. Then shall the righteous answer him, saying, Lord, when saw we thee and hungered and fed thee? Or thirsty, and gave thee drink?
44. When saw we thee a stranger, and took thee in? or naked and clothed thee?
45. Or when we saw thee sick, or in prison, and came unto thee?
46. And the King shall answer and say unto them, verily, I say unto you, inasmuch as ye have done it unto one of the least of these my brethren ye have done it unto me.

I was "one of the least of these" that the savior spoke about. I was "hungered" and "thirsty" for that warmth that exists in families. I was a "stranger" in Alaska, on Thanksgiving and the Robert Cacy family "took me in."

The Cacy family physically left my life that night of November 23rd, 1967, but there will always be a place for them in my heart as their extraordinary act of kindness continues to burn bright.

Extraordinary people.

The next morning we awoke, had breakfast in the hotel restaurant and boarded our plane to continue the journey.

Rick Ropele
E. Co, 1/6 198th LIB
67 – 68
Corona, California
rropele@earthlink.net

This is a note I got back from David Taylor. Dave is one of the editors for the Americal Journal and I sent him the article I submitted about Thanksgiving in Alaska for publication consideration

-----Original Message-----
From: David W. Taylor [SMTP:dwtaylor@neobright.net]
Sent: Friday, March 14, 2003 5:11 PM
To: rropele@earthlink.net
Subject: Road To Vietnam - Thanksgiving 1967

Rick, I just received an advance copy of the 1st Qtr 2003 Americal newsletter since I am the Contributing Editor. Let me tell you I was very touched and shed more than a few tears when reading your article. It was well written and I plan to send it to a number of people. Do you have a word file for it or did Gary Noller type set it? I want to thank you for writing it.

If I were a Priest (I'm Catholic) I would definitely find a way to use it in a homily. May Gods' Blessings be yours, now and forever!

Dave Taylor
C Co, 5th/46th, 198th LIB 1969

My response to Dave

-----Original Message-----
From: Rick Ropele [SMTP:rropele@earthlink.net]
Sent: Monday, February 24, 2003 10:03 PM
To: 'David W. Taylor'
Subject: RE: Road To Vietnam - Thanksgiving 1967

Dave: thanks for your kind words. It was one of those special experiences that we encounter in life that shapes character, outlook, and attitude. I was indeed fortunate.

I do have a word file. It's on my machine at work, I'll mail it to you on Monday.

Rick Ropele
RRopele@earthlink.net
Corona, CA

This is another note I got from someone who was on the same plane and had the same experience with another Alaskan family.

-----Original Message-----
From: HUGH S FITTS [SMTP:stevefitts3@juno.com]
Sent: Thursday, April 10, 2003 4:49 PM
To: rropele@earthlink.net
Subject: Vietnam Network (Americal Newsletter)

Hello Rick,

Read your article in the 1Q issue of the Newsletter. Quite interesting. I may have been on the same plane. We stopped in Anchorage, stayed in the terminal for a couple of hours and then went to a hotel. Went walking and I think it was two degrees that day with plenty of snow.

Went back to the hotel. I was assigned a room with a soldier from the Bronx, New York (I'm from Ringgold, VA). After eating a very nice meal, a group from the Mt. McKinley Lions Club showed up in the lobby. A radio station announced there was a planeload of soldiers enroute to VN. They broke us up in two and took us to their homes.

We went to the home of William Gates, a contractor in Anchorage. He and his wife were very nice to us. He had friends with the telephone company in Alaska and made a call that connected us to our families at home. I still have a small pennant he gave me from his club. Left the hotel the next morning for Cam Ranh Bay.

I wrote to Mr. Gates several times while in Nam. But we eventually lost contact because my personal mail, etc. was lost during a move (I was in the 3/16 Artillery, Que Son Valley, west of Chu Lai). I still think of them often for their concern and possibly thinking this may be the last holiday some of us would spend on this earth.
Again, enjoyed you article.

Steve Fitts, CW2, USAR, Retired
257 Old Cabin Trail
Ringgold, VA

My response to Hugh:

-----Original Message-----
From: Rick Ropele [SMTP:rropele@earthlink.net]
Sent: Saturday, April 12, 2003 7:21 AM
To: 'HUGH S FITTS'
Subject: RE: Vietnam Network (Americal Newsletter)

Hugh:
Thanks for the note. Yea, it was a special time and we were lucky there were so many good people willing to give of the time and family.

I wonder how many others on the plane went to the Americal. I wonder how many others didn't make it back home. We're the fortunate ones that both the experiences in Alaska and also those in Vietnam shaped our character and helped us to recognize there are good people all over this world.

Rick

This is another note I got from someone who also went through Alaska, although 2 years later. Obviously, not during the Thanksgiving period, but this guy connected because of those same feelings of loneliness and our lack of control over our futures.

-----Original Message-----
From: Wllyc511@aol.com [SMTP:Wllyc511@aol.com]
Sent: Saturday, April 26, 2003 1:00 PM
To: rropele@earthlink.net
Subject: Road to Vietnam 1967

Rick
I just finished reading your letter in the Americal newsletter. It really struck me emotionally. I also took the road through Anchorage, but our plane needed repairs and we had to stay overnight. It was 6 Jan 1971 and I was also 22 years old. As I read your letter I couldn't help but relive the loneliness and uncertainty that I felt at that time. Eight months earlier I had been playing Frisbee in front of my dorm at BC, while drinking a few beers. How did this happen?

Anyway, thank you for sharing your story. It was great, and I'm glad everything worked out for you.

God Bless,

Walter Cullen
A Co 4/3 11th Bde '71
Ipswich, Ma

Comment: I'm so glad that so many others were able to connect with my experience on that Thanksgiving day in 1967. It shows how the brotherhood among us is based on so many shared experiences, both good and not so good – experiences that are always with us and are close to the surface as we let them.

A Simple Act of kindness – Helen Shives

This is the fourth article I wrote that was published in my veterans magazine, the Americal Journal

When we were kids and Christmas was just days away, the anticipation of finding out what was under the Christmas tree was an exciting time. We didn't think we could last until Christmas morning. And finally when that moment arrived, we honed in on that big package, tore the paper off, scattering it all over the living room floor until we had that special gift in our hands. Usually, as an afterthought, we remembered who gave the gift to us and acknowledged them with a 'thank you' as we rode away on that new bike.

My Christmas experience in 1967 was nothing like that. However, it did serve as a key moment in life as I matured and realized the value of the people my life. It was my first Christmas away from home. Hell, it was my first Christmas in a war zone. I was an FNG, assigned to Co. E, 1/6th Inf., 198th LIB on LZ Bayonet. I was working to learn my role as a rifleman in an infantry squad.

Most of December was spent in the field doing the usual things - working the AO, searching villages, ambushes at night, just looking for the bad guys. It was during this December that I earned a lot of 'firsts' in my life – first time I went out on an ambush; first time I walked point; first time I walked point to a night ambush position; first time I shot at someone.

We had been out in the field for about two weeks and sometime just before Christmas we came back to base camp. As you all remember, we would get our mail in the field, but packages were usually held back at base camp until we came in for them.

This time, I had a package waiting for me from Helen Shives. Helen Shives is the mother of my brother's best friend. My older brother Don had known Gary Shives since they were classmates in elementary school. Now here I was, half a world away in Vietnam, getting a package from Gary's mom for Christmas.

A package from home usually meant something to eat. What was it - canned fruit, kool aid mix, pudding cups? It didn't matter; anything was a treat because it took the edge off the C-Rations. This package was one of those shirt size boxes you get from the department store. It was wrapped and taped for mailing in brown paper.

I remember sitting on the steps of the hooch and just like that child at home in front of the Christmas tree, I ripped through the paper to reveal a wax paper lined box of chocolate fudge brownies. She even cut them into those little squares.

The fudge brownies were soft, sticky and gooey – just the way they should be. We all dipped in and ate like it was going to be taken away if we didn't finish it right then and there.

I like to think that my mom and dad raised a considerate boy, but truthfully, I don't remember if I wrote a note of thanks to her or not. I like to think I did, but. . . .

Now here it is, 39 Christmases later, and I still marvel how this simple act of kindness, a gift of fudge brownies, helped me to gain a clearer understanding of the meaning of Christmas and the spirit of giving. I can visualize Mrs Shives in her kitchen preparing the package, never quite sure if it would arrive at its intended destination or sure that I would be around to receive it. I'm humbled to know that this woman had thought of me and my situation and took the time out of her busy Christmas preparation to do this seemingly small act – to think of me.

As we get older and wiser, we realize that it's not the gift that counts, but the efforts and thoughts that others extend on our behalf. This simple box of fudge brownies was one of the best Christmas gifts I've ever received. It not only fed my body, it also nourished my soul. It was exactly what I needed.

Helen Shives is now in her late 80's and in the twilight of her years. But she is still one of the sweetest and kindest women I know. I'm a better man today because of her example. I've spoken with her son Gary and related this incident and my feelings to him so that he would know just how much his Mother's concern and compassion affected my life. Every Christmas season I reflect on how a simple box of fudge brownies was better than a new bike or a new baseball mitt.

I believe that the people of the World War II era were a special generation of valiant souls. They were sent to this earth at a time when our Heavenly Father knew they would be instrumental in saving the world from the evil intentions of the rulers of Germany and Japan. Essentially, the men went to war and the women took their place in the workforce. A combined effort on the war front and on the home front resulted in victory and restored freedom throughout the world.

I also believe that this same generation of people was our strongest supporters in Vietnam because they could easily relate to the mission and the circumstances in which we were involved. Their concern and compassion for soldiers at war was developed during the trying times in the 1940s and we benefited as a result.

As we all told ourselves after 9/11, I'm ready to go again and serve my country. I believe that the men and women of this World War II generation also stood ready to serve again if their country called for their services in Vietnam. If they couldn't participate on the war front, then they choose to support the troops in other ways. Helen Shives is one of these women of the 'greatest generation' that acted on the thought and took the time to bring a little bit of home and Christmas cheer into my life.

There are countless millions of people alive today throughout the world because of the sacrifice and dedication of the men and women of the United States Military.

Honored and great are they that wear the colors of the United States of America.

Rick Ropele
E. Co, 1/6 198th LIB
67 – 68
Corona, California 92879

Appendix XIII – Named as the ADVA Far West Chapter Commander

I had been a member of the Americal Division Veterans Association for about 12 years and enjoyed getting the quarterly magazine reading and reliving those Vietnam experiences. Several times I thought it would be good to go to the annual National Reunions and perhaps meet some of the guys with whom I served with in Vietnam, but I just couldn't justify spending the family money on something that was just for me because we always seemed to have more important things going on that had first call on our funds –but I always had it in the back of my mind that perhaps one day .. . . .

I had also joined the local ADVA Far West Chapter (FWC)and was enjoyed getting their quarterly newsletter. Rich Merlin a former MP with the 23rd Military Police group that served in the Chu Lai area was the local chapter commander and lived in Riverside. In one of his newsletters, he talked about a Chapter reunion to be held in Las Vegas, so Cathy and I thought it would be a nice weekend trip and we decided to go.

I was excited to finally meet men who served in Vietnam in the same area as I. As you all know, when I was hit by those rocket fragments and medievaced home, I never saw anyone from my unit. The last person I saw was Lt. Livingston when he pinned my Purple Heart on me in the hospital in Chu Lai. Maybe this time I'd see someone.

We checked into the Golden Nugget in North Las Vegas and I called on the guys in the hospitality suite. Not that I expected otherwise, but I didn't know anyone there, didn't find anyone that served at the same time that I was there, didn't find anyone that was infantry. Still it was a good time and I got to associate with other Vietnam veterans, where I could speak of my experiences and they would understand. These were men who were honorable servants to their country. There were about 12 Vietnam veterans and about 6 World War II veterans attending this meeting.

On the first day of the reunion, which is a business meeting for the chapter affairs, Rich and Gene McGrath (the chapter secretary/treasurer) called me aside and asked me if I would accept the position of the chapter newsletter editor as they knew I had submitted several stories to the National Journal.

I told them I would be glad to do that – why be a part of an organization if you're not going to participate. So, in this meeting they sustained a new Chapter Commander, a new Vice Commander, a new Secretary Treasurer, and me the Newsletter Editor.

So, I was all jazzed about pulling this newsletter together

After returning home, I sent an email to the new chapter commander asking him to write an opening message for my first newsletter. He responded back that he never really wanted to be the Chapter Commander and sent me an e-mail resigning his position.

No problem, I'll just get the information from the new Vice Commander. I wrote him an e-mail telling him that the Chapter Commander resigned and because he was the next in line, would he write a message for my first newsletter. He also responded back that he also never really wanted to be Vice Commander and sent me an e-mail also resigning his position.

I notified Rich Merlin that all his appointees had resigned and he'd better do something. So I set about putting together my first newsletter and let him worry about the leadership. I didn't have to wait long. . ..

So, I figure if you're going to volunteer to participate in an organization, you should be ready to take on the assignments as they are handed out. Due to the vacancies in our Chapter leadership, Rich Merlin (Past Chapter Commander and current National Jr. Vice Commander) asked and I accepted the position of Chapter Commander, and was subsequently appointed by Larry Watson, ADVA National Chairman:

> "By authority of the bylaws I appoint Richard Ropele to the position of Commander of the Far West Chapter. This appointment is for the balance of the vacated term or until the Far West Chapter holds elections. signed, Larry Watson, Commander, ADVA".

So, what does a Chapter Commander do? Well, I'm not exactly sure, but the Far West Chapter is only as strong as the membership is active. As of the first of April, we have 155 members on the active roster, with only 29 having not yet renewed for the 2007 year.

So, here I am. . . . .

The newsletters that I wrote follow.

The Cannon

Far West Chapter AZ CA CO HA NV NM UT
Americal Division Veterans Association

2007 – A New Year – A New Commitment

Well, here it is, the year 2007. 2006 has past by and a new year is before us with fresh challenges and goals. One of my challenges, as the new editor of The Cannon, is to continue to put together a quality newsletter that you'll enjoy, look forward to receiving, and one in which you'll want to share your thoughts and experiences.

You'll notice that one change I made is to the 'Cannon' graphic. This is a picture of an 8 inch gun firing from LZ Dottie that I found on http://1_14thfa.tripod.com/index.html. I think it's representative of our camaraderie as Americal Veterans: infantry in the field engaged with the enemy, relying on support from the artillery, which is dependent on the logistics and support staff keeping the rear secure and having the necessary components in the supply line at the right place at the right time. All these things play an equal role in ensuring success and safety for one another.

Success of the Far West Chapter is likewise dependent on all of us taking an active part in the Chapter business. I want this newsletter to be your voice to your fellow Americal vets. Let's share those military thoughts and experiences that shaped our characters and influenced our outlook on life.

Being in the military taught me so many lessons about life and about myself, One thing that I truly believe is:

There are countless millions of people alive today throughout the world because of the sacrifice and dedication of the men and women of the Unites States Military.
Honored and great are they that wear the colors of the United States of America

I'm proud to have served, I'm proud to have served with you. Welcome home everyone. . .

The Pledge of Allegiance

I first read this account several years ago when reading John McCain's book 'Faith of my Fathers'. It's worth going through again because it helps to restore in our minds those ideals in which we Veterans hold dear. As I think about those men held as prisoners in that filth of North Vietnam, subject to isolation, torture, and brutality, with their lives being reduced to the bare essentials of living, I marvel at their strength of character. The only thing their North Vietnamese captors couldn't take from them was their integrity and their commitment to higher ideals. What great examples they are as they expressed that commitment to duty, honor, country, and to one another through an act as simple as the Pledge of Allegiance.

Think of them the next time you have the opportunity to Pledge your Allegiance.

"The Pledge of Allegiance" - by Senator John McCain

As you may know, I spent five and one half years as a prisoner of war during the Vietnam War. In the early years of our imprisonment, the NVA kept us in solitary confinement or two or three to a cell. In 1971 the NVA moved us from these conditions of isolation into large rooms with as many as 30 to 40 men to a room.

This was, as you can imagine, a wonderful change and was a direct result of the efforts of millions of

Americans on behalf of a few hundred POWs 10,000 miles from home.

One of the men who moved into my room was a young man named Mike Christian. Mike came from a small town near Selma, Alabama. He didn't wear a pair of shoes until he was 13 years old. At 17, he enlisted in the US Navy. He later earned a commission by going to Officer Training School. Then he became a Naval Flight Officer and was shot down and captured in 1967.

Mike had a keen and deep appreciation of the opportunities this country and our military provide for people who want to work and want to succeed.

As part of the change in treatment, the Vietnamese allowed some prisoners to receive packages from home. In some of these packages were handkerchiefs, scarves and other items of clothing. Mike got himself a bamboo needle and over a period of a couple of months, he created an American flag and sewed it on the inside of his shirt. Every afternoon, before we had a bowl of soup, we would hang Mike's shirt on the wall of the cell and say the Pledge of Allegiance. I know the Pledge of Allegiance may not seem the most important part of our day now, but I can assure you that in that stark cell it was indeed the most important and meaningful event.

One day the Vietnamese searched our cell, as they did periodically, and discovered Mike's shirt with the flag sewn inside, and removed it. That evening they returned, opened the door of the cell, and for the benefit of all of us, beat Mike Christian severely for the next couple of hours. Then, they opened the door of the cell and threw him in.

We cleaned him up as well as we could. The cell in which we lived had a concrete slab in the middle on which we slept. Four naked light bulbs hung in each corner of the room.

As I said, we tried to clean up Mike as well as we could. After the excitement died down, I looked in the corner of the room, and sitting there beneath that dim light bulb with a piece of red cloth, another shirt and his bamboo needle, was my friend, Mike Christian. He was sitting there with his eyes almost shut from the beating he had received, making another American flag.

He was not making the flag because it made Mike Christian feel better. He was making that flag because he knew how important it was to us to be able to Pledge our Allegiance to our flag and country.

So the next time you say the Pledge of Allegiance, you must never forget the sacrifice and courage that thousands of Americans have made to build our nation and promote freedom around the world. You must remember our duty, our honor, and our country

"I pledge allegiance to the flag of the United States of America and to the republic for which it stands, one nation under God, indivisible, with liberty and justice for all."

<u>Americal Division Challenge Coin</u>

You know, when Rich Merlin asked me and I accepted the calling to be the editor of the Far West Chapter newsletter, he gave me an Americal Division Challenge Coin. I thought that this was a nice gesture on his part, but I was left wondering what purpose a Challenge Coin serves. So, I looked at http://wikipedia.org/wiki/challenge_coin for information, but didn't like the definition. So I made my own:

The reason that I carry my Challenge Coin everyday is to remind me:

- I'm an American and when my country called, I served honorably.
- Of the brotherhood I enjoyed by serving with some of the greatest men and women of my generation.
- That those serving us today need our support and acknowledgement.

Challenge coins are available from the Americal PX (http://Americal/.org/px).

Far West Chapter Membership

Check your mailing label on this newsletter issue, if it has an '06', then you need to send your dues of $10.00 per year to our Secretary-Treasurer:

Tom Packard
6613 Birch Park Dr.
Galloway, OH 43119

Make your checks payable to 'ADVA – Far West Chapter'.

FYI: in accordance with the Chapter by-laws, if dues aren't paid by April1st for the previous year, a reminder notice is sent. Then, if not paid by May 1st, then the member is dropped from the roster

World War II Vets

Let's let others in the Chapter know of some of your experiences. Send me a note and tell me:

> Where you were and what you were doing when you heard of the Japanese attack on Pearl Harbor.
>
> Or
>
> What were your thoughts when you heard about the atomic bomb being dropped on Japan.

Send your submissions to my home address or to my e-mail address.

Here's an excerpt from the writings of Fernando Vera about his first night on Bougainville:

"Our first night we were greeted by the Japanese with an airplane bombing raid. Our defensive units locked him in with their searchlights and were shooting at him with tracers, and whatever. I don't remember but I think he dropped one bomb but it probably fell somewhere in the jungle.

In the meantime, I was in my very, very shallow slit trench foxhole with my knees shaking and my teeth actually chattering as this was going on. I remember that I had absolutely no feeling of fear. Guess that all the knee-shaking and chattering teeth absorbed all the fear adrenalin.

Your thoughts can be in the next issue, let me know!

2 Americal MIAs Accounted For

The DoD POW/Missing Personnel Office recently announced that the remains of 1LT Fredrick Ransbottom and PFC William E. Skivington, missing in action from the Vietnam War have been positively identified and returned to their families for burial with full military honors.

1LT Ransbottom and PFC Skivington were part of the 2nd Battalion, 1st Infantry, 196th LIB., and were KIA during the battle of Kham Duc on 12 March 1968 as the Special Forces camp and its surrounding observation posts were overrun. Their bodies could not be retrieved as the remaining soldiers had to abandon the camp.

Services for 1LT Ransbottom will be held on 12 January 2007 and internment in Edmonds OK.

Services for PFC Skivington will be held on 23 January 2007 and internment in Arlington National Cemetery.

Recommended Reading

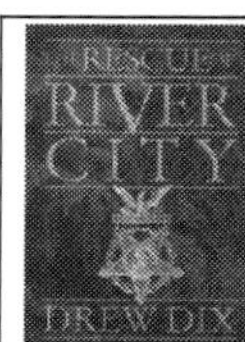

The Rescue of River City

By
Drew Dix
Winner of the Congressional Medal of Honor

A riveting account of a Special Forces soldier, working with indigenous troops to take back the city of Chau Phu during the Tet Offensive of 1968.

An inspiring testament of courageous men and their commitment to the mission and to the people they're tasked to protect.

2007 Far West Chapter Reunion

Our next Far West Chapter reunion is scheduled for September in Riverside CA. The specific date has not been established, but the reunion committee is working on it.

Tentative activities include a visit to the Riverside National Cemetery where we will conduct a wreath laying ceremony and a visit to the Medal of Honor Memorial, the Veterans Memorial, and the POW/MIA National Memorial.

The committee is also working to set up a tour at the March Air force Base Museum, home to some 60 historic aircraft, the P-38 Museum, and the War Dog Memorial.

This Chapter Reunion is a good chance to once again renew those bonds of brotherhood we experienced while on active duty. We have 156 members in this Chapter, let's get together and get acquainted.

Past Chapter Commander Rich Merlin is pulling this event together. If you would like to assist him, let me know
(rropele@yahoo.com)

Far West Chapter Officers

Commander

Vice Commander

Secretary/Treasurer
Tom Packard
(6140878-5197
Packard@aol.com

Sergeant At Arms
Curt Rothacker
(925)784-5391

Chaplain
Don Squire
(801)635-2547

Newsletter Editor
Rick Ropele
246 Coronado, Dr
Corona, CA 92879
(951)218-3071
rropele@yahoo.com

You'll notice that we have vacancies in our Chapter leadership. Both John Riley and Jim Craig, nominated as Commander and Vice Commander, respectively have declined to accept their positions. We wish them well and look forward to their participation in Chapter activities as their time permits.

In accordance with our Chapter by-laws, a special election will be held at our Chapter meeting in September in Riverside, CA.

History from the Old Guard

164th INFANTRY ASSOCIATION RECORDS

The 164th Infantry was operational from 1885-1955. During that time it's title was changed several times. It began in 1885 as the First Regiment, Dakota National Guard. It was redesignated the First Infantry Regiment, North Dakota National Guard on November 2, 1889 when North Dakota became a state. On May 20, 1898 it entered federal service as the First North Dakota Volunteer Infantry for the Spanish American War and the Philippine Insurrection. After being dismissed from federal service on September 25, 1899, it was reorganized in the North Dakota National Guard as First Infantry Regiment in November 1899. It was called into federal service on June 18, 1916 for the Mexican Border Conflict. On Saint Valentine's day, 1917, the regiment reverted to state control. In 1917 the regiment entered federal service for World War I. It was redesignated on October 4, 1917 as the 164th Infantry Regiment assigned to the 41st division. The regiment was demobilized on February 28, 1919. On May 16, 1923 the 164th was reorganized and federally recognized and then assigned to the 34th division and returned to state control.

The regiment entered federal service on February 10, 1941 for World War II. The regiment was assigned to the Americal Division on May 24, 1942. It was given back to state control on June 10, 1946 and assigned to the 47th division. The regiment was called into service on January 16, 1951 for the Korean War. On December 2, 1954 the regiment reverted to state control. The 164th Infantry Regiment was disbanded April 15, 1955 and converted into engineering battalions.

The Regiment's most notable time was when its service in World War II.

- At Guadalcanal in October 1942, it became the first U.S. Army unit to engage in offensive action against the enemy.
- It was involved in the heaviest fighting of this campaign and was congratulated by the Marine unit it reinforced.
- The Americal Division was awarded the Navy's Presidential Unit Citation.
- During its existence the unit and its members saw almost 600 days of combat, earned 199 Bronze Stars, 89 Silver Stars, six Legions of Merit, ten Soldiers Medals, six Distinguished Service Crosses, one Navy Cross and about 2,000 Purple Hearts.

My fellow Americal Veterans, this is the stock that set the bar for us. These are the men, who stepped up when their country called and by their actions said: I'm ready, I'm willing and I'm able.

I'm proud to say that I'm a Veteran of the Americal Division.

Memories from 1967

Welcome to Fort Polk, Louisiana – No doubt as to what our MOS is going to be

View of An Tan, looking south from the Tower

Richard Ropele
246 Coronado Dr.
Corona, CA 92879

National Reunions

2007 National Reunion
Buffalo, New York

The dates of next year's Americal Reunion will be from Thursday, June 21 to Sunday June 24 2007. The hotel is the Adam's Mark, (716)845-5100, room rates are $89.00 per night. Tell them you are with the ADVA for special room rates (http://www.americal.org/reunion.shtml).

Friday tours will include the Buffalo & Erie Co, Naval & Servicesman's Park where you can experience how sailors lived during a tour of the USS Little Rock missile cruise, the USS Sullivans destroyer, and the USS Croaker submarine. The park is the largest floating museum in America. A memorial service is planned for our group during the visit. Other Friday tours will include a Buffalo City Tour and a Niagara Fall Tours and Casino.

Saturday tours will include the Niagara Falls Experienced. Your will travel to the US side of the falls to visit Goat Island and Terapin Point for a view of the upper Niagara River Rapids and the American Falls from the brink. Price includes touring, maid of the mist boat tour and luncheon overlooking the Falls. Other Saturday tours include Galleria Mall Transportation and Ladies Tour.

National Reunion Summary

2007	Buffalo, New York	June 21 - 24	Adam Mark Hotel

2008	Jacksonville, Florida	June 26 - 29	Wyndham Riverwalk Hotel
2009	Shreveport, Louisiana		

Make your plans now to join with your fellow Americal veterans at this annual event. Enjoy the brotherhood and fellowship that we experienced when we were on active duty.

The Cannon

Far West Chapter AZ CA CO HA NV NM UT

Americal Division Veterans Association

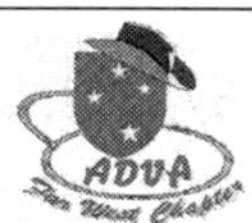

2007 – A New Year – A New Commitment

So, I figure if you're going to volunteer to participate in an organization, you should be ready to take on the assignments as they are handed out. Due to the vacancies in our Chapter leadership, Rich Merlin (Past Chapter Commander and current National Jr. Vice Commander) asked and I accepted the position of Chapter Commander, and was subsequently appointed by Larry Watson, ADVA National Chairman:

> By authority of the bylaws I appoint Richard Ropele to the position of Commander of the Far West Chapter. This appointment is for the balance of the vacated term or until the Far West Chapter holds elections. signed, Larry Watson, Commander, ADVA

So, what does a Chapter Commander do? Well, I'm not exactly sure, but the Far West Chapter is only as strong as the membership is active. As of the first of April, we have 155 members on the active roster, with only 29 having not yet renewed for the 2007 year.

The primary order of business for the Chapter is membership - both retention and recruitment

---

Men of the Americal

Before the mass murders of September 11th, the label 'hero' was handed out rather easily in our culture. Quite often, the media attached it to the athlete who scored the winning basket or touchdown.

After September 11th, the world was exposed to a different class of individuals who looked beyond self. These were those individuals who ran into the burning buildings at ground zero so that others would have a chance to live. That raised the bar for 'hero' in the eyes for most of the country.

However, we veterans always knew the real definition of hero; we served with many and saw their actions on a daily basis, these were men that went well beyond duty.

The Americal Division had its' share of heros. one from WW II and 12 men from Vietnam have been singled out and recognized for their actions by being awarded the Congressional Medal of Honor The citations of two of these extraordinary individuals follows

Staff Sergeant Jesse R. Drowley
Co. B, 132nd Inf Regt.
Bougainville, Solomon Islands

For gallantry and intrepidity at the risk of his life above and beyond the call of duty in action with the enemy at Bougainville, Solomon Islands, 30 January 1944. S/Sgt. Drowley, a squad leader in a platoon whose mission during an attack was to remain under cover while holding the perimeter defense and acting as a reserve for assaulting echelon, saw 3 members of the assault company fall badly wounded. When intense hostile fire prevented aid from reaching the casualties, he fearlessly rushed forward to carry the wounded to cover. After rescuing 2 men, S/Sgt. Drowley discovered an enemy pillbox undetected by assaulting tanks that was inflicting heavy casualties upon the attacking force and was a chief obstacle to the success of the advance.

Delegating the rescue of the third man to an assistant, he ran across open terrain to one of the tanks. Signaling to the crew, he climbed to the turret, exchanged his weapon for a submachine gun and voluntarily rode the deck of the tank directing it toward the pillbox by tracer fire. The tank, under constant heavy enemy fire, continued to within 20 feet of the pillbox where S/Sgt. Drowley received a severe bullet wound in the chest. Refusing to return for medical treatment, he remained on the tank and continued to direct its progress until the enemy box was definitely located by the crew. At this point he again was wounded by small arms fire, losing his left eye and falling to the ground.

He remained alongside the tank until the pillbox had been completely demolished and another directly behind the first destroyed. S/Sgt. Drowley, his voluntary mission successfully accomplished, returned alone for medical treatment.

Cpl Michael J. Crescenz

Co. A, 4/31st Inf., 196 LIB

20 November 1968

Hiep Duc Valley, RVN (Posthumous)

Cpl. Crescenz distinguished himself by conspicuous gallantry and intrepidity in action while serving as a rifleman with Company A. In the morning his unit engaged a large, well entrenched force of the North Vietnamese Army whose initial burst of fire pinned down the lead squad and killed the 2 point men, halting the advance of Company A.

Immediately, Cpl. Crescenz left the relative safety of his own position, seized a nearby machine gun and, with complete disregard for his safety, charged 100 meters up a slope toward the enemy's bunkers which he effectively silenced, killing the 2 occupants of each.

Undaunted by the withering machine gun fire around him, Cpl. Crescenz courageously moved forward toward a third bunker which he also succeeded in silencing, killing 2 more of the enemy and momentarily clearing the route of advance for his comrades. Suddenly, intense machine gun fire erupted from an unseen, camouflaged bunker. Realizing the danger to his fellow soldiers, Cpl. Crescenz disregarded the barrage of hostile fire directed at him and daringly advanced toward the position.

Assaulting with his machine gun, Cpl. Crescenz was within 5 meters of the bunker when he was mortally wounded by the fire from the enemy machine gun. As a direct result of his heroic actions, his company was able to maneuver freely with minimal danger and to complete its mission, defeating the enemy.

Cpl. Crescenz's bravery and extraordinary heroism at the cost of his life are in the highest traditions of the military service and reflect great credit on himself, his unit, and the U.S. Army

All the citations for all the MOH recipients are available at: http://www.army.mil/cmh-pg/moh1.htm

2007 Far West Chapter Reunion

Mark your Calendar
30 Sept - 02 Oct 2007
Riverside, CA

Final arrangements have been made for the 2007 Far West Chapter Annual Reunion

Where: Riverside Marriott Hotel
(951)784-8000

Planned Events:

Monday — Bus to Riverside National Cemetery
- Tour the Medal of Honor Memorial and the Fallen Soldiers/Veterans Memorial
- Wreath laying ceremony

March Air Force Base
- March Field Air Museum
- War Dog Memorial and Freedom Wall
- Lunch at the Museum

Tuesday — Annual Chapter Business Meeting
- Election of Officers
- Financial Report
- Planning for the 2008 Chapter Reunion
- Tour of the historic Mission Inn

Dinner and Dance

Contact the Riverside Marriott directly before 31 August for the special reservation rate of $109/night, mentioning the ADVA Far West Chapter. Additional information and reservations forms will be mailed soon.

This Chapter Reunion is a good chance to once again renew those bonds of brotherhood we experienced while on active duty. We have 155 members in this Chapter, let's get together and get acquainted.

Past Chapter Commander Rich Merlin is pulling this event together. If you would like to assist him, let me know
(rropele@yahoo.com)

Recommended Reading

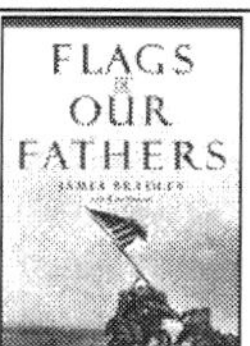	Flags of our Fathers By James Bradley Son of John Bradley, one of the 6 flag raisers
I read this book last year, not only is it an account of the battle for Iwo Jima, but it's also a focus study on the lives of the 6 flag raisers. 3 of whom lost their lives during that campaign. A good read to which we all can relate Admiral Chester Nimitz stated: 'Uncommon valor was a common virture at Iwo Jima'	

Social Security Information

The following information is from Social Security Administration publication No. 05-10017. You may be eligible for additional compensation. Contact your local SSA Office to confirm your eligibility.

Earnings for active duty military service or active duty training have been covered under Social Security since 1957. Social Security has covered inactive duty service in the armed forces reserves (such as weekend drills) since 1988. If you served in the military before 1957, you did not pay Social Security taxes, but we gave you special credit for some of your service.

Extra earnings

If you served in the military from 1940 through 1956, including attendance at a service academy, you did not pay Social Security taxes. However, we will credit you with $160 a month in earnings for military service from September 16, 1940, through December 31, 1956, if:

- You were honorably discharged after 90 or more days of service, or you were released because of a disability or injury received in the line of duty; or
- You are applying for survivors benefits based on a veteran's work and the veteran died while on active duty.

You cannot receive these special credits if you are receiving a federal benefit based on the same years of service, unless you were on active duty after 1956. If you were on active duty after 1956, you can get the special credit for 1951 through 1956, even if you are receiving a military retirement based on service during that period.

If you served in the military from 1957 through 1977, you are credited with $300 in additional earnings for each calendar quarter in which you received active duty basic pay.

If you served in the military from 1978 through 2001, you are credited with an additional $100 in earnings, up to a maxi-mum of $1,200 a year, for every $300 in active duty basic pay. After 2001, additional earnings are no longer credited.

If you began your service after September 7, 1980, and did not complete at least 24 months of active duty or your full tour, you may not be able to receive the additional earnings. Check with us for more information.

NOTE: In all cases, the additional earnings are credited to the earnings that we average over your working lifetime, not directly to your monthly benefit amount.

Far West Chapter Membership

Check the year above your name on the mailing label. If the year is "2006" then your dues are now due. Dues are $10.00 per year. You may also pay for more than one year at a time. Mail your dues to:

Tom Packard
6613 Birch Park Dr.
Galloway, OH 43119

Make your checks payable to 'ADVA – Far West Chapter'.

At this writing, membership renewals stand at 79%. It would be great to see 100% this year. We value your membership, so send in your dues today.

FYI: in accordance with the Chapter by-laws, if dues aren't paid by April 1st for the previous year, a reminder notice is sent. Then, if not paid by May 1st, then the member is dropped from the roster

Welcome back, reinstated members:
Jack Oglesby of Long Beach, CA
Thomas Molina of Madera, CA

Far West Chapter Roster

Enclosed with this issue of The Cannon is your copy of the Far West Chapter roster. I hope it will help you stay in touch with your friends from the chapter.

Send any corrections to the roster to Tom Packard.

While updating the roster I noticed that some of you are not on the ADVA national roster. Check your membership with National; it must be current to belong to a chapter.

Keep your family files current

Retired soldiers and surviving spouses; does your family know where your files and important papers are?

If you weren't here tomorrow, would they know where your bank account is, what insurance you carry and where the deed to your house is? I'm not a "retired" soldier but I found a very useful tool on the US Army post retirement website.

This three page form can be accessed online at:http://www.armyg1.army.mil/rso/PostRetirement.asp.

Look under information for Retired Soldiers and Family Members. Click on "Casualty Assistance Checklist". Complete the checklist and give it to your family to make thing just a little easier if you're not available.

(Reprinted from the Franklin County (Ohio) Veterans Service Commission newsletter, March, 07)

Far West Chapter Officers

Commander
Richard Ropele
(951)218-3071
rropele@yahoo.com

Vice Commander

Secretary/Treasurer
Tom Packard
(614)878-5197
Packard50@columbus.rr.com

Sergeant At Arms
Curt Rothacker
(925)784-5391

Chaplain
Don Squire
(801)635-2547

Newsletter Editor
Rick Ropele
246 Coronado, Dr
Corona, CA 92879
(951)218-3071
rropele@yahoo.com

You'll notice that we have a vacancy for the position of Vice Commander, if you're interested in serving with us, please contact me
The main responsibility of the Vice commander is Membership.

The final Thought

There are countless millions of people alive today throughout the world because of the sacrifice and dedication of the men and women of the Unites States Military.

Honored and great are they that wear the colors of the United States of America

Richard Ropele
246 Coronado Dr.
Corona, CA 92879

National Reunions

2007 National Reunion
Buffalo, New York

The dates of next year's Americal Reunion will be from Thursday, June 21 to Sunday June 24 2007. The hotel is the Adam's Mark, (716)845-5100, room rates are $89.00 per night. Tell them you are with the ADVA for special room rates (http://www.americal.org/reunion.shtml).

Friday tours will include the Buffalo & Erie Co, Naval & Servicesman's Park where you can experience how sailors lived during a tour of the USS Little Rock missile cruise, the USS Sullivans destroyer, and the USS Croaker submarine. The park is the largest floating museum in America. A memorial service is planned for our group during the visit. Other Friday tours will include a Buffalo City Tour and a Niagara Fall Tours and Casino.

Saturday tours will include the Niagara Falls Experienced. Your will travel to the US side of the falls to visit Goat Island and Terapin Point for a view of the upper Niagara River Rapids and the American Falls from the brink. Price includes touring, maid of the mist boat tour and luncheon overlooking the Falls. Other Saturday tours include Galleria Mall Transportation and Ladies Tour.

National Reunion Summary

2007	Buffalo, New York	June 21 - 24	Adam Mark Hotel
2008	Jacksonville, Florida	June 26 - 29	Wyndham Riverwalk Hotel
2009	Shreveport, Louisiana		

Make your plans now to join with your fellow Americal veterans at this annual event. Enjoy the brotherhood and fellowship that we experienced when we were on active duty.

The Cannon

Americal Division Veterans Association

Far West Chapter AZ CA CO HA NV NM UT

I had hoped that the primary topic of this issue of The Cannon would be a recap of my thoughts and impressions after attending my first ADVA National Reunion in Buffalo, New York. I was looking forward to connecting with some of those men with whom I had served way back in 1967 when I joined E Co. 1/6th 198th LIB in November of 1967 as a replacement.

Cathy and I had planned a whole east coast experience, but alas, it wasn't meant to be (this time). My wife's mothers' health has taken a turn such that wasn't advisable for us to be away from her at this time. All of us Vietnam Veterans are at this same stage in our lives where it's our turn to take care of our aging parents - a responsibility that we embrace.

So the primary theme for this issue of the newsletter is a brief exploration of the affects of Agent Orange. We were all over there when it was being used and need to be aware of the potential health risks we face.

This write-up is certainly not meant to be the definitive paper on Agent Orange, it is meant to stir our thoughts regarding something we should be aware of, and if necessary, take the appropriate action. I'm going to register with the VA and sign up for the Agent Orange Registry. I'll let you know about the process in subsequent newsletters

---

Agent Orange

Agent Orange was a herbicide used in Vietnam to kill unwanted plants and to remove leaves from trees that otherwise provided cover for the enemy. Between 1961 and 1971, the U.S. Military in South Vietnam used more than 19 million gallons for defoliation and crop destruction. Heavily sprayed areas included inland forests near the DMZ; inland forests at the junction of the borders of Cambodia, Laos, and South Vietnam; inland forests north and northwest of Saigon; mangrove forests on the southernmost peninsula of Vietnam.

One of the chemicals (2,4,5-T) in Agent Orange contained minute traces of 2,3,7,8-tetrachlorodibenzo-p-dioxin (also known as TCDD or dioxin), which has caused a variety of illnesses in laboratory animals. More recent studies have suggested that the chemical may be related to a number of malignancies and other disorders.

The following conditions are now presumptively recognized for service-connection for Vietnam veterans based on exposure to Agent Orange or other herbicides:

Condition	Description
Chloracne	A skin disorder. Chloracne is the one human effect universally linked to dioxin exposure. The presence of chloracne is considered a clinical sign of exposure. The VA has recognized Chloracne as the one human effect universally linked to dioxin exposure. The presence of Chloracne is considered a clinical sign of exposure as associated with (but not necessarily caused by) Agent Orange exposure
Porphyria Cutanea Tarda	When signs and symptoms occur, they usually begin in adulthood and result from the skin becoming overly sensitive to sunlight. Areas of skin exposed to the sun develop severe blistering, scarring, changes in pigmentation, and increased hair growth. Exposed skin becomes fragile and is easily damaged
Peripheral Neuropathy	Acute or subacute nerve disorder condition results from damage to the nerves that carry signals from the hands and feet
Type 2 Diabetes	There appears to be some relationship between Agent Orange exposure and increased insulin resistance, the precursor to type 2 diabetes
Numerous Cancers	Non-Hodgkin's Lymphoma, Soft tissue sarcoma, Hodgkin's disease, Multiple Myeloma, Prostate Cancer, and Respiratory Cancers: Lung Larynx Trachea Bronchus Lymphocytic Leukemia
Additionally, children of Vietnam Veterans' with the birth defect spinal bifida are eligible for certain benefits and services	
NOTE: these are just summary definitions that I extracted from various sources, please research further on your own for more definitive answers	

If you suspect that you have been exposed to Agent Orange (or other herbicides used in Vietnam (the three most common are Agent Orange, Agent White, and Agent Blue - mixtures identified by the colored stripe on the drum)), contact your nearest VA Medical Center for an examination under the Agent Orange Registry.

The examination consists of:

- A medical history
- A physical examination
- A series of basic laboratory tests
  - Chest X-Ray
  - Urinalysis
  - Blood tests
- If medically required, consultations with other health specialists are scheduled.

No special Agent Orange tests are offered because there is no way to show that Agent Orange caused individual medical problems.

The Department of Veterans affairs has set up a special examination program for Vietnam veterans who were worried about the long term health effects of exposure to Agent Orange. Contact your nearest VA medical center and ask about participating in the Agent Orange Registry.

Source: http://www1.va.gov/agentorange/, http://www1.va.gov/agentorange/page.cfm?pg=1

This map is a representation of herbicide spray missions in Vietnam.

The Orange areas represent concentrated spraying areas.

This map only represents fixed-wing aircraft spraying, and does not include helicopter spraying of perimeters, or other spray methods. The III Corps area received the heaviest concentrations of spraying, followed by I Corps, II Corps and IV Corps.

The product was tested in Vietnam in the early 1960's, and brought into ever widening use during the height of the war (1967-68), though its use was diminished and eventually discontinued in 1971.

The earliest health concerns about Agent Orange were about the product's contamination with TCDD, or dioxin. TCDD is one of a family of dioxins, some found in nature, and are cousins of the dibenzofurans and pcb's. The TCDD found in Agent Orange is harmful to man.

In laboratory tests on animals, TCDD has caused a wide variety of diseases, many of them fatal. TCDD is not found in nature, but rather is a man-made and always unwanted byproduct of the chemical manufacturing process.

The Agent Orange used in Vietnam was later found to be extremely contaminated with TCDD

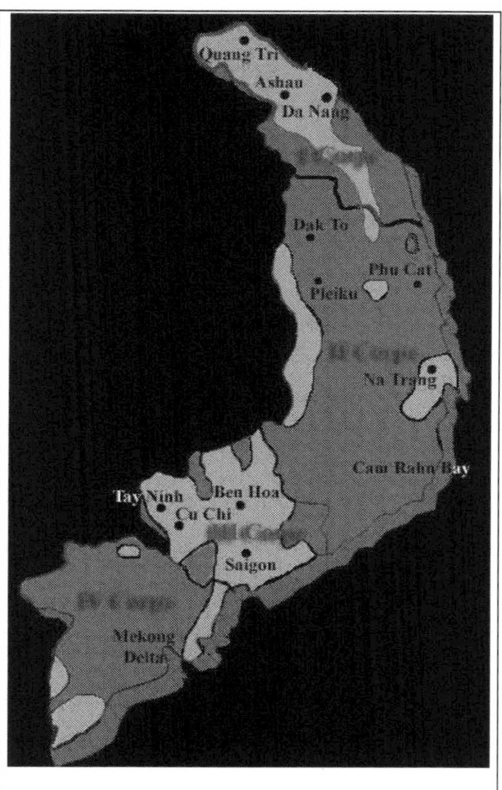

Welcome New Members

As a result of our on-going membership drive, please welcome our most recent Far West Chapter members, as of 06 July 2007.

WWII

Leonard Angus	Hayward, CA	Co. A, 1st Bn, 182nd Inf.
Fred F Drew, DPM	San Jose, CA	Co. C, 1st Med Bn, 164th Inf.
Kenneth C Lachmann	Albuquerque, NM	Co. G, 182nd Inf.

VIETNAM

SGM Volley H. Cole (USA Ret.)	Sun Lakes, AZ	16th Combat Aviation Group

Dr. Charles C. Mitchell	Valencia, CA	HHC, Div. Deputy IG
Lawrence Coldren	Denver, CO	HHC, 23rd Medical Bn.
Gregory W. Sanders	Cambria,CA	HHC, Div. G-5
Charles LaFlamme	Corning, CA	Delta Co. 1/20th, 11th LIB
Rueben L. Rojas	Escondido, CA	Co's D & E, 1/20th, 11th LIB
Leslie A. Gorsuch	Aurora, CO	Co. B, 8th Spt. BN, 196th LIB
Vincent M. McMenany	Henderson, NV	4/31 Inf, 196th LIB
Stephen D. Frausto	Costa Mesa, CA	Co. D, 5/46Inf, 198th LIB
Max D. Loffgren	Willows, CA	Co. B, 1/52 Inf, 198th LIB
Frank R. Yehle	San Clemente, CA	Co. B, 1/6 Inf, 198th LIB
Ronald Dunning	Porterville, CA	Co. B, 5/46 Inf, 198th LIB
Ronald R. Capek	Glendale, AZ	Co. D, 1/46 Inf, 198th LIB
James H Smith	Surprise, AZ	11th LIB
Colt Rymer	South Lake Tahoe, CA	26th Engrg
J. Mencor Valdez	Pagosa Springs, CO	1/82 Arty
Ostenberg, Robert MG	Woodside, CA	196/198 LIB

Men of the Americal

Continuing with the series of highlighting the exploits of the men of the Americal Division, following are two more citations of Americal men awarded the Congressional Medal of Honor.

SP4 Thomas J. McMahon
Co. A, 2/1, 196 LIB.
19 March 1969
Quang Tin Province, VN

For conspicuous gallantry and intrepidity in action at the risk of his life above and beyond the call of duty. Sp4c. McMahon distinguished himself while serving as medical aid man with Company A. When the lead elements of his company came under heavy fire from well fortified enemy positions, 3 soldiers fell seriously wounded. Sp4c. McMahon, with complete disregard for his safety, left his covered position and ran through intense enemy fire to the side of one of the wounded, administered first aid and then carried him to safety. He returned through the hail of fire to the side of a second wounded man. Although painfully wounded by an exploding mortar round while returning the wounded man to a secure position, Sp4c. McMahon refused medical attention and heroically ran back through the heavy enemy fire toward his remaining wounded comrade. He fell mortally wounded before he could rescue the last man.

Sp4c. McMahon's undaunted concern for the welfare of his comrades at the cost of his life are in keeping with the highest traditions of the military service and reflect great credit on himself, his unit, and the U.S. Army..

Staff Sgt Robert C. Murray
Co. B 4/31st Inf., 196 LIB
07 June 1970

Near the village of Hiep Duc, RVN
S/Sgt. Murray distinguished himself while serving as a squad leader with Company B. S/Sgt. Murray's squad was searching for an enemy mortar that had been threatening friendly positions when a member of the squad tripped an enemy grenade rigged as a booby trap. Realizing that he had activated the enemy booby trap, the soldier shouted for everybody to take cover. Instantly assessing the danger to the men of his squad, S/Sgt. Murray unhesitatingly and with complete disregard for his own safety, threw himself on the grenade absorbing the full and fatal impact of the explosion. By his gallant action and self sacrifice, he prevented the death or injury of the other members of his squad.

S/Sgt. Murray's extraordinary courage and gallantry, at the cost of his life above and beyond the call of duty, are in keeping with the highest traditions of the military service and reflect great credit on him, his unit, and the U.S. Army.

All the citations for all the MOH recipients are available at: http://www.army.mil/cmh-pg/moh1.htm

Still Serving

In case you missed it, there is a good article in the April, May, June issue of the Americal Journal. It's a story about Far West Chapter member, LTC Emory Clifton, an Americal Vietnam Veteran currently serving in Iraq and is due to return home in November, 2007.

Past Chapter Commander Rich Merlin is pulling this event together. If you would like to assist him, let me know
(rropele@yahoo.com)

2007 Far West Chapter Reunion

Mark your Calendar
30 Sept - 02 Oct 2007
Riverside, CA
Final arrangements have been made for the 2007 Far West Chapter Annual Reunion
Where: Riverside Marriott Hotel
(951)784-8000
Planned Events:

Monday Bus to Riverside National Cemetery

- Tour the Medal of Honor Memorial and the Fallen Soldiers/Veterans Memorial
- Wreath laying ceremony

March Air Force Base

- March Field Air Museum
- War Dog Memorial and Freedom Wall
- Lunch at the Museum

Tuesday Annual Chapter Business Meeting

- Election of Officers
- Financial Report
- Planning for the 2008 Chapter Reunion
- Tour of the historic Mission Inn

Dinner and Dance

Contact the Riverside Marriott directly before 31 August for the special reservation rate of $109/night, mentioning the ADVA Far West Chapter. Additional information and reservations forms will be mailed soon.

This Chapter Reunion is a good chance to once again renew those bonds of brotherhood we experienced while on active duty. We have 167 members in this Chapter, let's get together and get acquainted.

Recommended Reading

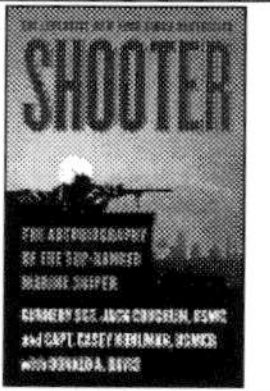

Shooter: The Autobiography of the Top-Ranked Marine Sniper
By
Jack Coughlin, Don Davis, & Casey Kuhlman

Coughlin has written a highly personal story about his deadly craft, taking readers deep inside an invisible society that is off-limits to outsiders. This is not a heroic battlefield memoir, but the careful study of an exceptional man who must keep his sanity while carrying forward one of the deadliest legacies in the U.S. military today

Far West Chapter Officers

Commander
Richard Ropele
(951)218-3071
rropele@yahoo.com

Vice Commander

Secretary/Treasurer
Tom Packard
(614)878-5197
Packard50@columbus.rr.com

Sergeant At Arms
Curt Rothacker
(925)784-5391

Chaplain
Don Squire
(801)635-2547

Newsletter Editor
Rick Ropele
246 Coronado, Dr
Corona, CA 92879
(951)218-3071
rropele@yahoo.com

Richard Ropele
246 Coronado Dr.
Corona, CA 92879

The final Thought

There are countless millions of people alive today throughout the world because of the sacrifice and dedication of the men and women of the Unites States Military.

Honored and great are they that wear the colors of the United States of America

Thanks you all for your service and dedication

The Cannon

Americal Division Veterans Association

Far West Chapter AZ CA CO HA NV NM UT

The 2007 Far West Chapter Reunion at the Riverside CA. Marriott Hotel was an unqualified success. Special thanks to Rich Merlin for putting it together and ensuring that everyone was taken care of.

Outside the Riverside Marriott Hotel: a group of WWII and Vietnam veterans that answered their countries call to serve.

We had a total of 16 chapter members attending, 4 from our World War II contingent.

There was a tour of the March Air Force Base Aircraft Museum where we had lunch and saw static displays of aircraft ranging from a WWII Bomber to the U2 Spy Plane. We were also treated to a special guided tour of Riverside National Cemetery where we saw and heard about their Medal of Honor Memorial, their POW/MIA Memorial and their Veterans Memorial - very moving.

The evening finished up with dinner and karaoke. We missed a lot of you and hope that you'll join us in Laughlin next year (details to follow in subsequent newsletters)

Memories from Don S. Squire

Note: Don is the Chaplain for the Far West Chapter. This article is a reprint of an interview he gave to the Hurricane Valley Journal, Hurricane Utah.

I was inducted into the Army April 11, 1943 at Fort Douglas, Utah. We were then shipped, via Union Pacific Railroad, to Camp Cook, California. I spent five long and miserable months there in basic training in the Second Armored Group. I was sent from

Camp Cook to Fort Ord, California, where I spent about one miserable month training as regular foot infantryman. Then late one night we boarded a train that took us to the docks of the Pacific Ocean, where we boarded the U.S.S. General George O. Squirer. This was October 28, 1943. Early the next morning we were on our way, moving out to sea, passing under the Golden Gate Bridge.

It was a long trip from San Francisco to the New Caledonia, arriving November 15. The eleven days we spent on the Island of New Caledonia we worked in the large warehouses loading and unloading supplies.

From there we went to Fiji and finally ended up on Bougainville Island, in the Solomon Islands, in January 1944. I was there for a little more than a year and this is where I first saw combat with the Americal Division. This Division got its name from combining America and Caledonia and was the Division that fought the battle on Guadualcanal.

Early in morning in the month of October, the year 1944, I Company of the 132nd Infantry Regiment, Americal Division, 3rd battalion fell out for a patrol that would take us deep into the jungles of Bougainville Island. Little did any of us realize what would happen the very first night out.

It rained hard that day, which definitely was not unusual; it made the trip that we had to take that much more miserable. The jungles of 'Bougie' (as it was referred to) seldom, if ever got dry. Then we had the swamps to contend with and the many streams.

The first evening we were getting ready to dig in for the night, all was calm and quiet until about five minutes after we arrived on this particular hill. Then all hell broke loose. Within about 30 minutes, one of our boys was killed and about eight wounded. Many of the Japanese soldiers were also killed. It was getting late, so we withdrew and set up a smoke signal and called for artillery. The artillery threw shells over us and onto this hill all during the night. The artillery shells were landing close enough that we could hear the shrapnel whistling through the trees around us. The next morning the shells had cleared out the enemy and we began patrolling another area.

A couple of months later we shipped out to Leyte Island in the Philippines. While there I went on a boat trip delivering supplies to Samar Island, where there was considerable gunfire, however we did not get fired on going or returning.

A few months after arriving on Leyte, I was put in the hospital because I was starting to lose control of the use of my right arm. I was moved from hospital to hospital until they finally sent me to a general hospital on New Guinea. I was there for almost a month and then, on April 24, 1945, my birthday, I was informed I would be leaving for the States the next day. After receiving several months of treatment, I was Honorable discharged on June 30 1945, with 40 percent disability. I was awarded the Asiatic Pacific Theater ribbon and Combat Infantry Badge and campaign stars for the Solomon and Philippines Islands.

Don S. Squire grew up in La Verkin, Utah. He is now a retired Superintendent of the U. S. National Parks Service and a resident of Hurricane, Utah

<u>2008 Far West Chapter Membership</u>

It's that time again......

Check the mailing label for the year above your name. This is the year your chapter dues are paid through. If it's 2007, then your annual dues are now due.

Chapter dues are still just $10.00 per year. You may renew for any number of years.

Make out your check to the FAR WEST CHAPTER and mail it to:

ADVA/Far West Chapter
c/o Tom Packard
6613 Birch Park Drive
Galloway, Ohio 43119.

<u>Men of the Americal</u>

Continuing with the series of highlighting the exploits of the men of the Americal Division, following is one more citation of Americal men awarded the Congressional Medal of Honor.

<u>Capt. James Allen Taylor</u>
Troop B, 1st Cavalry
09 November 1967
West of Que Son, RVN

Capt. Taylor, Armor, was serving as executive officer of Troop B, 1st Squadron. His troop was engaged in an attack on a fortified position west of Que Son when it came under intense enemy recoilless rifle, mortar, and automatic weapons fire from an enemy strong point located immediately to its front. One armored cavalry assault vehicle was hit immediately by recoilless rifle fire and all 5 crewmembers were wounded. Aware that the stricken vehicle was in grave danger of exploding, Capt. Taylor rushed forward and personally extracted the wounded to safety despite the hail of enemy fire and exploding ammunition. Within minutes a second armored cavalry assault vehicle was hit by multiple recoilless rifle rounds. Despite the continuing intense enemy fire, Capt. Taylor moved forward on foot to rescue the wounded men from the burning vehicle and personally removed all the crewmen to the safety of a nearby dike. Moments later the vehicle exploded. As he was returning to his vehicle, a bursting mortar round painfully wounded Capt. Taylor, yet he valiantly returned to his vehicle to relocate the medical evacuation landing zone to an area closer to the front lines. As he was moving his vehicle, it came under machine gun fire from an enemy position not 50 yards away. Capt. Taylor engaged the position with his machine gun, killing the 3 man crew. Upon arrival at the new evacuation site, still another vehicle was struck. Once again Capt. Taylor rushed forward and pulled the wounded from the vehicle, loaded them aboard his vehicle, and returned them safely to the evacuation site. His actions of unsurpassed valor were a source of inspiration to his entire troop, contributed significantly to the success of the overall assault on the enemy position, and were directly responsible for saving the lives of a number of his fellow soldiers.

His actions were in keeping with the highest traditions of the military profession and reflect great credit upon himself, his unit, and the U.S. Army.

Note: Capt Taylor is a member of our Far West Chapter of the ADVA.

2008 Far West Chapter Reunion

- Planned for Laughlin Nevada
- The date is tentative, but we're looking at the first or second week in October.

More information will be forth coming as soon as we firm the hotel and the schedule of events.

Please note: A significant part of our lives were spent in the service to our country and to one another. From this service we developed character and personality traits that we still carry with us today. Success of our Chapter reunions is directly dependent on the participation of our membership Please consider taking the time to join us next year in Laughlin. It's this fellowship and camaraderie that held us together in WWII and Vietnam and it's what makes our chapter successful today.

Far West Chapter Officers

Commander
Richard Ropele
(951)218-3071
rropele@yahoo.com

Vice Commander

Secretary/Treasurer
Tom Packard
(614)878-5197
Packard50@columbus.rr.com

Sergeant At Arms
Curt Rothacker
(925)784-5391

Chaplain
Don Squire
(801)635-2547

Newsletter Editor
Richard Ropele
246 Coronado, Dr
Corona, CA 92879
(951)218-3071
rropele@yahoo.com

The Veterans Memorial at Riverside National Cemetery

U2 Spy Plane: March Air Force Base Museum

The Historic Mission Inn, Riverside California

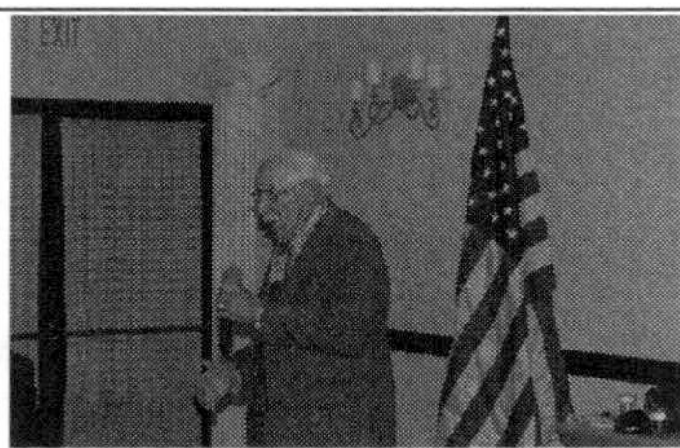

Paris Tognoli: the master of Karoake

POW/MIA Memorial: Riverside National Cemetery.
Bound and shackled, but head still high and proud

WWII Bomber: March Air Force Base Museum

B52 Bomber: March Airforce Base Museum

Medal of Honor Memorial

During our tour of Riverside National Cemetery, we spotted a small granite monument funded and placed on the grounds by the 3rd Infantry Division. This monument is a black granite block measuring 49 by 25 by 30 and holds a brass plaque identifying the campaigns in which the 3rd ID was involved.

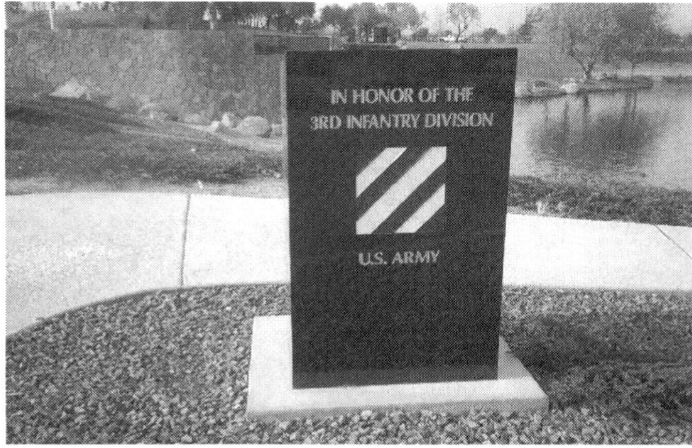

Part of the business meeting was devoted to a discussion of this monument and whether we could sponsor a similar edifice for the Americal Division. It was generally met with a positive response, but without cost and schedules details we couldn't make a commitment to move forward.

It was decided that we would put together a committee to do the research and put together a proposal for the memberships' consideration and vote

This proposal has not been started yet, but we'll get something on the table in the next couple of months.

Richard Ropele
246 Coronado Dr.
Corona, CA 92879

The final Thought

There are countless millions of people alive today throughout the world because of the sacrifice and dedication of the men and women of the Unites States Military.

Honored and great are they that wear the colors of the United States of America

Thank you all for your service and dedication

The Cannon

Americal Division Veterans Association

Far West Chapter AZ CA CO HA NV NM UT

For this issue of The Cannon, I did some internet research and found a number of sites that reported on WWII and Vietnam from a statistical point of view. As we all look back on our service, we see people, places, and events in the context in which we lived them. However, a statistical look back removes those personal aspects - sort of a '5000 foot perspective' of that time period and paints a broader perspective of the whole.

Most of these research sites on Vietnam extract data from the Combat Area Casualty Current File (CACCF) maintained by the National Archives and Records Administration (NARA).

Country of Casualty	Number of Records
Cambodia	520
Laos	733
North Vietnam	1,124
Communist China	10
Republic of Vietnam (South Vietnam)	55,629
Thailand	177
Total	**58,193**

See page 4 and 5 for additional data

Men of the Americal

Continuing with the series of highlighting the exploits of the men of the Americal Division, following are two more citation of Americal men awarded the Congressional Medal of Honor.

Sergeant Lester R. Stone, Jr.

Company B 1/20, 11th Infantry Brigade
31 March 1969
West of LZ Liz, RVN

For conspicuous gallantry and intrepidity in action at the risk of his life above and beyond the call of duty. Sgt. Stone, distinguished himself while serving as squad leader of the 1st Platoon. The 1st Platoon was on a combat patrol mission just west of Landing Zone Liz when it came under intense automatic weapons and grenade fire from a well concealed company size force of North Vietnamese regulars. Observing the platoon machine gunner fall critically wounded, Sgt. Stone remained in the exposed area to provide cover fire for the wounded soldier who was being pulled to safety by another member of the platoon. With enemy fire impacting all around him, Sgt. Stone had a malfunction in the machine gun, preventing him from firing the weapon automatically. Displaying extraordinary courage under the most adverse conditions, Sgt. Stone repaired the weapon and continued to place on the enemy positions effective suppressive fire which enabled the rescue to be completed. In a desperate attempt to overrun his position, an enemy force left its cover and charged Sgt. Stone. Disregarding the danger involved, Sgt. Stone rose to his knees and began placing intense fire on the enemy at pointblank range, killing 6 of the enemy before falling mortally wounded. His actions of unsurpassed valor were a source of inspiration to his entire unit, and he was responsible for saving the lives of a number of his fellow soldiers.

His actions were in keeping with the highest traditions of the military profession and reflect great credit on him, his unit, and the U.S. Army.

Private First Class Daniel John Shea

Headquarters Company, 3/21, 196th LIB
14 May 1969
Quang Tri Province, RVN

For conspicuous gallantry and intrepidity in action at the risk of his life above and beyond the call of duty. Pfc. Shea, Headquarters and Headquarters Company, 3d Battalion, distinguished himself while serving as a medical aidman with Company C, 3d Battalion, during a combat patrol mission. As the lead platoon of the company was crossing a rice paddy, a

large enemy force in ambush positions opened fire with mortars, grenades and automatic weapons. Under heavy crossfire from 3 sides, the platoon withdrew to a small island in the paddy to establish a defensive perimeter. Pfc. Shea, seeing that a number of his comrades had fallen in the initial hail of fire, dashed from the defensive position to assist the wounded. With complete disregard for his safety and braving the intense hostile fire sweeping the open rice paddy, Pfc. Shea made 4 trips to tend wounded soldiers and to carry them to the safety of the platoon position. Seeing a fifth wounded comrade directly in front of one of the enemy strong points, Pfc. Shea ran to his assistance. As he reached the wounded man, Pfc. Shea was grievously wounded. Disregarding his welfare, Pfc. Shea tended his wounded comrade and began to move him back to the safety of the defensive perimeter. As he neared the platoon position, Pfc. Shea was mortally wounded by a burst of enemy fire. By his heroic actions Pfc. Shea saved the lives of several of his fellow soldiers.
Pfc. Shea's gallantry in action at the cost of his life were in keeping with the highest traditions of the military service and reflect great credit upon himself, his unit, and the U.S. Army.

<u>2008 Far West Chapter Membership</u>

It's that time again......

Check the mailing label for the year above your name. This is the year your chapter dues are paid through. If it's 2007, then your annual dues are now due.

Chapter dues are still just $10.00 per year. You may renew for any number of years.

Make out your check to the FAR WEST CHAPTER and mail it to:

ADVA/Far West Chapter
c/o Tom Packard
6613 Birch Park Drive
Galloway, Ohio 43119.

VFW URGES RUSSIA TO RESTORE FULL ACCOUNTING SUPPORT

WASHINGTON (Nov. 14, 2007) – The Veterans of Foreign Wars of the U.S. national commander's trip last week to assist Russian veterans with their goal of creating a system similar to the U.S. Department of Veterans Affairs was made more urgent because American researchers have been banned from Russia's central military archives for the past 13 months.

According to U.S. officials in the Defense POW/Missing Personnel Office, the archives are vitally important to America's Full Accounting Mission because archival material could help to determine the fate of some of the 88,000 missing and unaccounted-for Americans going back to World War II.

VFW Commander-in-Chief George Lisicki now wants the Russian veterans' groups to use their collective influence on their government so that America can resume its mission to account for missing Americans.

Lisicki, a Vietnam combat veteran from Carteret, N.J., traveled to Russia last week on the invitation of retired Russian Gen. Lt. Ruslan Aushev, the chairman of the Commonwealth of Independent States Committee of Warrior Internationalists.

Speaking at a joint veterans' conference Nov. 6, Lisicki urged the 65 leaders to use their combined influence to bring their government back to the U.S.-Russia Joint Commission. The commission was created in 1992, but has been largely ineffective since June 2004 due to a reduction in the size of the Russian government's executive branch. The U.S. government was told it was an oversight, but no correction has yet been made.

"Helping Russian veterans to create a system similar to our VA is something we are doing out of respect for them as military veterans," he said. "I now need their help to move their government from inaction to action on the full accounting issue."

Lisicki told the audience that the U.S. had provided the Russian government dozens of reports and intelligence data on the capture, imprisonment or deaths of former Soviet military personnel in Afghanistan. "To my knowledge, this information has enabled Russia to account for 63 soldiers who were formerly listed as missing in action. More important is that information helped to bring closure to 63 Russian families," he said.

The VFW national commander now wants that same assistance for American families. "Our wars are over, but these families relive their wars every hour of every day," he said. "The Full Accounting Mission is a humanitarian issue for the families of our dead comrades in arms."

In an unprecedented gesture, Lisicki also met with several members from both houses of Russia's parliament, where he urged them to restore their side of the bilateral commission and to restore U.S. research access to their archives.

Lisicki believes the veteran-to-veteran exchange in Russia will prove just as beneficial to the Full Accounting Mission as the relationship the VFW has forged with Vietnamese veterans' organizations. The VFW is the only American veterans' organization to return to Vietnam every year since 1991.

"We are veterans ... not politicians or diplomats," he explained. "We understand the true nature of war, and we and our families understand the sacrifices that are sometimes required. The Full Accounting Mission fulfills a soldier's pledge that we will never live a fallen comrade behind on the battlefield. This is one issue that all military veterans from all nations can support."

To read VFW National Commander George Lisicki's Nov. 6 speech to the Russian veterans, go to: http://www.vfw.org/resources/pdf/speechrussianveteransconference2007.pdf.

2008 Far West Chapter Reunion

- Planned for Laughlin Nevada
- The date is tentative, but we're looking at the first or second week in October.

More information will be forth coming as soon as we firm the hotel and the schedule of events.

Note: A significant part of our lives were spent in the service to our country and to one another. From this service we developed character and personality traits that we still carry with us today. Success of our Chapter reunions is directly dependent on the participation of our membership Please consider taking the time to join us next year in Laughlin. It's this fellowship and camaraderie that held us together in WWII and Vietnam and it's what makes our chapter successful today.

Far West Chapter Officers

Commander
Richard Ropele
(951)218-3071
rropele@yahoo.com

Vice Commander

Secretary/Treasurer
Tom Packard
(614)878-5197
Packard50@columbus.rr.com

Sergeant At Arms
Curt Rothacker
(925)784-5391

Chaplain
Don Squire
(801)635-2547

Newsletter Editor
Richard Ropele
246 Coronado, Dr
Corona, CA 92879
(951)218-3071
rropele@yahoo.com

WW II and Vietnam Causalities Statistics

Over the years I have seen many sites on the internet reporting these kinds of statistics, some have disappeared over the years, others are still around. For this issue, I used a combination of old and new.

Http://www.archives.gov/research/vietnam-war/casualty-statistics.html.

Http://www.ddaymuseum.org/education/education_numbers.html

If you Google 'Vietnam War Casualty Statistics' or 'WWII Casualty Statistics' you'll be offered a lot of choices to review. The numbers may vary between, but overall the totality of their story is essentially the same.

Losses in Southeast Asia by Rank - Jan 1961 thru Dec 1976

Enlisted

Grade	Army	Navy	Cst Grd	Marines	Air Force	Consolidated	Total
E-9	20/21	1/3	0/0	11/6	9/5	41/35	76
E-8	123/62	5/6	0/0	17/13	8/10	153/91	244
E-7	712/239	29/34	1/0	88/19	20/32	850/324	1,174
E-6	1,697/436	99/83	1/0	255/38	57/57	2,109/614	2,723
E-5	4,123/1,000	202/120	0/1	610/108	99/97	5,034/1,328	6,380
E-4	9,252/2,242	434/179	0/0	2,031/275	103/97	11,820/2,793	14,613
E-3	11,041/1,762	414/219	1/0	3,848/491	51/80	15,355/2,552	17,907
E-2	295/178	21/44	0/0	5,089/526	3/3	5,408/751	6,159
E-1	87/55	1/2	0/0	312/66	0	400/123	523

Officers

Rank	Army	Navy	Cst Grd	Marines	Air Force	Consolidated	Totals
General - Admiral	0/0	0/0	-/-	0/0	0/0	0/0	
Lt. General - Vice Admiral	0/0	0/0	-/-	0/0	0/0	0/0	
Major General - Rear Admiral	2/0	0/0	0/0	1/0	1/1	4/1	5
Brigadier General - Rear Admiral	2/3	0/1	0/0	0/0	1/0	3/4	7
Colonel - Captain	8/9	12/1	0/0	1/3	52/3	73/18	89
Lt. Colonel - Commander	81/50	48/23	0/0	17/8	39/21	195/100	295
Major - Lt. Commander	142/8	80/43	0/0	51/15	223/50	493/200	696
Captain - Lieutenant	748/281	84/70	1/0	183/39	450/82	1,448/452	1898
1st Lieutenant - Lieutenant JG	1,222/248	81/70	1/1	248/57	157/54	1,707/428	2135
2nd Lieutenant - Ensign	483/33	9/8	0/0	288/18	7/1	745/80	805
Chief Warrant Officer W-4	0/4	0/0	0/0	1/1	0/4	1/9	10
Chief Warrant Officer W-3	14/15	0/0	0/0	2/0	0/0	18/15	31
Chief Warrant Officer W-2	138/141	0/0	0/0	7/0	0/0	143/141	284
Warrant Officer W-l	554/350	2/2	0/0	3/3	0/0	559/355	914

Killed in Action/Non-Hostile Death

Reason (Cause of Casualty)	Number of Records
Gun, Small Arms Fire	18,518
Multiple Fragmentary Wounds	8,456
Air Loss, Crash on Land	7,992
Other Explosive Devices	7,450
Artillery, Rocket or Mortar	4,914
Other Accident	1,371
Misadventure	1,326
Drowned, Suffocated	1,207
Vehicle Loss, Crash	1,187
Accidental Homicide	944
Accidental Self Destruction	842
Other Causes	754
Air Loss, Crash in Sea	577
Burns	530
Illness, Disease	482
Suicide	382
Heart Attack	273
Intentional Homicide	234
Malaria	118
Bomb Explosion	52
Stroke	42
Hepatitis	22
Unknown, Not Reported	520
Total	**58,193**

Military Service Branch	Number of Records
Air Force	2,584
Army	38,209
Coast Guard	7
Marine Corps	14,838
Navy	2,555
Total	**58,193**

Military Component	Number of Records
Military Reserves	5,760
National Guard	97
Regular Military	34,475
Selective Service	17,672
Unknown	189
Total	**58,193**

Race	Number of Records
American Indian	226
Caucasian	50,120
Malayan	252
Mongolian	116
Negro	7,264
Unknown, Not Reported	215
Total	**58,193**

World War II Numbers	
Total deaths in WWII	54,770,000
Number of civilian deaths	38, 573, 000
Number of American deaths	292,131
Number of Americans deaths on D Day	3,393
Number of casualties on D-Day (deaths, wounded, prisoners)	6, 603
Number of American deaths on Iwo Jima	7,000
Number of American deaths on Okinawa	12,000
Number of American deaths in the Pacific	51,983
Number of Japanese military deaths	1,130,429
Number of Japanese civilian deaths	Estimates between 700,000 - 10,000,000
Number of Soviets deaths	7,720,000
Number of British deaths	300,000
Number of French deaths	173,260
Number of Italian deaths	93,000
Number of Polish deaths	6,028,000

Number of Americans serving in the Military in 1944	
Army	7,994,750
Navy	2,981,365
Marines	475,604
Number of Americans drafted	11,535,000 (61.2%)
Number of Americans volunteered	6,333,000 (38%)
Peak strength of U.S. forces	12,364,000
Peak strength of German forces	10,000,000 (includes Austrians)
Peak strength of French forces	5,000,000
Peak strength of Soviet forces	12,500,000
Peak strength of British forces	4,683,000
Peak strength of Japanese forces	6,095,000

Number of Women who served	350,000
Number of Women who served in the Defense Industry	6,500,000
Number of African-American women who served	4,000
Number of African-American men who served	1,200,000
Number of African-American Medal of Honor awardees	7 Total: 6 posthumously
Number of Hispanics men who served	Between 250,000 and 500,000
Number of Japanese-American who served	33,000

Number of Jews killed under Nazi rule	5,993,900
Number of non-Jews killed under Nazi rule	Between 16,000,000 and 20,000,000 (includes elderly, Gypsies, Jehovah's Witnesses, Homosexuals, etc.

Richard Ropele
246 Coronado Dr.
Corona, CA 92879

The final Thought

There are countless millions of people alive today throughout the world because of the sacrifice and dedication of the men and women of the Unites States Military.

Honored and great are they that wear the colors of the United States of America

Thank you all for your service and dedication

The Cannon

Americal Division Veterans Association

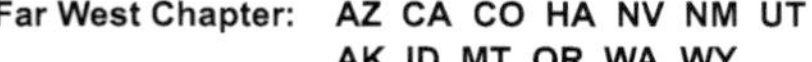

Far West Chapter: AZ CA CO HA NV NM UT AK ID MT OR WA WY

As we go to print with this issue of The Cannon, one of the agenda items at the National Organization meeting in Jacksonville Florida this year, was a discussion and approval of the consolidation of our Far West Chapter with the Northwest Chapter to be known collectively as the Far West Chapter, and Dave Hammond accepting the appointment as Vice Commander of the newly consolidated organization. We'd like to welcome our brothers from the north into our fraternity and look forward to their continued participation in the Chapter. Tom Packard will be putting together a 'Welcome Aboard' package and we will begin contacting everyone as soon as possible.

Here we are at the 4th of July, where we celebrate and recognize the inspiration and sacrifice of the founding fathers as they set that standard of liberty 232 years ago. We also recognize your service and sacrifice in giving people around the world peace, freedom and democracy.

The Signers of the Declaration of Independence

Independence Day is here and we celebrate the courage and tenacity of those individuals that built the basic foundation of our country. Who were these men? Did they gain land, wealth and prestige for their efforts? Were they revered by their fellow country men? True patriots serve because the cause is right and just. Read on. . .

Five signers were captured by the British as traitors, and tortured before they died. Twelve had their homes ransacked and burned. Two lost their sons serving in the Revolutionary Army; another had two sons captured. Nine of the 56 fought and died from wounds or hardships of the Revolutionary War. They signed and they pledged their lives, their fortunes, and their sacred honor.

What kind of men were they? Twenty-four were lawyers and jurists. Eleven were merchants, nine were farmers and large plantation owners; men of means, well educated. But they signed the Declaration of Independence knowing full well that the penalty would be death if they were captured.

Carter Braxton of Virginia, a wealthy planter and trader, saw his ships swept from the seas by the British Navy. He sold his home and properties to pay his debts, and died in rags.

Thomas McKeam was so hounded by the British that he was forced to move his family almost constantly. He served in the Congress without pay, and his family was kept in hiding. His possessions were taken from him, and poverty was his reward.

Vandals or soldiers looted the properties of Dillery, Hall, Clymer, Walton, Gwinnett, Heyward, Ruttledge, and Middleton.

At the battle of Yorktown, Thomas Nelson Jr, noted that the British General Cornwallis had taken over the Nelson home for his headquarters. He quietly urged General George Washington to open fire. The home was destroyed, and Nelson died bankrupt.

Francis Lewis had his home and properties destroyed. The enemy jailed his wife, and she died within a few months.

John Hart was driven from his wife's bedside as she was dying. Their 13 children fled for their lives. His fields and his gristmill were laid to waste. For more than a year he lived in forests and caves, returning home to find his wife dead and his children vanished. A few weeks later he died from exhaustion and a broken heart.

Norris and Livingston suffered similar fates.

Such were the stories and sacrifices of the American Revolution. These were not wild-eyed, rabble-rousing ruffians. They were soft-spoken men of means and education. They had security, but they valued liberty more. Standing tall, straight, and unwavering, they pledged: "For the support of this declaration, with firm reliance on the protection of the divine providence,,we mutually pledge to each other, our lives, our fortunes, and our sacred honor." They gave you and me a free and independent America.

We didn't fight just the British. We were British subjects at that time and we fought our own government!

Take a few minutes this year during your 4th of July holiday to teach your families that freedom is not free, that someone has always paid the price. Remember the sacrifices made by others in our behalf. Thank these patriots for their sacrifices by stepping up to the opportunities presented by your country to preserve these liberties for ourselves and others less fortunate.

Recommended Reading

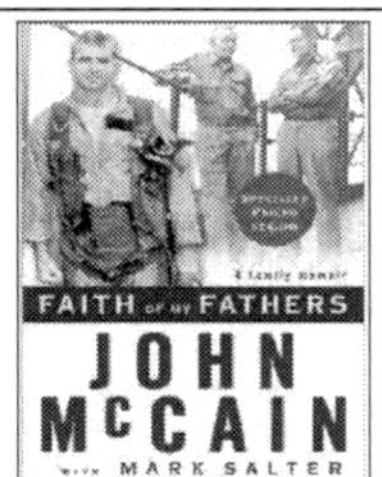 	**Faith of my Fathers** **By** **John McCain**

A good time to read about the life of one of our own, now that Senator John McCain is running for the Presidency of the United States.

New Members of the Far West Chapter

John M Corte	Goodyear,AZ	VN, 198th Inf
Al Diederich	Vista, CA	WWII, 132nd Inf
John Wachter	Surprise, AZ	VN Task Force Oregon
Rueben Martinez	Las Cruces, NM	VN, 198th Inf
Carmine C Iosue	Sun Lakes, AZ	VN, 11th Inf

Welcome to the chapter. We look forward to hearing from you and hope to see you in Laughlin this year at the reunion

ON A SADDER NOTE: we lost a member of our Chapter this year as Fernando Vera passed away. You may have read his articles published in the last two issues of the Americal Journal. To his family, we express our condolences and say, 'your loss is our loss' as a great American takes his rest. Thanks Fernando for your service.

2008 Far West Chapter Membership

Just so you'll know

Check the mailing label for the year above your name. This is the year your chapter dues are paid through. If it's 2007, then your annual dues are now due.

Chapter dues are still just $10.00 per year. You may renew for any number of years.

Make out your check to the FAR WEST CHAPTER and mail it to:

ADVA/Far West Chapter
c/o Tom Packard
6613 Birch Park Drive
Galloway, Ohio 43119.

2008 Far West Chapter Reunion

- **Pending concurrence from the Riverside Resort**
- Where: Riverside Resort & Casino, Laughlin, NV
- When: 12 - 14 October
- A special mailing will be sent to all when the details are finalized.

Note: A significant part of our lives were spent in the service to our country and to one another. From this service we developed character and personality traits that we still carry with us today. Success of our Chapter reunions is directly dependent on the participation of our membership Please consider taking the time to join us this year in Laughlin. It's this fellowship and camaraderie that held us together in WWII and Vietnam and it's what makes our chapter successful today.

Far West Chapter Officers

Commander
Richard Ropele
(951)218-3071
rropele@yahoo.com

Vice Commander
Dave Hammond
pacwesthi@aol.com

Secretary/Treasurer
Tom Packard
(614)878-5197
Packard50@columbus.rr.com

Sergeant At Arms
Curt Rothacker
(925)784-5391

Chaplain
Don Squire
(801)635-2547

Newsletter Editor
Richard Ropele
246 Coronado, Dr
Corona, CA 92879
(951)218-3071
rropele@yahoo.com

Men of the Americal

Continuing with the series of highlighting the exploits of the men of the Americal Division, following is one more citation of Americal men awarded the Congressional Medal of Honor.

Private First Class David F. Winder

Headquarters Company, 3/1 Inf, 11th Infantry Brigade
13 May 1970

Pfc. Winder distinguished himself while serving in the Republic of Vietnam as a senior medical aidman with Company A. After moving through freshly cut rice paddies in search of a suspected company size enemy force, the unit started a thorough search of the area. Suddenly they were engaged with intense automatic weapons and rocket propelled grenade fire by a well entrenched enemy force. Several friendly soldiers fell wounded in the initial contact and the unit was pinned down. Responding instantly to the cries of his wounded comrades, Pfc. Winder began maneuvering across approximately 100 meters of open, bullet swept terrain toward the nearest casualty. Unarmed and crawling most of the distance, he was wounded by enemy fire before reaching his comrades. Despite his wounds and with great effort, Pfc. Winder reached the first casualty and administered medical aid. As he continued to crawl across the open terrain toward a second wounded soldier he was forced to stop when wounded a second time. Aroused by the cries of an injured comrade for aid, Pfc. Winder's great determination and sense of duty impelled him to move forward once again, despite his wounds, in a courageous attempt to reach and assist the injured man. After struggling to within 10 meters of the man, Pfc. Winder was mortally wounded. His dedication and sacrifice inspired his unit to initiate an aggressive counter assault which led to the defeat of the enemy.

Pfc. Winder's conspicuous gallantry and intrepidity in action at the cost of his life were in keeping with the highest traditions of the military service and reflect great credit on him, his unit and the U.S. Army.

The End of World War II in the Pacific

The following is the text of remarks of General Douglas MacArthur, made on the deck of the U.S.S. Missouri in Tokyo Bay upon the signing of the surrender document ending the war in the Pacific with Japan (quoted from the book, 'Reminscences' (page 275) by General Douglas MacArthur, Supreme Commander).

'We are gathered here, representatives of the major warring powers, to conclude a solemn agreement whereby peace may be restored. The issues, involving divergent ideals and ideologies, have been determined on the battlefields of the world and hence are not for discussion or debate. Nor is it for us here to meet, representing as we do a majority of the people of the earth, in a spirit of distrust, malice, or hatred, But rather is it for us, both victors and vanquished to rise to that higher dignity which alone befits the sacred purposes we are about to serve, committing all our people unreservedly to faithful compliance with the obligation they are here formally to assume.'

'It is my earnest hope and indeed the hope of all mankind that from this solemn occasion a better world shall emerge out of the blood and carnage of the past - a world founded upon faith and understanding - a world dedicated to the dignity of man and the fulfillment of this most cherished wish - for freedom, tolerance and justice.'

'The terms and conditions upon which the surrender of the Japanese Imperial Forces is here to be given and accepted are contained in the instrument of surrender now before you.'

'As Supreme Commander of the Allied Powers, I announce it my firm purpose in the tradition of the countries I represent, to proceed in the discharge of my responsibilities with justice and tolerance, while taking all necessary dispositions to insure that the terms of surrender are fully, promptly and faithfully complied with.'

When all the representatives had finished signing, General MacArthur announces slowly:

'Let us pray that peace be now restored to the world and that God will preserve it always. These proceedings are closed.'

Articles from the Los Angeles Herald, dated, September 3rd, 1945.

I thought it appropriate to continue the discussion of the war in the Pacific as we approach VJ day in August. The following picture and article were scanned from an original copy of the September 3rd 1945 edition of the Los Angeles Herald newspaper. My mother had the foresight to save this edition of the paper as it was issued 6 days after I was born. As I'm able to scan more, I'll publish them in future editions of The Cannon.

General MacArthur signs the Surrender Document

Caption: FOR ALLIES - General Douglas MacArthur, seated at desk signs as the triumphant Allied commander, the Japanese surrender documents aboard the U.S.S. Missouri. Behind him are Lieutenant Gen. Jonathan M. Wainwright, left, who surrendered Corregidor and Lieut. Gen Sir Archibald Percival

FOR ALLIES—General Douglas MacArthur, seated at desk, signs, as the triumphant Allied commander, the Japanese surrender documents aboard the U. S. S. Missouri. Behind him are Lieutenant Gen. Jonathan M. Wainwright, left, who surrendered Corregidor, and Lieut. Gen. Sir Archibald Percival.

Surrender Sidelights

Wainwright's Stare Coldest
McCain's Laugh Loudest at Surrender Ceremony
By Julian Hartt

ABOARD THE U.S.S. MISSOURI, TOKYO BAY Sept 2 - Surrender sidelights:

The most colorful figure was ruddy, rotund mustached General Sir Thomas Blamey of Australia

The loudest and happiest laugh from the greatest gathering of the worlds high-ranking military men was Vice Admiral John S. McCain's as the generals and admirals milled, joked and bantered on the gallery deck before the Japs arrived.

THE COLDEST STARE AT THE JAP EMISSARIES WAS LEVELLED BY LIEUTENANT GENERAL JOHNATHAN M. WAINWRIGHT, WHO STOOD GRIMLY OPPOSITE THEM WITH ARMS FOLDED, BONEY HANDS GRIPPING HIS ELBOWS.

The most unexpected figure in the crowd ws Rear Admiral Richard Evelyn Byrd, pioneer of naval aviation that contributed so largely to victory.

The voice of Commander Roland W. Faulk of Sherveport La. and Missouri's chaplain called all to prayer.

Admiral William F, 'Bull' Halsey and McCain were caught suddenly alone.

Their heads bowed reverently as Faulk intoned. . .'Remembering another Sabbath desecrated by the beginning of this brutal war, we are thankful that those who loved peace have been rewarded with victory over those who loved war. . .'

When the Japs arrived, the dapper Frenchman, General Jacques Le Celere appraised them with cold eyes, leaning nonchalantly on a cane he held behind his back. Le Celere absently exercised his game left leg as Foreign Minister Mamoru Shigemitsu adjusted his wooden right leg to stand up position with a yellow-gloved hand.

China's General Hsu ignored his old enemy to watch instead busy photographers among the 238 newsmen aboard.

WAINWRIGHT RUBBED THE SIDE OF HIS NOSE AS GENERAL DOUGLAS MACARTHUR SIGNED THE SURRENDER INSTRUMENT. HE HELD THE GIFT PEN MACARTHUR GAVE HIM AT HIS SIDE BUT SINGAPORES PERCIVAL POCKETED HIS BEFORE SALUTING THE SUPREME ALLIED COMMANDER.

MacArthur's hands and legs were trembling with emotion at the beginning, but his always firm deep-toned Lincolnesque voice could be heard by everyone.

There was a tense moment when MacArthur peremptorily beckoned Lieutenant General Richard Sutherland to step up to the table when the Japs fumbled in delay at the start of the ceremony.

MacArthur's brisk chief of staff soon straightened out the difficulties.

Shigemitsu's pen, probably made in Japan, wouldn't work.

Wainwright's Stare Coldest

McCain's Laugh Loudest at Surrender Ceremony

By Julian Hartt

Staff Correspondent International News Service

ABOARD THE U. S. S. MISSOURI, TOKYO BAY, Sept. 2.—Surrender sidelights:

The most colorful figure was ruddy, rotund, mustached General Sir Thomas Blamey of Australia.

* * *

The loudest and happiest laugh from the greatest gathering of the world's high-ranking military men was Vice Admiral John S. McCain's as the generals and admirals milled, joked and bantered on the gallery deck before the Japs arrived.

* * *

THE COLDEST STARE AT THE JAP EMISSARIES WAS LEVELLED BY LIEUTENANT GENERAL JOHNATHAN M. WAINWRIGHT, WHO STOOD GRIMLY OPPOSITE THEM WITH ARMS FOLDED, BONEY HANDS GRIPPING HIS ELBOWS.

* * *

The most unexpected figure in the crowd was Rear Admiral Richard Evelyn Byrd, pioneer of naval aviation that contributed so largely to victory.

* * *

The voice of Commander Roland W. Faulk of Shreveport, La., and Missouri's chaplain, called all to prayer.

Admiral William F. "Bull" Halsey and McCain were caught suddenly alone.

Their heads bowed reverently as Faulk intoned . . . "Remembering another Sabbath desecrated by the beginning of this brutal war, we are thankful that those who loved peace have been rewarded with victory over those who loved war . . ."

* * *

When the Japs arrived, the dapper Frenchman, General Jacques Le Clerc, appraised them with cold eyes, leaning nonchalantly on a cane he held behind his back. Le Clerc absently exercised his game left leg as Foreign Minister Mamoru Shigemitsu adjusted his wooden right leg to stand-up position with a yellow-gloved hand.

* * *

China's General Hsu ignored his old enemy to watch instead busy photographers among 238 newsmen aboard.

* * *

WAINWRIGHT RUBBED THE SIDE OF HIS NOSE AS GENERAL DOUGLAS MACARTHUR SIGNED THE SURRENDER INSTRUMENT. HE HELD THE GIFT PEN MACARTHUR GAVE HIM AT HIS SIDE BUT SINGAPORE'S PERCIVAL POCKETED HIS BEFORE SALUTING THE SUPREME ALLIED COMMANDER.

* * *

MacArthur's hands and legs were trembling with emotion at the beginning, but his always firm, deep-toned Lincolnesque voice could be heard by everyone.

There was a tense moment when MacArthur peremptorily beckoned Lieutenant General Richard Sutherland to step up to the table when the Japs fumbled in delay at the start of the ceremony.

MacArthur's brisk chief of staff soon straightened out the difficulties.

Shigemitsu's pen, probably made in Japan, wouldn't work.

Traitor's Pay--Tokyo Rose Got 100 Yen a Month--$6.60

By Clark Lee

Staff Correspondent [illegible] News Service

TOKYO, [illegible] (Delayed).—The one a[illegible] "Tokyo Rose," a Los Angeles-born American of Japanese ancestry, is "willing to take her medicine."

But Iva Ikuko Toguri, 30-year-old graduate of the University of California at Los Angeles, does not feel that she was a traitor to the United States.

For the job of trying to make American troops homesick she was paid a miserable 100 yen monthly—$6.60 at the present exchange rate.

In an exclusive interview with this correspondent, Iva admitted she did not think it through when she took the job nor did she consider the possibilities of being adjudged a traitor to her country.

She said she believed Americans would enjoy her music and laugh at her propaganda.

Miss Toguri said that circumstances forced her into broadcasting on Tokyo radio's "Zero Hour" program.

She was caught in Japan on her first visit in 1941, shortly after her graduation as a zoologist at U. C. L. A., she said, and rather than impose on relatives she went to work—first for Domei then Radio Tokyo.

Richard Ropele
246 Coronado Dr.
Corona, CA 92879

The Final Thought

There are countless millions of people alive today throughout the world because of the sacrifice and dedication of the men and women of the Unites States Military.

Honored and great are they that wear the colors of the United States of America

Thank you all for your service and dedication

The Cannon

Americal Division Veterans Association

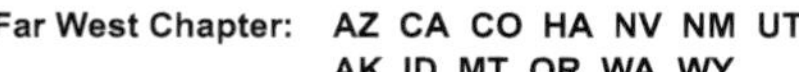

Far West Chapter: AZ CA CO HA NV NM UT AK ID MT OR WA WY

Annual Far West Chapter Reunion: As we go to print with this issue of The Cannon, we like to formally welcome those individuals previously associated with Northwest Chapter and welcome them as full registered members of the Far West Chapter. We look forward to seeing many of you at our annual Far West Chapter Reunion on 12 – 14 October at the Aquarius Casino Resort/Hotel in Laughlin, NV. If you haven't already registered, there is still time. The relevant information is contained herein.

2008 Far West Chapter Reunion

You all should have received the following registration information for the reunion. There is still time to join us in Laughlin

AMERICAL DIVISION VETERANS ASSOCIATION
FAR WEST CHAPTER
REUNION REGISTRATION FORM
LAUGHLIN, NEVADA OCTOBER 12-14, 2008

Please return your registration by the cutoff date of September 13, 2008

Last name ____________ First name ____________

Guest(s) name ____________

Address ____________

City ____________ State ______ Zip Code ____________

Phone Number or E-Mail address ____________

Unit served with ____________

REGISTRATION
$20 per person times the number of people ( ) $ ________

DINNER / DANCE (Tuesday Night)
$35 per person times the number of people ( ) $ ________

TOTAL AMOUNT REMITTED $ ________

Make your check payable to "ADVA Far West Chapter" and mail to:
Tom Packard 6613 Birch Park Drive Galloway, Ohio 43119-9386

Dinner will consist of a Mixed Green Salad, Breast of Chicken Piccata with Oven Roasted Rosemary Red Potatoes, Fresh Seasonal Vegetables, Dinner Rolls and Butter and Carrot Cake for dessert.
NOTE: Tours this year will be on your own. Suggestions for activities during your stay in Laughl are enclosed.

Don't forget to bring something from your area for our annual raffle.

FAR WEST CHAPTER LAUGHLIN REUNION EVENT INFORMATION
October 12-14, 2008

HOTEL RESERVATIONS
Make your reservations directly with the Aquarius Casino Resort (the former Flamingo). Ca 800-662-5825.
Ask for group rate code "C-AMR08" or tell them you are with the Americal-Far West Chapter Room rates are $29.00 + tax per night Sunday - Thursday and $65.00 - tax per night Friday a Saturday. The Aquarius Casino Resort is located at 1900 South Casino Dr. **Reservations must made by September 28, 2008 to receive the group rate.**

HOSPITALITY ROOM AND REUNION CHECK-IN
Our hospitality room will open at 4 PM on Sunday, Oct 12. The Front Desk will direct you to th room when you check in. Reunion check in will be in the hospitality room.

TUESDAY EVENING BANQUET
Our annual dinner will take place at the Aquarius in the Pisces or Gemini Room and will begin at 6:45 PM. Our Hospitality Room will be open for cocktails at 5:45 PM. After dinner, music will provided by a DJ for your dancing or karaoke pleasure.

TOURS www.visitlaughlin.com
Tours this year will be on your own. Suggested activities include:

Colorado River tours: A 90 minutes aquatic tour w/drink service that leaves from the Aquari dock. $15/ Call 702-298-1047.
River Jetz Tours to Lake Havasu and the London Bridge. This trip also leaves from the Aquari dock and lasts about six hours. A 2 hour ride in an enclosed speed boat to Lake Havasu stoppin for 2 hours at the London Bridge for lunch and shopping at the English Village, then returning the Aquarius. $60 Adult $56 Senior - Call 800-327-2386.
This company also offers boat and jet ski rentals.

Golf Golf at a 9 hole par 3 course at the Chaparral County Club At 928-758-6330 or 18 hole courses at the Mohave Resort 702-535-4653 and Desert Lakes 928-768-1000.

- More than 1300 slots & video poker machines at the Aquarius along with Laughlin's widest selection of table games.
- Don Laughlin's Classic Car Collection at the Riverside Casino - Free
- Shopping at the Preferred Outlets Mall - Free
- Tour Oatman, AZ - Old mining community where wild burros roam the streets. Free
- Lake Mohave with its 200 miles of shoreline and the Katherine Mine nearby.
- Old #7 offers train rides around the 27 acre Tropicana Express property - Free
- Hoover Dam - 75 miles north of Laughlin. At 726 feet high makes it the US's highest da

This time of the year marks the 63rd anniversary of the end of World War II. I thought it appropriate that we mark that milestone and read President Truman proclamations to American people. The war in Europe ended in May 1945 and the war in the Pacific ended in September 1945. His remarks follow:

President Truman proclaimed the war over in Europe in May 1945 and in the Pacific in September 1945.

May 8th 1945: By the President of the United States of America.

The Allied armies, through sacrifice and devotion and with God's help, have wrung from Germany a final and unconditional surrender. The western world has been freed of the evil forces which for five years and longer have imprisoned the bodies and broken the lives of millions upon millions of free-born men. They have violated their churches, destroyed their homes, corrupted their children, and murdered their loved ones. Our Armies of Liberation have restored freedom to these suffering peoples, whose spirit and will the oppressors could never enslave.

Much remains to be done. The victory won in the West must now be won in the East. The whole world must be cleansed of the evil from which half the world has been freed. United, the peace-loving nations have demonstrated in the West that their arms are stronger by far than the might of dictators or the tyranny of military cliques that once called us soft and weak. The power of our peoples to defend themselves against all enemies will be proved in the Pacific was as it has been proved in Europe.

For the triumph of spirit and of arms which we have won, and of its promise to peoples everywhere who join us in the love of freedom, it is fitting that we, as a nation, give thanks to Almighty God, who has strengthened us and given us the victory.

NOW, THEREFORE, I, HARRY S. TRUMAN, President of the United States of America, do hereby appoint Sunday, May 13, 1945 to be a day of prayer.

I call upon the people of the United States, whatever their faith, to unite in offering joyful thanks to God for the victory we have won and to pray that He will support us to the end of our present struggle and guide us into the way of peace.

I also call upon my countrymen to dedicate this day of prayer to the memory of those who have given their lives to make possible our victory.

IN WITNESS WHEREOF, I have hereunto set my hand and caused the seal of the United States of America to be affixed.

Done at the City of Washington this eighth day of May in the year of our Lord nineteen hundred and forty-five and of the Independence of the United States of America the one hundred and sixty-ninth.

By the President: Harry S. Truman

September 1, 1945: Radio Address to the American People After the signing the Terms of Unconditional Surrender by Japan. Broadcast from the White House at 10 p.m.

My fellow Americans, and the Supreme Allied Commander, General MacArthur, in Tokyo Bay:

The thoughts and hopes of all America--indeed of all the civilized world--are centered tonight on the battleship Missouri. There on that small piece of American soil anchored in Tokyo Harbor the Japanese have just officially laid down their arms. They have signed terms of unconditional surrender.

Four years ago, the thoughts and fears of the whole civilized world were centered on another piece of American soil--Pearl Harbor. The mighty threat to civilization which began there is now laid at rest. It was a long road to Tokyo--and a bloody one.

We shall not forget Pearl Harbor.

The Japanese militarists will not forget the U.S.S. Missouri.

The evil done by the Japanese war lords can never be repaired or forgotten. But their power to destroy and kill has been taken from them. Their armies and what is left of their Navy are now impotent.

To all of us there comes first a sense of gratitude to Almighty God who sustained us and our Allies in the dark days of grave danger, who made us to grow from weakness into the strongest fighting force in history, and who has now seen us overcome the forces of tyranny that sought to destroy His civilization.

God grant that in our pride of the hour, we may not forget the hard tasks that are still before us; that we may approach these with the same courage, zeal, and patience with which we faced the trials and problems of the past 4 years.

Our first thoughts, of course--thoughts of gratefulness and deep obligation--go out to those of our loved ones who have been killed or maimed in this terrible war. On land and sea and in the air, American men and women have given their lives so that this day of ultimate victory might come and assure the survival of a civilized world. No victory can make good their loss.

We think of those whom death in this war has hurt, taking from them fathers, husbands, sons, brothers, and sisters whom they loved. No victory can bring back the faces they longed to see.

Only the knowledge that the victory, which these sacrifices have made possible, will be wisely used, can give them any comfort. It is our responsibility--ours, the living--to see to it that this victory shall be a monument worthy of the dead who died to win it.

We think of all the millions of men and women in our armed forces and merchant marine all over the world who, after years of sacrifice and hardship and peril, have been spared by Providence from harm.

We think of all the men and women and children who during these years have carried on at home, in lonesomeness and anxiety and fear.

Our thoughts go out to the millions of American workers and businessmen, to our farmers and miners--to all those who have built up this country's fighting strength, and who have shipped to our Allies the means to resist and overcome the enemy.

Our thoughts go out to our civil servants and to the thousands of Americans who, at personal sacrifice, have come to serve in our Government during these trying years; to the members of the Selective Service boards and ration boards; to the civilian defense and Red Cross workers; to the men and women in the USO and in the entertainment world--to all those who have helped in this cooperative struggle to preserve liberty and decency in the world.

We think of our departed gallant leader, Franklin D. Roosevelt, defender of democracy, architect of world peace and cooperation.

And our thoughts go out to our gallant Allies in this war: to those who resisted the invaders; to those who were not strong enough to hold out, but who, nevertheless, kept the fires of resistance alive within the souls of their people; to those who stood up against great odds and held the line, until the United Nations together were able to supply the arms and the men with which to overcome the forces of evil.

This is a victory of more than arms alone. This is a victory of liberty over tyranny.

From our war plants rolled the tanks and planes which blasted their way to the heart of our enemies; from our shipyards sprang the ships which bridged all the oceans of the world for our weapons and supplies; from our farms came the food and fiber for our armies and navies and for our Allies in all the corners of the earth; from our mines and factories came the raw materials and the finished products which gave us the equipment to overcome our enemies.

But back of it all were the will and spirit and determination of a free people--who know what freedom is, and who know that it is worth whatever price they had to pay to preserve it.

It was the spirit of liberty which gave us our armed strength and which made our men invincible in battle. We now know that that spirit of liberty, the freedom of the individual, and the personal dignity of man, are the strongest and toughest and most enduring forces in all the world.

And so on V-J Day we take renewed faith and pride in our own way of life. We have had our day of rejoicing over this victory. We have had our day of prayer and devotion. Now let us set aside V-J Day as one of renewed consecration to the principles which have made us the strongest nation on earth and which, in this war, we have striven so mightily to preserve.

Those principles provide the faith, the hope, and the opportunity which help men to improve themselves and their lot. Liberty does not make all men perfect nor all society secure. But it has provided more solid progress and happiness and decency for more people than any other philosophy of government in history. And this day has shown again that it provides the greatest strength and the greatest power which man has ever reached.

We know that under it we can meet the hard problems of peace which have come upon us. A free people with free Allies, who can develop an atomic bomb, can use the same skill and energy and determination to overcome all the difficulties ahead.

Victory always has its burdens and its responsibilities as well as its rejoicing.

But we face the future and all its dangers with great confidence and great hope. America can build for itself a future of employment and security. Together with the United Nations, it can build a world of peace rounded on justice, fair dealing, and tolerance.

As President of the United States, I proclaim Sunday, September the second, 1945, to be V-J Day--the day of formal surrender by Japan. It is not yet the day for the formal proclamation of the end of the war nor of the cessation of hostilities. But it is a day which we Americans shall always remember as a day of retribution--as we remember that other day, the day of infamy.

From this day we move forward. We move toward a new era of security at home. With the other United Nations we move toward a new and better world of cooperation, of peace and international good will and cooperation.

God's help has brought us to this day of victory. With His help we will attain that peace and prosperity for ourselves and all the world in the years ahead.

NOTE: The President's address was part of the broadcast of the surrender ceremonies on board the U.S.S. Missouri.

Tiger Yamashita Surrenders Today T\to Wainwright

The following picture and text is from an article in the Los Angeles Examiner newspaper, dated September 3rd 1945

Blustering Ends General Tomoyki Yamashita, Famed Tiger of Malaya who has given himself up to Americal troops and will surrender formally today to Jonathan Wainwright, hero of Corregidor, at Baugio. Yamashita's former blustering, boastful attitude has been replaced by smiling courteous manner.

With the U.S. 32nd Division, Luzon Island.

A tamed and docile Japanese 'Tiger of Malaya,' Lieutenant General Tomoyki Yamashita, gave himself up to American troops today and prepared to surrender formally tomorrow to Lieutenant General Jonathan Wainwright, hero of Corregidor.

Another drama of the pacific was scheduled to be written at Baguio, Philippines summer capital, where arrogant and boastful Yamashita, captor of Malaya and Singapore, will formally surrender what remains of his shattered armies in this archipelago.

Facing Yamashita will be the famous 'Skinny' Wainwright as the representative of triumphant America. Back in the spring of 1942, it was Wainwright who in the face of overwhelming odds, surrendered his heroic band of Corregidor defenders to Japanese General Homma.

The formal surrender ceremony was scheduled for 9:30 a.m., Monday.

Yamashita came from his mountain hideout in the northern Luzon mountains and surrendered himself this morning to a special American guard force near Klangan, Four other Nipponese generals gave up simultaneously.

Yamashita's smiling, pleasant and courteous manner was a marked changed from the blustering, boastful attitude he consistently maintained before the Yanks recaptured the Philippines.

Clad in a clean but worn uniform and with his Samurai sword buckled at his side, Yamashita was accompanied by 11 Japanese, including for Generals. The enemy group was met on a rugged mountain trail by 24 picked members of the 32nd Division, led by Lieutenant Russell Bauman of Glenbeulah, Wisc.

Bauman and Yamashita exchanged salutes after which the American Lieutenant told the Japanese: 'I have been charged with bringing you and your party through our lines without hindrance, delay or molestation'.

Yamashita replied through an interpreter: 'I want to tell you how much I appreciate the courtesies and good treatment you have shown us.' He repeated that expression several times later.

After brief formalities were exchanged, the entire group turned and hiked the three miles to Klangan where the Japanese were met in a schoolhouse by Colonel Ernest A. Barlow, of Salt Lake City, Utah, 32nd Division Chief of Staff and Lieutenant Colonel Alex Robinet, of Thomas Ky. Commander of the 128th Regiment.

Yamashita, whose weight had dropped from 200 to 165 pounds, appeared in good condition during the walk out of the mountains. He only puffed slightly but stopped infrequently to wipe his closely shaven head. He wore few of the trappings of his high rank. Only two decorations were pinned on his chest.

The Japanese supreme Philippines commander was put aboard a plane in the afternoon en route to Baguio for the surrender ceremony.

While waiting in the school house one of the Nipponese generals asked Barlow what the Red Arrow through a line meant in the Division insignia. Barlow explained it represented the divisions breaking of the Hindenburg line in the First World War

'Yes', responded the general 'and Yamashita's line in the second World War'.

The 32nd, one of the veteran outfits of the fighting in the Pacific, pursued the Japanese all the way from Buna in New Guinea to the mountains of Northern Luzon.

2008 Far West Chapter Membership

Just so you'll know

Check the mailing label for the year above your name. This is the year your chapter dues are paid through. If it's 2007, then your annual dues are now due.

Chapter dues are still just $10.00 per year. You may renew for any number of years.

Make out your check to the FAR WEST CHAPTER and mail it to:

ADVA/Far West Chapter
c/o Tom Packard
6613 Birch Park Drive
Galloway, Ohio 43119.

Far West Chapter Officers

Commander
Richard Ropele
(951)218-3071
rropele@yahoo.com

Vice Commander
Dave Hammond
pacwesthi@aol.com

Secretary/Treasurer
Tom Packard
(614)878-5197
Packard50@columbus.rr.com

Sergeant At Arms
Curt Rothacker
(925)784-5391

Chaplain
Don Squire
(801)635-2547

Newsletter Editor
Richard Ropele
246 Coronado, Dr
Corona, CA 92879
(951)218-3071
rropele@yahoo.com

23rd Recon Group plans a cruise to Panama

Jack Rudder, a member of the Far West Chapter and a veteran of the Americal 23rd Recon group that served in Panama is part of a committee putting together a cruise to Panama. If you are interested in participating, please contact him directly:

23rd Recon Company Reunion

ON THE

CORAL PRINCESS

VOYAGE TO PANAMA

Jack Rudder (23rd Recon 1954-1955)

19 DAYCRUISE

DEPART SUNDAY APRIL 26, 2009

SAILING ROUND TRIP FROM SAN PEDRO (LA HARBOR)

PORTS OF CALL: MEXICO PORTS- CABO SAN LUCAS, PUERTO VALLARTA, ACAPULCO, HUATULCO, IXTAPA, and PUNTARENAS, (COSTA RICA), PUERTO CORINTO (NICARAGUA), PUERTO QUETZAL, (GUATAMALA)

and

Spend a full day cruising the Panama Canal and a day docked at

FORT AMADOR (with shore leave)

[Ft Amador is adjacent to Panama City near Balboa]

	Per Person* Double Occupancy
INSIDE CABIN	$ 2,[illegible]- $ [illegible]
OCEAN VIEW (obstructed view)	$ [illegible]- $ [illegible]
OCEAN VIEW	$ [illegible]- $ [illegible]
BALCONY	$ [illegible]- $ [illegible]
MINI-SUITE	$ [illegible]- $ [illegible] (wait listed only)

*rates are per person, double occupancy, cruise only, and subject to change and availability includes fuel surcharge of $126. Please add Port and Government Fees of $[illegible] per person. Gratuities are not included. It is recommended that you purchase optional Cruise Insurance.

ADDITIONAL INFORMATION AVAILABLE: CONTACT

JACK RUDDER (310) 519-1522 "jack.rudder@[illegible]"

BOOK EARLY TO RESERVE YOUR SPACE

(This cruise only happens twice a year)

AIR TRANSPORTATION RATES AVAILABLE ON REQUEST

DEPOSITS-PAYMENTS: (Fully refundable until January 28, 2009) $600 per person ($1,200 per cabin) needed to hold your cabin. [add travel insurance if any] Final payment due by January 28, 2009 (Prepayments toward final payment accepted). Make checks payable to Age of Travel. Mail to AGE OF TRAVEL, 28 Montecillo Dr., Rolling Hills Est., CA. 90274 (For more info or to make credit card payments call Jack at (310) 519-1522. "jack.rudder@[illegible]"

FOR SOME PIX OF JACK'S 2007 PANAMA CRUISE GO TO "http://[illegible]"

Richard Ropele
246 Coronado Dr.
Corona, CA 92879

The Final Thought

There are countless millions of people alive today throughout the world because of the sacrifice and dedication of the men and women of the Unites States Military.

Honored and great are they that wear the colors of the United States of America

Thank you all for your service and dedication

	**The Cannon** **Americal Division Veterans Association** **Far West Chapter: AZ CA CO HA NV NM UT AK ID MT OR WA WY**	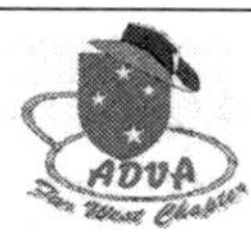

Well, here it is, the end of another year; 2008 is coming to an end and 2009 welcomes us to yet another year in this great country, the United States of America. I know we all had those lingering doubts those 40 and 60 some years ago when we were running through the jungles of the world, that we would be welcoming the next year, let alone 2009. I'm glad you're all back and we can celebrate life and family again this new.

We had another very successful Far West Chapter Reunion in October at Laughlin Nevada. Tom's recap in the 4th quarter issue of the Americal Journal is very good and should be read by all. We appreciate all those that traveled and participated. We had 5 World War II veterans and 16 Vietnam era veterans. One of our chapter members from the northwest shared his slides of his recent trip back to Vietnam, where we saw the country again, this time not from the same perspective as we had seen it 40 years earlier.

CHAPTER NEWSLETTER IS GOING ELECTRONIC

In an effort to save some chapter funds and to continue producing a quality publication we want to distribute The Cannon electronically to your e-mail address beginning with the first quarter issue of 2009.

Over the past two years we have incurred about $2000 in expenses to print and mail individual copies to our Chapter membership. We feel that this move to electronic distribution is a more prudent use of our chapter funds which is a benefit for all our Chapter members.

Please help us now by sending your email address to:

Tom Packard
packard50@columbus.rr.com

Tom will begin to update the addresses we already have and to collect new addresses in January, 2009. As usual, this e-mail information will only be used for the distribution of our newsletter and will be protected as all your address information is protected

Don't worry if you don't have an email address, you will continue to receive your printed copy each quarter.

CHAPTER DUES NOTICE

Chapter dues are payable on January 1st, 2009 for members whose dues expire in 2008. If you have either a "2008" or a "08" after your name on the mailing label on the front of this newsletter your membership expired on December 31, 2008. Dues remain at just $10.00 per year. You may pay for any number of years.

ADVA members who reside in the former Northwest Chapter area were welcomed into the reorganized chapter in June of 2008 as current active members for the remainder of the year We hope you have enjoyed the benefits of membership in the Far West Chapter and will continue as an active member. You will receive a membership application along with a letter inviting you to continue with your membership in the chapter. Look for the invitation in January.

Make your check payable to: "ADVA Far West Chapter" at mail to:

Tom Packard
6613 Birch Park Drive
Galloway, Ohio 43119

Men of the Americal

Continuing with the series of highlighting the exploits of the men of the Americal Division, following are two more citations of Americal men awarded the Congressional Medal of Honor.

Major Kern W. Dunagan.
Company A, 1/46 Inf, 198th LIB
13 May 1969
Quang Tin Province, RVN

For conspicuous gallantry and intrepidity in action at the risk of his life above and beyond the call of duty. Maj. (then Capt.) Dunagan distinguished himself during the period May 13 and 14, 1969, while serving as commanding officer, Company A. On May 13, 1969, Maj. Dunagan was leading an attack to relieve pressure on the battalion's forward support base when his company came under intense fire from a well-entrenched enemy battalion. Despite continuous hostile fire from a numerically superior force, Maj. Dunagan repeatedly and fearlessly exposed himself in order to locate enemy positions, direct friendly supporting artillery, and position the men of his company. In the early evening, while directing an element of his unit into perimeter guard, he was seriously wounded during an enemy mortar attack, but he refused to leave the battlefield and continued to supervise the evacuation of dead and wounded and to lead his command in the difficult task of disengaging from an aggressive enemy. In spite of painful wounds and extreme fatigue, Maj. Dunagan risked heavy fire on 2 occasions to rescue critically wounded men. He was again seriously wounded. Undaunted, he continued to display outstanding courage, professional competence, and leadership and successfully extricated his command from its untenable position on the evening of May 14. Having maneuvered his command into contact with an adjacent friendly unit, he learned that a 6 man party from his company was under fire and had not reached the new perimeter. Maj. Dunagan unhesitatingly went back and searched for his men. Finding one soldier critically wounded, Maj. Dunagan, ignoring his wounds, lifted the man to his shoulders and carried him to the comparative safety of the friendly perimeter. Before permitting himself to be evacuated, he insured all of his wounded received emergency treatment and were removed from the area. Throughout the engagement, Maj. Dunagan's actions gave great inspiration to his men and were directly responsible for saving the lives of many of his fellow soldiers.

Maj. Dunagan's extraordinary heroism above and beyond the call of duty, are in the highest traditions of the U.S. Army and reflect great credit on him, his unit, and the U.S. Army.

Staff Sergeant Nicky Daniel Bacon
Company B, 4/21 Inf, 11th Infantry Brigade
26 August 1968
West of Tam Ky, RVN

For conspicuous gallantry and intrepidity in action at the risk of his life above and beyond the call of duty. S/Sgt. Bacon distinguished himself while serving as a squad leader with the 1st Platoon, Company B, during an operation west of Tam Ky. When Company B came under fire from an enemy bunker line to the front, S/Sgt. Bacon quickly organized his men and led them forward in an assault. He advanced on a hostile bunker and destroyed it with grenades. As he did so, several fellow soldiers including the 1st Platoon leader, were struck by machine gun fire and fell wounded in an exposed position forward of the rest of the platoon. S/Sgt. Bacon immediately assumed command of the platoon and assaulted the hostile gun position, finally killing the enemy gun crew in a single-handed effort. When the 3d Platoon moved to S/Sgt. Bacon's location, its leader was also wounded. Without hesitation S/Sgt. Bacon took charge of the additional platoon and continued the fight. In the ensuing action he personally killed 4 more enemy soldiers and silenced an antitank weapon. Under his leadership and example, the members of both platoons accepted his authority without question. Continuing to ignore the intense hostile fire, he climbed up on the exposed deck of a tank and directed fire into the enemy position while several wounded men were evacuated. As a result of S/Sgt. Bacon's extraordinary efforts, his company was able to move forward, eliminate the enemy positions, and rescue the men trapped to the front.

S/Sgt. Bacon's bravery at the risk of his life was in the highest traditions of the military service and reflects great credit upon himself, his unit, and the U.S. Army.

Far West Chapter Officers

Commander
Richard Ropele
(951)218-3071
rropele@yahoo.com

Vice Commander
Dave Hammond
pacwesthi@aol.com

Secretary/Treasurer
Tom Packard
(614)878-5197
Packard50@columbus.rr.com

Sergeant At Arms
Curt Rothacker
(925)784-5391

Chaplain
Gene McGrath
(775)751-1861
Mc2some@sbcglobal.net

Newsletter Editor
Richard Ropele
246 Coronado, Dr
Corona, CA 92879
(951)218-3071
rropele@yahoo.com

2009 Far West Chapter Annual Reunion

The 2009 Far West Reunion will be held in:

Reno, Nevada
October 18 thru 20 2009

The Atlantis Casino Resort Spa
3800 South Virginia St., Reno, NV. 89502
(800) 723-6500.
http://www.atlantiscasino.com/

Our special Room rate for these three days will be $62.00 a night.

Rooms can be booked starting December 1, 2008, the cut off date is September 17, 2009. Tell them that you are with the Americal Veterans Association to receive this special room rate.

The Atlantis is located only 3.3 miles from the Reno Tahoe International Airport with free shuttle service available. Valet and self parking is also free at the Atlantis.

Information about tours and registration forms will be available in the near future.
All Veterans are invited.

Richard Ropele
246 Coronado Dr.
Corona, CA 92879

The Final Thought

There are countless millions of people alive today throughout the world because of the sacrifice and dedication of the men and women of the Unites States Military.

Honored and great are they that wear the colors of the United States of America

Thank you all for your service and dedication

The Cannon

Americal Division Veterans Association
Far West Chapter

AZ CA CO HA NV NM UT AK ID MT OR WA WY

Coming into 2009 marks the Far West Chapter's entrance into the electronic communication age as this issue of The Cannon earmarks our first distribution via electronic mail. Over the last couple of month, our Chapter Secretary/Treasurer Tom Packard has been collecting and validating e-mail addresses from many of you as we seek to find ways to reduce our overall production cost. Please let us know of any problems.

Also note in the piece which I transcribed from the Los Angeles Examiner regarding the surrender ceremony aboard the U.S.S. Missouri, the flag flying that day on the famed battlewagon was the same flag that was flying over the U.S. Capitol building some 4 years earlier on December 7, 1941, indicative of the fact that the U.S. came full circle that day - the 'sleeping giant' that they awoke on December7 1941 finally held the Japanese accountable for their deceitful act.

2009 Far West Chapter Annual Reunion

The 2009 Far West Reunion will be held in:

Reno, Nevada
October 18 thru 20 2009

The Atlantis Casino Resort Spa
3800 South Virginia St., Reno, NV. 89502
(800) 723-6500.
http://www.atlantiscasino.com/

Our special Room rate for these three days will be $62.00 a night.

Rooms can be booked starting December 1, 2008; the cut off date is September 17, 2009. Tell them that you are with the Americal Veterans Association to receive this special room rate.

The Atlantis is located only 3.3 miles from the Reno Tahoe International Airport with free shuttle service available. Valet and self parking is also free at the Atlantis.

More information about tours and registration forms will be available in the near future as Reno Rich Merlin continues to pull together the details –

All Veterans are invited – hope to see you there.

CHAPTER NEWSLETTER IS GOING ELECTRONIC

This is it – this issue of The Cannon will be distributed to a majority of our Far West Chapter member via e-mail.

Thanks to all those who have responded to Tom's inquiries for your e-mail information. This looks to be a major cost saving for us as we judiciously seek to be prudent managers of your dues.

Don't worry if you don't have an email address, you will continue to receive your printed copy each quarter.

As always, this e-mail information will only be used for the distribution of our newsletter and other chapter related correspondence and will be protected as all your address information is protected

If you haven't already done so, please continue to work with Tom by sending your email address to:

Tom Packard
packard50@columbus.rr.com
or

You can reach him via postal mail at:

6613 Birch Drive
Galloway, Ohio, 43119

Men of the Americal

Concluding our series of highlighting the exploits of the men of the Americal Division, following are the final two citations of Americal men awarded the Congressional Medal of Honor.

It's good to reacquaint ourselves with the deeds of these 'ordinary' soldiers. It's true what they say: 'Heroes walk among us'

Platoon Sergeant, Finnis D. McCleery
Company A, 1 Battalion, 6th Infantry, 198th LIB
Quang Tin province, RVN
14 May 1968

For conspicuous gallantry and intrepidity in action at the risk of his life above and beyond the call of duty. p/Sgt. McCleery, U.S. Army, distinguished himself while serving as platoon leader of the 1st platoon of Company A. A combined force was assigned the mission of assaulting a reinforced company of North Vietnamese Army regulars, well entrenched on Hill 352, 17 miles west of Tam Ky. As p/Sgt. McCleery led his men up the hill and across an open area to close with the enemy, his platoon and other friendly elements were pinned down by tremendously heavy fire coming from the fortified enemy positions. Realizing the severe damage that the enemy could inflict on the combined force in the event that their attack was completely halted, p/Sgt. McCleery rose from his sheltered position and began a I man assault on the bunker complex. With extraordinary courage, he moved across 60 meters of open ground as bullets struck all around him and rockets and grenades literally exploded at his feet. As he came within 30 meters of the key enemy bunker, p/Sgt. McCleery began firing furiously from the hip and throwing hand grenades. At this point in his assault, he was painfully wounded by shrapnel, but, with complete disregard for his wound, he continued his advance on the key bunker and killed all of its occupants. Having successfully and single-handedly breached the enemy perimeter, he climbed to the top of the bunker he had just captured and, in full view of the enemy, shouted encouragement to his men to follow his assault. As the friendly forces moved forward, p/Sgt. McCleery began a lateral assault on the enemy bunker line. He continued to expose himself to the intense enemy fire as he moved from bunker to bunker, destroying each in turn. He was wounded a second time by shrapnel as he destroyed and routed the enemy from the hill. p/Sgt. McCleery is personally credited with eliminating several key enemy positions and inspiring the assault that resulted in gaining control of Hill 352.

His extraordinary heroism at the risk of his life, above and beyond the call of duty, was in keeping with the highest standards of the military service, and reflects great credit on him, the Americal Division, and the U.S. Army.

Major Patrick Henry Brady
Medical Service Corps, 54th Medical Detachment, 67th Medical Group, 44th Medical Brigade
Near Chu Lai, RVN
06 Jan 1968

For conspicuous gallantry and intrepidity in action at the risk of his life above and beyond the call of duty, Maj. Brady distinguished himself while serving in the Republic of Vietnam commanding a UH-1H ambulance helicopter, volunteered to rescue wounded men from a site in enemy held territory which was reported to be heavily defended and to be blanketed by fog. To reach the site he descended through heavy fog and smoke and hovered slowly along a valley trail, turning his ship sideward to blow away the fog with the backwash from his rotor blades. Despite the unchallenged, close-range enemy fire, he found the dangerously small site, where he successfully landed and evacuated 2 badly wounded South Vietnamese soldiers. He was then called to another area completely covered by dense fog where American casualties lay only 50 meters from the enemy. Two aircraft had previously been shot down and others had made unsuccessful attempts to reach this site earlier in the day. With unmatched skill and extraordinary courage, Maj. Brady made 4 flights to this embattled landing zone and successfully rescued all the wounded. On his third mission of the day Maj. Brady once again landed at a site surrounded by the enemy. The friendly ground force, pinned down by enemy fire, had been unable to reach and secure the landing zone. Although his aircraft had been badly damaged and his controls partially shot away during his initial entry into this area, he returned minutes later and rescued the remaining injured. Shortly thereafter, obtaining a replacement aircraft, Maj. Brady was requested to land in an enemy minefield where a platoon of American soldiers was trapped. A mine detonated near his helicopter, wounding 2 crewmembers and damaging his ship. In spite of this, he managed to fly 6 severely injured patients to medical aid. Throughout that day Maj. Brady utilized 3 helicopters to evacuate a total of 51 seriously wounded men, many of whom would have perished without prompt medical treatment.

Maj. Brady's bravery was in the highest traditions of the military service and reflects great credit upon himself and the U.S. Army.

Protocol on Displaying the Flag of the United States of America

We've all seen the flag displayed inappropriately at poinst in our lives, most of the time it's by well meaning people who are not familiar with the proper procedures. Every since my son has been on active duty and most especially since he's been serving in Iraq, I display my flag daily and I seem to be more aware when flags are not displayed correctly. I thought it might be good to review a few of these procedures

- When the flag is displayed over the middle of the street, it should be suspended vertically with the union to the north in an east and west street or to the east in a north and south street.
- When flags of States, cities, or localities, or pennants of societies are flown on the same halyard with the flag of the United States, the latter should always be at the peak. When the flags are flown from adjacent staffs, the flag of the United States should be hoisted first and lowered last. When the flag is half-masted, both flags are half-masted, with the US flag at the mid-point and the other flag below.
- When the flag is suspended over a sidewalk from a rope extending from a house to a pole at the edge of the sidewalk, the flag should be hoisted out, union first, from the building.
- When the flag of the United States is displayed from a staff projecting horizontally or at an angle from the window sill, balcony, or front of a building, the union of the flag should be placed at the peak of the staff unless the flag is at half-staff.
- When the flag is used to cover a casket, it should be so placed that the union is at the head and over the left shoulder. The flag should not be lowered into the grave or allowed to touch the ground.
- When the flag is displayed in a manner other than by being flown from a staff, it should be displayed flat, whether indoors or out. When displayed either horizontally or vertically against a wall, the union should be uppermost and to the flag's own right, that is, to the observer's left. When displayed in a window it should be displayed in the same way, that is with the union or blue field to the left of the observer in the street.
- That the flag, when carried in a procession with another flag, or flags, should be either on the marching right; that is, the flag's own right, or, if there is a line of other flags, in front of the center of that line.
- The flag of the United States of America should be at the center and at the highest point of the group when a number of flags of States or localities or pennants of societies are grouped and displayed from staffs.
- When flags of two or more nations are displayed, they are to be flown from separate staffs of the same height. The flags should be of approximately equal size. International usage forbids the display of the flag of one nation above that of another nation in time of peace.
- When displayed from a staff in a church or public auditorium on or off a podium, the flag of the United States of America should hold the position of superior prominence, in advance of the audience, and in the position of honor at the clergyman's or speaker's right as he faces the audience. Any other flag so displayed should be placed on the left of the clergyman or speaker (to the right of the audience).
- When the flag is displayed on a car, the staff shall be fixed firmly to the chassis or clamped to the right fender.
- When hung in a window, place the blue union in the upper left, as viewed from the street.

CHAPTER DUES NOTICE

Chapter dues are payable on January 1st, 2009 for members whose dues expire in 2008. If you have either a "2008" or a "08" after your name on the mailing label on the front of this newsletter your membership expired on December 31, 2008. Dues remain at just $10.00 per year. You may pay for any number of years.

ADVA members who reside in the former Northwest Chapter area were welcomed into the reorganized chapter in June of 2008 as current active members for the remainder of the year We hope you have enjoyed the benefits of membership in the Far West Chapter and will continue as an active member. You will receive a membership application along with a letter inviting you to continue with your membership in the chapter. Look for the invitation in January.

Make your check payable to: "ADVA Far West Chapter" at mail to:

Tom Packard
6613 Birch Park Drive
Galloway, Ohio 43119

Far West Chapter Officers

Commander
Richard Ropele
(951)218-3071
rropele@yahoo.com

Vice Commander
Dave Hammond
pacwesthi@aol.com

Secretary/Treasurer
Tom Packard

(614)878-5197
Packard50@columbus.rr.com

Sergeant At Arms
Curt Rothacker
(925)784-5391

Chaplain
Gene McGrath
(775)751-1861
Mc2some@sbcglobal.net

Newsletter Editor
Richard Ropele
246 Coronado, Dr
Corona, CA 92879
(951)218-3071
rropele@yahoo.com

Transcribed from the Los Angeles Examiner, date September 3, 1945

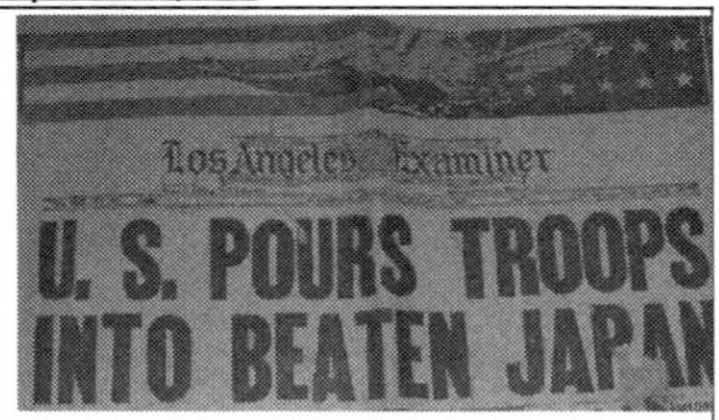

Los Angeles Examiner

U. S. POURS TROOPS INTO BEATEN JAPAN

YOHOHAMA, Sept 3 (Monday) Surrendered Japan, stripped of all conquests and arms, was under stern foreign military rule today (Sunday, U.S. time) for the first time in her long and pugnacious history.

Thirty minute after Japan signed the surrender on the battleship Missouri at 9:18 a.m., yesterday (5:18 p.m. Saturday, P.W.T.) a 42 ship convoy steamed into Tokyo Bay and began disgorging troops.

By nightfall, the U.S. Eight Army had landed 13,000 troops swelling occupation forces to beyond 35,000 and only a signal from General MacArthur was awaited for a march on Tokyo.

When this order might come was not indicated, but a spokesman made it clear that no troops would cross the Tama River at Tokyo's southern outskirts until the supreme Allied commander gave the word.

Japanese imperial headquarters under MacArthur's first order radioed all field commanders to surrender at once.

NATION WARNED---

This same order at a single stroke surrendered all Japanese arms and war making potential, and the beaten country was warned that all failure or delay would mean 'drastic and summary punishment.'

Premier Prince Higashi–Kuni told the Japanese people to obey the terms of surrender on all orders.

Only Japanese police charged with maintaining order now may bear arms. All aircraft are grounded, and all Japanese merchantmen must remain at anchor until further orders.

Japan was returned inexorably to the size at which Commodore Matthew C. Perry found her when he sailed into Tokyo Bay in 1853, opened the mysterious land to the Occident and unlocked Pandora's box of trouble.

And the fact that with surrender and the first occupation order all factories and research laboratories fell under MacArthur's control showed clearly that the Allies do not intend to let Japan rearm.

On this first day after his empire's surrender, Emperor Hirohito prepared to worship at three Shinto shrines in the imperial palace grounds, Domei agency reported.

For the moment, the occupation forces remained in a 700 square mile area stretching south of Tokyo, but that condition will not long prevail.

MacArthur's orders call for the immediate surrender to him of all four main home islands, adjacent islands, southern Korea and the Philippines.

Storms of typhoon proportions between Okinawa and the main island of Honshu interrupted the further airborne landing and in turn affected the move on Tokyo, and Eighth Army spokesman said.

Until yesterday's formal surrender, international law provided that the only troops to enter the country were to act as guard for the supreme Allied Commander.

The crack Eleventh Airborne Division and the American and British Marines and the bluejackets performed that function.

CALVERY LANDS---

But with the signing, the flood gates were opened and for days now troops will be swarming ashore until an occupation army possibly 500,000 strong is landed.

In the first wave landing at Yokohama from the convoy was the First Calvary Division, including the famed First Brigade, liberators of the Santo Tomas internment camp at Manila.

They hit the beaches as demobilized Japanese troops in ragged lines walked past impassively.

Out beyond the beaches, the Japanese could see the imposing line of men-o'war and transports, symbolic of the power that defeated them.

The ceremony which restored peace to a weary world lasted but 20 minutes yesterday aboard the battle ship Missouri.

Over the battlewagon flew the American Flag that fluttered from Washington's capitol on the day of infamy, December 7, 1941.

Also displayed aboard was the Flag which Perry unfurled 92 years ago, it 31 stars faded.

The Japanese delegation faced a table upon which lay two large copies of the articles of surrender, the Allies copy bound in green, the Japanese bound in black – symbolic of the mournful day for Japan.

Shigemitsu was the first to sign and after signatories of all the Allies had followed, MacArthur declared:

> 'Peace is now restored to the world. May God preserve it always'.

MacArthur gave one of the pens with which he signed in behalf of all the Allies to Lieutenant General Jonathan M. Wainwright, liberated defender of Corregidor.

Wainwright was bound southward today for another pleasant duty – the acceptance of the surrender of all Japanese forces in the Philippines from Lieutenant General Tomoyuki Yamashita, swaggering conqueror of Singapore.

There was rigid formality throughout. The Japanese stood aloof with no show of emotion during the proceedings. They had been the last to board the battleship.

With the foreign minister were General Yoshijiro Umezu, who signed as chief of the imperial staff and nine other Japanese.

The signatories of the Allied Nations had assembled earlier in the cabin of Admiral Halsey and filed out in order of their rank, led by Admiral Nimitz who signed for the United States.

MacArthur strode to the small table covered with green felt place on the starboard side of the great No. 2 turret of three 16 inch guns pointed towards the overcast skies.

Silence fell over the crowd of dignitaries as MacArthur at 8:58 a.m. (4:58 p.m. Saturday P.W.T.) began slowly, clearly, and with dramatic emphasis:

> 'We are gathered here, representatives of the major warring power to conclude a solemn agreement. . '

Every top-flight American general and admiral in the Pacific was present. They were dressed in Khaki with shirts open at the neck in the fighting tradition established by Halsey early in the war.

They wore neither decorations nor ribbons as did the colorfully uniformed British, French, Dutch, Russian, and Chinese delegations.

An Open Letter to Veterans

March 13, 2009

Secretary of Veterans Affairs Eric K. Shinseki

My name is Ric Shinseki, and I am a Veteran. For me, serving as Secretary of Veterans Affairs is a noble calling. It provides me the opportunity to give back to those who served with and for me during my 38 years in uniform and those on whose shoulders we all stood as we grew up in the profession of arms.

The Department of Veterans Affairs has a solemn responsibility to all of you, today and in the future, as more Veterans join our ranks and enroll to secure the benefits and services they have earned. I am fully committed to fulfilling President Obama's vision for transforming our department so that it will be well-positioned to perform this duty even better during the 21st Century. We welcome the assistance and advice of our Veterans Service Organizations, other government departments and agencies, Congress, and all VA stakeholders as we move forward, ethically and transparently, so that Veterans and citizens can understand our efforts.

Creating that vision for transforming the VA into a 21st Century organization requires a comprehensive review of our department. We approach that review understanding that Veterans are central to everything VA does. We know that results count, that the department will be measured by what we do, not what we promise, and that our best days as an organization supporting Veterans are ahead of us. We will fulfill President Lincoln's charge to care for ". . . him, who shall have borne the battle, and for his widow, and his orphan .. . ." by redesigning and reengineering ourselves for the future.

Transforming any institution is supremely challenging; I know this from my own experience in leading large, proud, complex, and high-performing organizations through change. But the best organizations must be prepared to meet the challenging times, evolving technology and, most importantly, evolving needs of clients. Historically, organizations that are unwilling or unable to change soon find themselves irrelevant. You and your needs are not irrelevant.

Veterans are our clients, and delivering the highest quality care and services in a timely, consistent and fair manner is a VA responsibility. I take that responsibility seriously and have charged all of the department's employees for their best efforts and support every day to meet our obligations to you. Our path forward is challenging, but the President and Congress support us. They have asked us to do this well—for you. Veterans are our sole reason for existence and our number one priority—bar none. I look forward to working together with all VA employees to transform our department into an organization that reflects the change and commitment our country expects and our Veterans deserve.

Thank you, and God bless our military, our Veterans, and our Nation.

Eric K Shinseki: VA Official Biography

Secretary Shinseki served as Chief of Staff, United States Army, from 1999 to June 11, 2003, and retired from active duty on August 1, 2003.

Following the September 11, 2001 terrorist attacks, he led the Army during Operations Enduring Freedom and Iraqi Freedom.

Prior to becoming the Army's Chief of Staff, Secretary Shinseki served as the Vice Chief of Staff from 1998 to 1999. He previously served simultaneously as Commanding General, United States Army, Europe and Seventh Army; Commanding General, NATO Land Forces, Central Europe, both headquartered in Heidelberg, Germany; and Commander of the NATO-led Stabilization Force, Bosnia-Herzegovina, headquartered in Sarajevo.

He was commissioned a second lieutenant of Artillery upon graduation from the United States Military Academy in June 1965 and was attached to Company A, 1st Battalion, 14th Infantry Regiment, 25th Infantry Division as a forward observer from December 1965 to September 1966, when he was wounded in combat in the Republic of Vietnam. He returned to Tripler Army Medical Center, Honolulu, Hawaii to recuperate and subsequently was assigned as Assistant Secretary, then Secretary to the General Staff, U.S. Army, Hawaii, Schofield Barracks, from 1967-1968. He transferred to Armor Branch and attended the Armor Officer Advanced Course at Fort Knox, Kentucky, before returning to Vietnam a second time in 1969. While serving as Commander, Troop A, 3d Squadron, 5th Cavalry Regiment, he was wounded a second time in 1970.

Other assignments include Commander, 3rd Squadron, 7th Cavalry, 3rd Infantry Division; Commander, 2nd Brigade, 3rd Infantry Division; Deputy Chief of Staff, Support for Allied Land Forces Southern Europe; Assistant Division Commander-Maneuver, 3rd Infantry Division; Commander, 1st Cavalry Division, as well as G-3, 3rd Infantry Division, 1984-1985; G-3, VII US Corps, 1989-1990; and Deputy Chief of Staff for Operations and Plans, Headquarters, Department of the Army, 1996-1997.

Shinseki holds a BS degree from the U.S. Military Academy at West Point, a MA degree from Duke University, and is a graduate of the National War College. Secretary Shinseki was awarded the Defense Distinguished Service Medal, Distinguished Service Medal, Legion of Merit (with Oak Leaf Clusters), Bronze Star Medal with "V" Device (with 2 Oak Leaf Clusters), Purple Heart (with Oak Leaf Cluster), Defense Meritorious Service Medal, Meritorious Service Medal (with 2 Oak Leaf Clusters), Air Medal, Parachutist Badge, Ranger Tab, Joint Chiefs of Staff Identification Badge, and the Army Staff Identification Badge.

Richard Ropele
246 Coronado Dr.
Corona, CA 92879

The Final Thought

There are countless millions of people alive today throughout the world because of the sacrifice and dedication of the men and women of the Unites States Military.

Honored and great are they that wear the colors of the United States of America

Thank you all for your service and dedication

	**The Cannon** **Americal Division Veterans Association** **Far West Chapter** **AZ CA CO HA NV NM UT AK ID MT OR WA WY**	

Far West Chapter Annual Reunion
18 – 20 October 2009

'The Biggest Little City in the World', Reno Nevada, will be the host site for this years' 2009 annual Chapter reunion. An excellent time to reacquaint yourselves with your fellow veterans, meet new friends, and enjoy that camaraderie that can only exist among veterans.

Headquarters for this reunion will be:

The Atlantis Casino Resort Spa
3800 S. Virginia Street
Reno, Nevada 89502-6082
(800)723-6500
Http://www.atlantiscasino.com

Room reservations can be placed now at our negotiated daily rate of $62/night. The hotel has set 17 September 2009 as the cut off date for this special room rate. Let the reservation clerk know you are with the Americal Division Veteran Association to get this special rate.

Attached on the following pages is our Registration form for you and your guest/spouse as well as details of the hotel/bus trip, etc.

Please make your check payable to: "Americal Far West Chapter" and mail to:

Rich Merlin
6820 Indiana Ave, Suite 260
Riverside, CA 92506
951-781-3700 (Bus)
951-785-9816 (Res)
Rmerlin425@aol.com

We have been assured by our reunion chairman, 'Reno' Rich Merlin, that there will be a multitude of activities scheduled to hold your interest. Be sure you bring that special gift from your area for the raffle that takes place at the dinner– it's a fun activity and is just another way we can offset some of our expenses.

We need you to commit your attendance as soon as possible as we have to size and select the activities and commit Chapter funds that lock in our reservations.

Located in the downtown Reno area is the Truckee River Whitewater Park . The Riverwalk District offers entertainment, dining and shopping opportunities. The National Automobile Museum, featuring the 'Harrah Collection' is also nearby. If you'd like to take a little road trip through the Rocky Mountains, Historic Virginia City celebrates its 150th birthday this year and is just a short drive southeast of Reno. Additionally, scenic Lake Tahoe offering 70 miles of pristine shoreline is less than one hour drive away.

Looking forward to seeing you all again in Reno

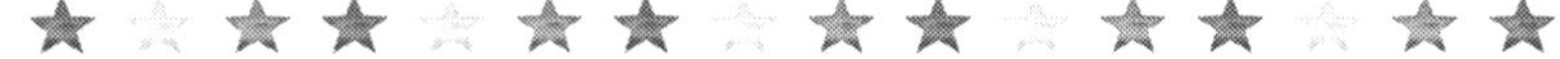

AMERICAL DIVISION VETERANS ASSOCIATION
FAR WEST CHAPTER
REUNION REGISTRATION FORM
RENO, NEVADA OCTOBER 18-21, 2009

Last Name______________________**First name**__________________________

Guest Name____

Address___________________**City**_________**State**_______**Zip**___________

Phone__________________**War & Unit served with**______________________

REGISTRATION
$20 PER PERSON X # OF PEOPLE ( ) **$**________

MONDAY BUS TRIP
$38 PER PERSON X # OF PEOPLE ( ) **$**________

DINNER/DANCE (Tuesday night)
$45 PER PERSON X # OF PEOPLE ( ) **$**________

TOTAL **$**________

Cut off date for registration is October 10, 2009

Tuesday Night Dinner Buffet

Tossed Garden Salad with Dressings
Mediterranean Pasta Salad
Chilled Prawns served with Cocktail Sauce
Marinated Mushroom & Artichoke Salad
Sliced Seasonal Fruit

Tortellini Alfredo
Pacific Salmon in Lemon-Chardonnay
Chicken Bouquet Garni

CARVING STATION WITH CHEF CARVING:
Slow-Roasted Prime Rib of Beef
With Au Jus & Creamy Horseradish

Red Roasted Potatoes
Sautéed Vegetable Medley
Rolls with Butter

Assorted Pies, Cakes, & Mini Pastries

FAR WEST ADVA RENO, NV REUNION EVENT DESCRIPTIONS
October 18-21, 2009

HOTEL RESERVATIONS

Make your reservations directly with the Atlantis Casino Resort Spa located at 3800 South Virginia St., Reno, NV. 89502. Call 800-723-6500 and identify yourself as being with the Americal Division Veterans Association. Room rates are $62.00 per night.

HOSPITALITY & REUNION CHECK IN

Our headquarters and hospitality room will open up at 4 pm on Sunday, October 18th. We will have a welcome reception with plenty to drink and eat. We will be located in one of the Atrium Paradise Suites. Room number will be available when you check in for your room. Hospitality Suite will be in the name of "Rich Merlin".

MONDAY BUS TRIP

VIRGINIA CITY TOUR & RED'S OLD 395 GRILL: 9:30 am to 2:30 pm (Includes Lunch) $38.00 per person
We will travel by bus with a Tour Guide to Virginia City, where we will be given a guided tour of the town and then have some free time to explore and visit the many shops, old time bars, and gambling halls. On the way back we will stop at Carson City, where we will have lunch at the famous "Red's Old 395 Grill" On the way back to Reno we will tour past some Historic Victoria Homes for a view of the Governor's Mansion and then head back to Reno through the Washoe Valley.

TUESDAY, October 19th

We will meet in the Emerald Meeting Room at 10am, where we will take our group picture and then conduct our annual membership meeting.

TUESDAY NIGHT DINNER/DANCE

Our annual dinner will take place in the Treasures Banquet Room starting at 6 pm. We will have a great dinner with wine at each table. Music and dancing will be available. For dinner, we will be treated to a great Buffet, see the registration form for the complete buffet menu.

Make check payable to: "Americal Far West Chapter" and mail to:
Rich Merlin — 951-785-9816 (Res)
6820 Indiana Ave, Suite 260 — 951-781-3700 (Bus)
Riverside, CA 92506 — Rmerlin425@aol.com

"Don't forget that special gift from your area for our raffle"

CHAPTER DUES NOTICE

Chapter dues are payable on January 1st, 2009 for members whose dues expire in 2008. If you have either a "2008" or a "08" after your name on the mailing label on the front of this newsletter your membership expired on December 31, 2008. Dues remain at just $10.00 per year. You may pay for any number of years.

ADVA members who reside in the former Northwest Chapter area were welcomed into the reorganized chapter in June of 2008 as current active members for the remainder of the year We hope you have enjoyed the benefits of membership in the Far West Chapter and will continue as an active member. You will receive a membership application along with a letter inviting you to continue with your membership in the chapter. Look for the invitation in January.

Make your check payable to: "ADVA Far West Chapter" at mail to:

Tom Packard
6613 Birch Park Drive
Galloway, Ohio 43119

Missing Albert Re

Since our last publication of The Cannon, we lost one those valiant souls that served so honorable with the 182nd INF during World War II. We extend our condolences to the family of Albert Re.

Far West Chapter Officers

Commander
Richard Ropele
(951)218-3071
rropele@yahoo.com

Vice Commander
Dave Hammond
pacwesthi@aol.com

Secretary/Treasurer
Tom Packard
(614)878-5197
Packard50@columbus.rr.com

Sergeant At Arms
Curt Rothacker
(925)784-5391

Chaplain
Gene McGrath
(775)751-1861
Mc2some@sbcglobal.net

Newsletter Editor
Richard Ropele
246 Coronado, Dr
Corona, CA 92879
(951)218-3071
rropele@yahoo.com

Information of interest for Veterans

The following are a few excerpts from the VFW Washington Weekly publication that would be interest to our membership. More information is available by checking their site at: http://www.vfw.org/washingtonweekly/2009/ww06192009.pdf.

1. Priority 8 Enrollment Update: VA changed enrollment eligibility rules on June 15 to make it easier for more veterans to enroll in VA's health care system. Under this new provision, they expect about 266,000 more veterans to enroll this year and possibly 500,000 in the next four years. VA relaxed income restrictions on enrollment for health benefits. While this new provision does not remove consideration of income, it does increase income thresholds. A web-based calculator is available for veterans to enter personal data at http://www.va.gov/healtheligibility/apps/enrollmentcalculator/. Veterans may also contact VA's health resource center at 1-877-222-8387 or visit the VA health eligibility website at http://www.va.gov/healtheligibility/

2. Endoscopic Procedures Hearing: The House VA Subcommittee on Oversight and Investigations held hearing following reports that three VA medical facilities failed to use proper safeguards in the cleaning of endoscopic equipment. A recent VA Inspector General report said fewer than half of 42 VA facilities selected for no-notice inspections last month had proper training and guidelines in place. The report came after VA uncovered procedural errors at medical centers in Georgia, Florida and Tennessee that potentially exposed more than 10,00 veterans to HIV and other infections, such as

Hepatitis B and C. Members of the committee expressed outrage and disbelief at the findings, and tasked VA to ensure that proper policies and training programs are in place. They also questioned the care and treatment of those exposed and how they are going to regain the trust of the veterans they serve. For prepared testimony and to listen to audio from the hearing, go to: http://veterans.house.gov/hearings/hearing.aspx?newsid=417

3. VA Appropriations Update: This week, the House Appropriations Subcommittee on Military Construction and VA moved advanced appropriations closer to final approval when it cleared a $77.9 billion bill. The bill, as approved, contains $48.2 billion in advanced funding for VA medical accounts for FY 2011. VFW testified before the committee several times in support of the concept, as we believe this will allow VA to better plan for the future, attract and recruit high-quality health care professionals, and allow them to better target gaps in care among other enhancements. For the subcommittee press release, go to: http://appropriations.house.gov/pdf/Milcon-FY2010-EdwardsStatement-9-16-10.pdf

Homecoming Celebrations for Returning Servicemen

My son Rod, is serving in the Army in Iraq and is due to return to the U.S.A. after his tour ends in August. Before I tell you about his experience returning home for R & R, let me frame it in context with a small episode from my homecoming.

I came back as a medievac patient as a result of the Tet Offensive of 1968, ultimately ending up at the hospital at Fort Ord. You hear the stories about returning soldiers being castigated by crowds of people calling them names and spitting, I never was overtly set upon by anyone, but when opportunities arose for assistance, no one bothered:

> I remember returning to Fort Ord after my first convalescent leave. I was in my Class A uniform, on crutches and the plane landed at San Jose so that I could get a connecting flight to Monterey and get back to the post Hospital. Well, it was raining in San Jose, the flight was late and I missed the last connecting flight to Monterey.
>
> I'm crutching around the San Jose airport trying to figure out how to get back to Fort Ord before my leave expires at midnight. A cabbie says he'll drive me there for $100. Crap, I don't have that kind of money. I finally connect with a train and for $20 it has a stop directly across from the main gate.
>
> It's still raining, it's dark, I get off the train, crutch my way across the coast highway, get on post, but I can't get a cab to the post hospital. So the only alternative was to crutch my way down the road back to the hospital. I'm absolutely soaked through my uniform. Fortunately, some other soldier stops and gives me a ride.

It's hard to believe that it still bothers me that no one at San Jose would go out of their way to assist an obviously wounded soldier.

Now, in contrast, read my Sons' experience when he came home on R & R.

Rod left Kuwait with all the others going on leave where they were routed to Germany and divided into an east coast group and a west coast group and put on commercial airliners.

After leaving Germany, he landed in Dallas to get his connecting flight to California. The attached picture is a postcard, but this is just the first indication of how the returning troops are first greeted upon returning to American soil.

:

The caption on the postcard reads:

Dallas/fort Worth International Airport
Welcome Home Our Troops
Each day, the DFW Airport community welcomes home U.S. troops returning from the Middle East for Rest and Recuperation. Upon arrival, DFW Fire and Rescue officers salute the arriving flight with its traditional 'Shower of Affection'. The water salute consists of two water turrets with nozzles that discharge 1,500 gallons of water per minute arching over the plane.

Rod said that after going through customs and leaving the International Terminal and moving through the main airport to their various gates, all the other waiting passengers stopped what they were doing, turned, and applauded the troops as they walked through the airport. He said that all throughout the airport along the way there were groups of people, men, women, teenagers, children, scouts, were applauding and cheering for them.

I know it was hard for them to be the center of attention, but I also know they appreciated the recognition for their service. Rod said something to the affect: 'Man, those people in Texas are the real Americans'.

I guess I'm jealous that the country recognizes and acknowledges their service and contribution, but our same contribution was pushed to the side as though everyone was ashamed. It's hard to believe that after 40 years, I can still let these things affect me.

I think it's great that the country recognizes that the contribution and sacrifice the men and women of the military make to the peace and stability of our country and to other countries throughout the world. I'm proud to have worn the uniform and represented the United States of America in time of war. I'm proud and stand with my fellow Vietnam Veterans and say to those returning from Iraq, Afghanistan, and other places, 'Thanks for your service, you are my heroes'.

Since the first gulf war, troops returning from the Middle East have been hailed as heroes and given the recognition they deserve for their world wide peach keeping efforts

How grateful I am for these experiences for him

Richard Ropele
246 Coronado Dr.
Corona, CA 92879

The Final Thought

There are countless millions of people alive today throughout the world because of the sacrifice and dedication of the men and women of the Unites States Military.

Honored and great are they that wear the colors of the United States of America

Thank you all for your service and dedication

	**The Cannon** **Americal Division Veterans Association** **Far West Chapter** **AZ CA CO HA NV NM UT AK ID MT OR WA WY**	

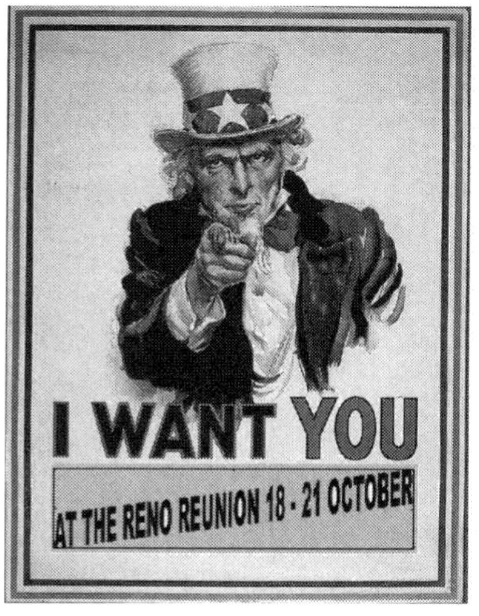

Far West Chapter Annual Reunion
18 – 20 October 2009

Time is running out. The annual reunion is right around the corner. We need you in Reno

'The Biggest Little City in the World', Reno Nevada, will be the host site for this years' 2009 annual Chapter reunion. An excellent time to reacquaint yourselves with your fellow veterans, meet new friends, and enjoy that camaraderie that can only exist among veterans.

Headquarters for this reunion will be:
The Atlantis Casino Resort Spa
3800 S. Virginia Street
Reno, Nevada 89502-6082
(800)723-6500
Http://www.atlantiscasino.com

Please make your check payable to: "Americal Far West Chapter" and mail to:
Rich Merlin
6820 Indiana Ave, Suite 260
Riverside, CA 92506
951-781-3700 (Bus)
951-785-9816 (Res)
Rmerlin425@aol.com

AMERICAL DIVISION VETERANS ASSOCIATION
FAR WEST CHAPTER
REUNION REGISTRATION FORM
RENO, NEVADA OCTOBER 18-21, 2009

Last Name______________ First name______________

Guest Name______________

Address________ City______ State____ Zip______

Phone__________ War & Unit served with__________

REGISTRATION
$20 PER PERSON X # OF PEOPLE ( ) $______

MONDAY BUS TRIP
$38 PER PERSON X # OF PEOPLE ( ) $______

DINNER/DANCE (Tuesday night)
$45 PER PERSON X # OF PEOPLE ( ) $______

TOTAL $______

Cut off date for registration is October 10, 2009

Tuesday Night Dinner Buffet

Tossed Garden Salad with Dressings
Mediterranean Pasta Salad
Chilled Prawns served with Cocktail Sauce
Marinated Mushroom & Artichoke Salad
Sliced Seasonal Fruit

Tortellini Alfredo
Pacific Salmon in Lemon-Chardonnay
Chicken Bouquet Garni

CARVING STATION WITH CHEF CARVING:
Slow-Roasted Prime Rib of Beef
With Au Jus & Creamy Horseradish

Red Roasted Potatoes
Sautéed Vegetable Medley
Rolls with Butter

Assorted Pies, Cakes, & Mini Pastries

FAR WEST ADVA RENO, NV REUNION EVENT DESCRIPTIONS
October 18-21, 2009

HOTEL RESERVATIONS

Make your reservations directly with the Atlantis Casino Resort Spa located at 3800 South Virginia St., Reno, NV. 89502. Call 800-723-6500 and identify yourself as being with the Americal Division Veterans Association. Room rates are $62.00 per night.

HOSPITALITY & REUNION CHECKIN

Our headquarters and hospitality room will open up at 4 pm on Sunday, October 18th. We will have a welcome reception with plenty to drink and eat. We will be located in one of the Atrium Paradise Suites. Room number will be available when you check in for your room. Hospitality Suite will be in the name of "Rich Merlin".

MONDAY BUS TRIP

VIRGINIA CITY TOUR & RED'S OLD 395 GRILL: 9:30 am to 2:30 pm (Includes Lunch) $38.00 per person
We will travel by bus with a Tour Guide to Virginia City, where we will be given a guided tour of the town and then have some free time to explore and visit the many shops, old time bars, and gambling halls. On the way back we will stop at Carson City, where we will have lunch at the famous "Red's Old 395 Grill" On the way back to Reno we will tour past some Historic Victoria Homes for a view of the Governor's Mansion and then head back to Reno through the Washoe Valley.

TUESDAY, October 19th

We will meet in the Emerald Meeting Room at 10am, where we will take our group picture and then conduct our annual membership meeting.

TUESDAY NIGHT DINNER/DANCE

Our annual dinner will take place in the Treasures Banquet Room starting at 6 pm. We will have a great dinner with wine at each table. Music and dancing will be available. For dinner, we will be treated to a great Buffet, see the registration form for the complete buffet menu.

Make check payable to: "Americal Far West Chapter" and mail to:
Rich Merlin — 951-785-9816 (Res)
6820 Indiana Ave. Suite 260 — 951 781-3700 (Bus)
Riverside, CA 92506 — Rmerlin425@aol.com

"Don't forget that special gift from your area for our raffle"

Room reservations can be placed now at our negotiated daily rate of $62/night. The hotel has set 17 September 2009 as the cut off date for this special room rate. Let the reservation clerk know you are with the Americal Division Veteran Association to get this special rate.

Society of The Honor Guard – Tomb of the Unknown Soldier

The Society works toward preserving and maintaining records, educating the public concerning the history of the Tomb and the Unknown Soldiers, as well as the history of the Guards who have stood watch over them since 1926.

The unknown soldiers buried in the Plaza represent the missing and unknown service members for four different wars. Being buried at Arlington gives these families a place to grieve and pray. We stand watch over their graves in humble reverence, ensuring they rest in peace. These Americans have not only given their lives, but their identities for our freedom and way of life.

General George S. Patton, Jr. said it best:

> *"The soldier is the Army. No army is better than its soldiers. The Soldier is also a citizen. In fact, the highest obligation and privilege of citizenship is that of bearing arms for one's country.*
>
> *"Hence it is a proud privilege to be a soldier – a good soldier ... [with] discipline, self-respect, pride in his unit and his country, a high sense of duty and obligation to comrades and to his superiors, and a self confidence born of demonstrated ability."*

Reference : http://www.tombguard.org

How does the Guard rotation work? Is it an 8 hour shift?

Currently, the Tomb Guards work on a three Relief (team) rotation - 24 hours on, 24 hours off, 24 hours on, 24 hours off, 24 hours on, 96 hours off. However, over the years it has been different. The time off isn't exactly free time. It takes the average Sentinel 8 hours to prep his/her uniform for the next work day. Additionally, they have Physical Training, Tomb Guard training, and haircuts to complete before the next work day.

How many steps does the Guard take during his walk across the Tomb of the Unknowns and why?

21 steps. It alludes to the twenty-one gun salute, which is the highest honor given any military or foreign dignitary.

How long does the Sentinel hesitate after his about face to begin his return walk and does he carry his rifle on the same shoulder all the time, and if not, why not?

He does not execute an about face. He stops on the 21st step, then turns and faces the Tomb for 21 seconds. Then he turns to face back down the mat, changes his weapon to the outside shoulder, counts 21 seconds, then steps off for another 21 step walk down the mat. He faces the Tomb at each end of the 21 step walk for 21 seconds. The Sentinel then repeats this over and over until he is relieved at the Guard Change.

Why are his gloves wet?

His gloves are moistened to improve his grip on the rifle.

How often are the Guards changed?

The Guard is changed every thirty minutes during the summer (April 1 to Sep 30) and every hour during the winter (Oct 1 to Mar 31). During the hours the cemetery is closed, the guard is changed every 2 hours. The Tomb is guarded, and has been guarded, every minute of every day since 1937.

Is it true they must commit 2 years of life to guard the Tomb, live in a barracks under the tomb, and cannot drink any alcohol on or off duty for the rest of their lives.

No, this is a false rumor. The average tour at the Tomb is about a year. There is NO set time for service there. The Sentinels live either in a barracks on Ft. Myer (the Army post located adjacent to the cemetery) or off base if they like. They do have living quarters under the steps of the amphitheater where they stay during their 24 hour shifts, but when they are off, they are off. And if they are of legal age, they may drink anything they like, except while on duty.

Is it true they cannot swear in public for the rest of their lives?

Again, another false rumor.

Is it true after two years, the guard is given a wreath pin that is worn on their lapel signifying they served as Guard of the Tomb, that there are only 400 presently worn, and that the Guard must obey these rules for the rest of their lives or give up the wreath pin?

The Tomb Guard Identification Badge is awarded after the Sentinel passes a series of tests. The Badge is permanently awarded after a Sentinel has served 9 months as a Sentinel at the Tomb. Over 500 have been awarded since its creation in the late 1950's. And while the Badge can be revoked, the offense must be such that it discredits the Tomb. Revocation is at the Regimental Commander's discretion. But you can drink a beer and even swear and still keep the Badge. The Badge is a full size award, worn on the right pocket of the uniform jacket, not a lapel pin.

Are the shoes specially made with very thick soles to keep the heat and cold from their feet?

The shoes are standard issue military dress shoes. They are built up so the sole and heel are equal in height. This allows the Sentinel to stand so that his back is straight and perpendicular to the ground. A side effect of this is that the Sentinel can "roll" on the outside of the build up as he walks down the mat. This allows him to move in a fluid fashion. If he does this correctly, his hat and bayonet will appear to not "bob" up and down with each step. It gives him a more formal and smooth look to his walk, rather than a "marching" appearance.

The soles have a steel tip on the toe and a "horseshoe" steel plate on the heel. This prevents wear on the sole and allows the Sentinel to move smoothly during his movements when he turns to face the Tomb and then back down the mat.

Then there is the "clicker". It is a shank of steel attached to the inside of the face of the heel build-up on each shoe. It allows the Sentinel to click his heels during certain movements. If a guard change is really hot, it is called a "smoker" because all the heel clicks fall together and sound like one click. In fact, the guard change is occasionally done in the "silent" mode (as a sign of devotion to the Unknowns"). No voice commands - every thing is done in relation to the heel clicks and on specific counts.

How many times will a Soldier be on duty during the shift?

Each Relief (team) has a rotation during the 24 hour work day. This rotation is dependent on the number of Soldier-Sentinels who are proficient enough to guard the Tomb. The standard is 3-4 qualified Sentinels, 1-2 Relief Commander/Assistant Relief Commander, and 1-2 Sentinels in training. Generally, the Sentinel will be on guard duty for a tour and have two tours off in between - then go out for another tour. However, in extreme cases, Sentinels have been known to go back-to-back for the entire 24 hour shift.

How do the Soldiers get to and from the quarters without being seen?

Most wear civilian clothes - although the short, tight haircuts tend to give us away.

There is a small green shack next to the Tomb. What is it for?

"The Box" is used primarily during wreath-laying ceremonies for the Sentinel to retreat to while flowers and Taps are being presented. There also is a phone with a direct line downstairs to the Tomb Guard Quarters - this is used in times of emergencies or just to notify the next shift of something.

Has anyone ever tried to get past the Tomb guards, or attempted to deface the Tomb?

Yes, that is the reason why we now guard the Tomb. Back in the early 1920's, we didn't have guards and the Tomb looked much different People often came to the cemetery in those days for picnics during which time some would actually use the Tomb as a picnic area (probably because of the view). Soon after, 1925, they posted a civilian guard; in 1926, a military guard was posted during cemetery hours; and on July 1, 1937, this was expanded to the 24-hour watch. Since then, the ceremony has developed throughout the years to what we have today. Today, most of the challenges faced by the Sentinels are tourists who want to get a better picture or uncontrolled children (which generally is very frightening for the parent when the Soldier challenges the child).

What happened to the soldier that was in the Tomb from the Vietnam War?

The remains of the Vietnam Unknown Soldier were exhumed May 14, 1998. Based on mitochondrial DNA testing, DoD scientists identified the remains as those of Air Force 1st Lt. Michael Joseph Blassie, who was shot down near An Loc, Vietnam, in 1972. It has been decided that the crypt that contained the remains of the Vietnam Unknown will remain vacant. (Further Background)(News Article from the Department of Defense)

What is it like to guard in bad weather?
The guards at the Tomb of the Unknown Soldier (we call ourselves "Sentinels") are completely dedicated to their duty of guarding the Tomb. Because of that dedication, the weather does not bother them. In fact, they consider it an honor to stand their watch (we call it "walking the mat"), regardless of the weather. It gets cold, it gets hot - but the Sentinels never budge. And they never allow any feeling of cold or heat to be seen by anyone.

Do you guard in a blizzard or a bad thunderstorm?
YES, BUT the accomplishment of the mission and welfare of the Soldier is never put at risk. The Tomb Guards have contingencies that are ready to be executed IF the weather conditions EVER place the Soldiers at risk of injury or death – such as lightning, high winds, etc. This ensures that Sentinels can maintain the Tomb Guard responsibilities while ensuring soldier safety. It is the responsibility of the Chain of Command from the Sergeant of the Guard to the Regimental Commander to ensure mission accomplishment and soldier welfare at all times
It was erroneously reported that during Hurricane Isabel, the Sentinels were ordered to abandon their posts for shelter and that they refused. No such order was ever given. All proper precautions were taken to ensure the safety of the Sentinels while accomplishing their mission. Risk assessments are constantly conducted by the Chain of Command during changing conditions to ensure that soldier welfare is maintained during mission accomplishment.

Do you guard all night long, even when the cemetery is closed?
The Tomb is guarded 24 hours a day, 7 days a week. In fact, there has been a Sentinel on duty in front of the Tomb every minute of every day since 1937. And the Sentinel does not change the way he guards the Tomb, even at night when there is no one around. The Sentinels do this because they feel that the Unknown Soldiers who are buried in the Tomb deserve the very best they have to give.

How many Sentinels have been female?
There have been 3 female Sentinels.

For More Information

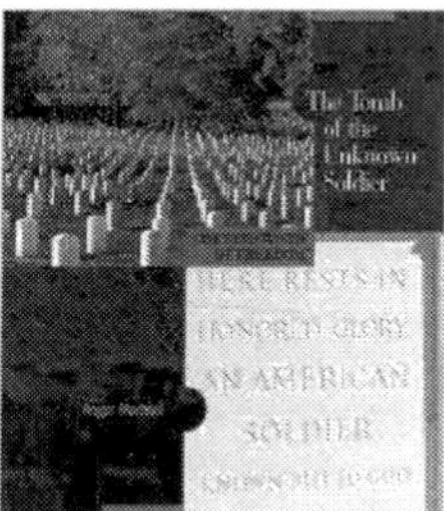

A description of the history and characteristics of the national monument known as the Tomb of the Unknown Soldier at Arlington National Cemetery, Arlington, Virginia, which was established after World War I to honor an unidentified soldier from each war

Far West Chapter Officers

Commander
Richard Ropele
(951)218-3071
rropele@yahoo.com

Vice Commander
Dave Hammond
pacwesthi@aol.com

Secretary/Treasurer
Tom Packard
(614)878-5197
Packard50@columbus.rr.com

Sergeant At Arms
Curt Rothacker
(925)784-5391

Chaplain
Gene McGrath
(775)751-1861
Mc2some@sbcglobal.net

Newsletter Editor
Richard Ropele
246 Coronado, Dr
Corona, CA 92879
(951)218-3071
rropele@yahoo.com

Richard Ropele
246 Coronado Dr.
Corona, CA 92879

The Final Thought

There are countless millions of people alive today throughout the world because of the sacrifice and dedication of the men and women of the Unites States Military.

Honored and great are they that wear the colors of the United States of America

My Turn in the Barrel

Thank you all for your service and dedication

Appendix XIII – Various E-Mail Correspondence

This is the first message I got from Ed Bartel in response to the Thanksgiving day stopover in Alaska article that I wrote and was published in the January – March edition of the Americal Newsletter :

-----Original Message-----
From: Ed Bartel [SMTP:edbartel@pldi.net
Sent: Monday, April 21, 2003 1:59 PM
To: rropele@earthlink.net
Subject: Vietnam-1967

Hi Rick,

You have a TREMENDOUS memory about things that happened a long time ago!!!

I too was on that airplane, and experienced the same things. However, I don't have names, and etc. anymore, the way you do. I went to Vietnam after training at Fort Polk (Tiger Land). I was in the 196th LIB, and months later was infused into 198th LIB. Small world.

I live in Oklahoma.

Ed Bartel
edbartel@pldi.net

This is the response I wrote to Ed after reading that he was at Fort Polk:

From: "Rick Ropele" <rropele@earthlink.net>
To: "'Ed Bartel'" <edbartel@pldi.net>
Sent: Tuesday, April 22, 2003 8:27 PM
Subject: RE: Vietnam-1967

Ed: good to get your note. I also got a response from a Steve Fitts, who was on the plane also and remembered the same situation. Your name doesn't ring a bell. I also went to AIT at Fort Polk, I don't remember the company, but we were located in barracks directly across the street from the EM club. I hung around with Tom Jordan, Ed Cahill (both from Oklahoma, in the Oklahoma City area) and Ted Smith, also from Oklahoma. A guy named Bodey was our trainee platoon Sgt.

I was there from 9/67 to 11/67. I took the attached photo when the bus came in to the base, and then knew for sure we weren't going to clerk typist school :-).

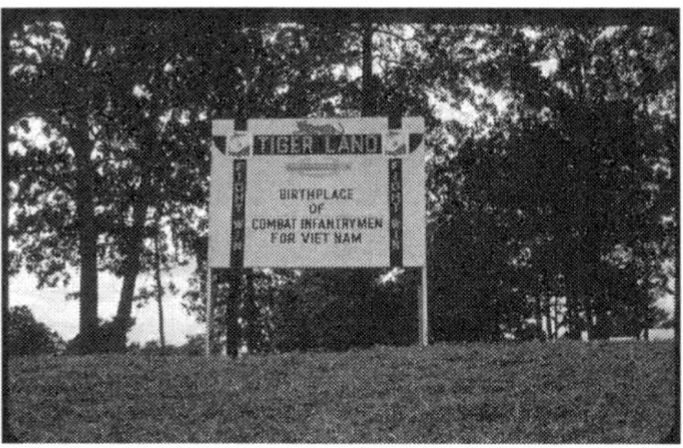

Where in OK are you located? My wife is from Okemah and has relatives in Bixby, Okemah, and McAlister. Small world huh?

Rick
rropele@earthlink.net
Corona, CA

Ed's response:

-----Original Message-----
From: Ed Bartel [SMTP:edbartel@pldi.net]
Sent: Wednesday, April 23, 2003 10:51 AM
To: rropele@earthlink.net
Subject: Re: Vietnam-1967

Rick, I was in the same barracks. Those guys were my friends. A bunch of us went through Boot Camp together at Fort Bliss, TX, and then straight to Fort Polk. Tom Jordan and I bunked together at Fort Bliss (he was bottom and I was top). I am from Oklahoma City, and almost the entire company at Fort Bliss was from OK.

I can't believe this.

Great picture, thanks.

I now live about 100 miles N.W. of OKC, near a small town named Longdale.

Ed

My note back to Ed:

-----Original Message-----
From: Rick Ropele [SMTP:rropele@earthlink.net]
Sent: Wednesday, April 23, 2003 6:51 PM
To: 'Ed Bartel'
Subject: RE: Vietnam-1967

Ed: holy cow! At Polk, I bunked either under Tom Jordan or in the rack next to him. I remember one time Tom got into a fight with one of the African Americans in our platoon while we were policing the company area (near the road), Tom just cleaned his clock. Do you remember the instance when Tom flew home one weekend and came back with a 56 Chevy?

After finishing AIT, Tom, and I and Ed Cahill drove back to Oklahoma City, I met my Dad there in Tulsa and that's the last time I saw Tom. I did see and talk to Ed Cahill over in Vietnam in January 68. I saw him on highway 1, just north of the river by An Tan. My platoon was assigned to the bridge during TET. I think Ed was with some guys and they were going back to the 196th LIB base camp, I think it was near Tam Ky.

I got hit with rocket frags that first night of TET there at the bridge and was medievac'd home by the end of February.

Attached is picture of someone from Polk. I don't remember who he is, perhaps you recognize him. Also, I posted some pictures of Polk on my family's web site (http://home.earthlink.net/~rropele/).

Rick

My note to Ed and his response (I put his remarks in italics, as he interspersed his comments throughout my note to him).

-----Original Message-----
From: Ed Bartel [SMTP:edbartel@pldi.net]
Sent: Saturday, April 26, 2003 1:50 PM
To: Rick
Subject: Vietnam-1967

Ed: attached is another copy of the picture of the guy standing in front of orderly room. We enlarged it and changed the contrast so it's lighter. If that's you, what a coincidence, huh. .*(Well, it isn't me in the picture after all)*. . I don't remember getting a picture of the entire company from Polk. *(I did get a picture of our company. It was an 8 x 11, and I remember it had Cahill and everyone in it. If I find it, I'll get a copy to you.)*

I bunked upstairs about halfway down the row on the right side (if your back is to the stairs). *(I was downstairs, close to the door. You talk about digging down deep into the memory.)* I remember having to pull KP from 4:00 am to midnight. *(I did too. Although I don't remember exactly the times. How do you do it?)*

I've lived in SoCal
all my life. *(The guy I mentioned before, Bill Pohl, was from CA also. I went to Navy boot camp in 1982 in San Diego, and was stationed there, North Island Naval Air Station, from 1989 - 1991. We liked CA. That's right, I joined the Navy later)* After VN, I spent my last year in Colorado at Fort Carson. *(I re-enlisted for 2 more years in the Army, spent 20 months in Vietnam, and then 22 months at Fort Hood, TX.)* We had an XO named Lt Trujillo, as I recall, he said he was from the 198th and was a mortar platoon leader.

Rick
rropele@earthlink.net

(Ed)

Printed in Great Britain
by Amazon

34713273R00167